Deconstructing Zionism

About the Series

The **Political Theory and Contemporary Philosophy** series stages an ongoing dialogue between contemporary European philosophy and political theory. Following Hannah Arendt's and Leo Strauss's repeated insistence on the qualitative distinction between political *theory* and political *philosophy*, the series showcases the lessons each discipline can draw from the other. One of the most significant outcomes of this dialogue is an innovative integration of 1) the findings of twentieth- and twenty-first-century phenomenology, existentialism, hermeneutics, psychoanalysis, and deconstruction (to name but a few salient currents) and 2) classical as well as modern political concepts, such as sovereignty, polity, justice, constitution, statehood, self-determination, etc.

In many instances, the volumes in the series both re-conceptualize age-old political categories in light of contemporary philosophical theses and find broader applications for the ostensibly non- or apolitical aspects of philosophical inquiry. In all cases, political thought and philosophy are featured as equal partners in an interdisciplinary conversation, the goal of which is to bring about a greater understanding of today's rapidly changing political realities.

The series is edited by Michael Marder, Ikerbasque Research Professor in the Department of Philosophy at the University of the Basque Country, Vitoria-Gasteiz.

Other volumes in the series include:

Humanity at Risk edited by Daniel Innerarity and Javier Solana
Heidegger on Hegel's Philosophy of Right by Marcia Sa Cavalcante Schuback, Michael Marder and Peter Trawny
The Metaphysics of Terror by Rasmus Ugilt
Negative Revolution by Artemy Magun
The Voice of Conscience by Mika Ojakangas

Deconstructing Zionism

A Critique of Political Metaphysics

Edited by

Gianni Vattimo and Michael Marder

BLOOMSBURY ACADEMIC
NEW YORK • LONDON • OXFORD • NEW DELHI • SYDNEY

BLOOMSBURY ACADEMIC
Bloomsbury Publishing Inc
1385 Broadway, New York, NY 10018, USA
50 Bedford Square, London, WC1B 3DP, UK
29 Earlsfort Terrace, Dublin 2, Ireland

BLOOMSBURY, BLOOMSBURY ACADEMIC and the Diana logo are trademarks of
Bloomsbury Publishing Plc

First published in 2014

Copyright © Gianni Vattimo, Michael Marder, and Contributors 2014

All rights reserved. No part of this publication may be reproduced or transmitted in any form or by any means, electronic or mechanical, including photocopying, recording, or any information storage or retrieval system, without prior permission in writing from the publishers.

Bloomsbury Publishing Inc does not have any control over, or responsibility for, any third-party websites referred to or in this book. All internet addresses given in this book were correct at the time of going to press. The author and publisher regret any inconvenience caused if addresses have changed or sites have ceased to exist, but can accept no responsibility for any such changes.

Library of Congress Cataloging-in-Publication Data
Deconstructing Zionism : a critique of political metaphysics / edited by Gianni Vattimo, Michael Marder.
    pages cm. – (Political theory and contemporary philosophy)
    Includes bibliographical references and index.
    ISBN 978-1-4411-4345-7 (hardback) – ISBN 978-1-4411-0594-3 (paperback) 1. Zionism–Historiography. I. Vattimo, Gianni, 1938- editor of compilation. II. Marder, Michael, 1980- editor of compilation. III. Vattimo, Gianni, 1938- editor of compilation. How to become an Anti-Zionist.
    DS149.D33 2013
    320.54095694–dc23
    2013023952

ISBN: HB: 978-1-4411-4345-7
         PB: 978-1-4411-0594-3
         ePDF: 978-1-4411-1556-0
         eBook: 978-1-4411-1477-8

Series: Political Theory and Contemporary Philosophy

Typeset by Fakenham Prepress Solutions, Fakenham, Norfolk NR21 8NN

To find out more about our authors and books visit www.bloomsbury.com and sign up for our newsletters.

For Jacques Derrida

Contents

Contributors ... ix

Introduction: "If Not Now, When?" *Gianni Vattimo and Michael Marder* ... xi

1. Anti-Semitism and its Transformations *Slavoj Žižek* ... 1
2. How to Become an Anti-Zionist *Gianni Vattimo* ... 15
3. Is Judaism Zionism? Or, Arendt and the Critique of the Nation-State *Judith Butler* ... 23
4. Decolonizing the Nation-State: Zionism in the Colonial Horizon of Modernity *Walter D. Mignolo* ... 57
5. Karl Marx and Hannah Arendt on the Jewish Question: Political Theology as a Critique *Artemy Magun* ... 75
6. Notes on the Prophetic Instability of Zionism *Marc H. Ellis* ... 99
7. The Spirit of Zionism: Derrida, *Ruah*, and the Purloined Birthright *Christopher Wise* ... 113
8. Rex, or the Negation of Wandering *Ranjana Khanna* ... 133
9. The Hermeneutical Stance: Being Discharged at the Margins of Political Zionism *Santiago Zabala* ... 147
10. The Zionist Synecdoche *Michael Marder* ... 155
11. Sharing Humanity: Towards Peaceful Coexistence in Difference *Luce Irigaray* ... 169

Index ... 181

Contributors

Judith Butler is an American philosopher who has contributed to the fields of feminist philosophy, queer theory, political philosophy, and ethics. An author of numerous books, she is a Professor in the Rhetoric and Comparative Literature Departments at the University of California Berkeley, as well as the Hannah Arendt Professor of Philosophy at the European Graduate School.

Marc H. Ellis is an American author, liberation theologian, and a retired University Professor of Jewish Studies at Baylor University. He is currently a visiting professor at the United Nations University for Peace in Costa Rica.

Luce Irigaray is a French philosopher, linguist, psychoanalyst, and cultural theorist. One of the most influential feminist thinkers in the world, she is best known for her works *The Speculum of the Other Woman* (1974) and *This Sex Which Is Not One* (1977).

Ranjana Khanna Professor at Duke University, works on Anglo- and Francophone Postcolonial Theory and Literature, Psychoanalysis, and Feminist Theory. She has published articles on transnational feminism, psychoanalysis, autobiography, postcolonial agency, multiculturalism in an international context, postcolonial Joyce, Area Studies and Women's Studies, and Algerian film. She is the author of *Dark Continents: Psychoanalysis and Colonialism* (2003) and *Algeria Cuts: Women and Representation 1830 to the present* (2008).

Artemy Magun is Professor of Democratic Theory and Chair of the Department of Political Science and Sociology at the European University at Saint-Petersburg, Russia. He is the author and editor of several books, including, most recently, *Negative Revolution* published by Bloomsbury in 2013.

Michael Marder is IKERBASQUE Research Professor in the Department of Philosophy at the University of the Basque Country (UPV-EHU), Vitoria-Gasteiz. He is the Associate Editor of *Telos: A Quarterly Journal of Critical Thought* and the author of *The Event of The Thing: Derrida's Post-Deconstructive Realism* (2009); *Groundless Existence: The Political Ontology of Carl Schmitt* (2010); and *Plant-Thinking: A Philosophy of Vegetal Life* (2013).

Walter D. Mignolo is an Argentine semiotician and Professor at Duke University, who has published extensively on semiotics and literary theory, and worked on different aspects of the modern and colonial world, exploring concepts such as global coloniality, the geopolitics of knowledge, transmodernity, border thinking, and pluriversality.

Gianni Vattimo is Emeritus Professor of Philosophy at the University of Turin and a member of the European Parliament. He is the author of *Hermeneutic Communism* (co-authored with S. Zabala), *A Farewell to Truth; The Responsibility of the Philosopher; Christianity, Truth, and Weakening Faith* (with R. Girard); *Not Being God: A Collaborative Autobiography* (with P. Paterlini); *Art's Claim to Truth; After the Death of God* (with John D. Caputo); *Dialogue with Nietzsche; The Future of Religion* (with Richard Rorty); *Nihilism and Emancipation: Ethics, Politics, and Law;* and *After Christianity*.

Christopher Wise is a Professor of English and Comparative Literature at Western Washington University in Bellingham. He is the author of several books, including *Derrida, Africa, and the Middle East* (2009) and *Chomsky and Deconstruction* (2011).

Santiago Zabala is ICREA Research Professor of Philosophy at the University of Barcelona. His books include *The Hermeneutic Nature of Analytic Philosophy* (2008), *The Remains of Being* (2009), and, most recently, *Hermeneutic Communism* (2011, co-authored with Gianni Vattimo).

Slavoj Žižek is a Slovene philosopher and cultural critic. He is a senior researcher at the Institute for Sociology and Philosophy at the University of Ljubljana and a Professor of Philosophy and Psychoanalysis at the European Graduate School. He writes widely on a diverse range of topics, including political theory, film theory, cultural studies, and psychoanalysis.

Introduction

"If Not Now, When?"

Gianni Vattimo and Michael Marder

The final sequence of the poignant film *Lemon Tree* (Eran Riklis, 2008), based on actual events, is symptomatic of the hidden dynamics of the Israeli–Palestinian conflict. Israel's defense minister, who moves with his family to a new house on the occupied West Bank, deems the neighboring lemon grove of a Palestinian widow, Salma Zidane (Hiam Abbass), a security threat. His legal team files a motion to uproot Zidane's lemon trees in a case that reaches Israel's Supreme Court. The Court's decision is truly Kafkaesque: the trees are to be "pruned" to a height that would not exceed 50 centimeters off the ground in order to allow for an unobstructed view of the territory. In the final sequence we see the defense minister standing in front of a concrete wall separating his backyard from his Palestinian neighbor's grove. As the camera zooms into and sweeps over the wall—in a cinematic transgression of boundaries, "separation fences," and apartheid lines—it reveals Salma Zidane wistfully walking on the other side, amidst the maimed stumps of her trees.

The symbolic identification between the lemon grove and the stateless Palestinian people is obvious. But what does the Supreme Court decision mean in this context? Does it not imply that, whenever they are not altogether uprooted, expelled from their houses, and forcibly removed from their land, Palestinians find themselves in an impossible situation of *barely remaining* alive, no more than 50 centimeters off the ground? Does it not suggest that, even if they are to keep the roots tethering them to Palestine, their growth will be stunted and they will bear no fruit? The concrete wall casts everything around it in its own image, rendering the world it divides uninhabitable and hence world-less, lifeless, and sterile. And so, the film reconfigures the entire Palestinian–Israeli conflict as a standoff between the inorganic (and deadening) force concentrated in the wall and the vanishing presence of the organic realm condensed in the lemon trees. The Israeli national myth of "having made the desert bloom" reveals the dark underside that has made it possible in the first place: Zionism has turned, and continues to turn, blossoming tree groves into a desert.

Lemon tree stumps are the traces of the trees themselves, reminders of something that is no longer there but that, nonetheless, persists in its virtual effects. Like the mangled corpses of soldiers and horses strewn over a battlefield—a scene which Maurice Blanchot described so vividly in "The Moment of My Death" and Jacques Derrida later analyzed in his *Demeure*[1]—they are the ruined witnesses of past violence.

Testimonies that silently appeal to the survivors—the stumps and the corpses are the places where the loss of immediate biological life is converted into a traumatic memory, which lives on as a sign of violence, both past and all too present.

The trace of survival and the vanishing presence we find in *Lemon Tree* are also the threads that bind together two twentieth-century philosophical movements: deconstruction and weak thought, *pensiero debole*. Against the "strong" categories of metaphysics, with their conceptual border police and ideal separation fences between the "inside" and the "outside," deconstruction and weak thought embrace the fragile, threatened, finite existence on the point of disappearing, neither fully present nor entirely absent. For Derrida, a trace—or what Santiago Zabala calls "the remains of Being," constituting the possibility of emancipation from metaphysics[2]—is neither in nor outside of Being. On the verge of disappearing, it is always "under erasure," *sous rature*.[3]

At the bottom of mutually incompatible land claims simmers the desire to erase the trace of the Other, along with the traces of this very erasure. The Israeli Occupation endeavors to reduce the Palestinian trace to a pure absence, while claiming for itself the honor of strong and undisputed historical origins, the genuine (biblical) rootedness in the Land of Israel. Indeed, in the mindset of Zionism, the two things are inseparable: the presence of Jewish origins and the absence of Palestinian traces are two sides of the same counterfeit coin. Still, as tree stumps, expropriated houses, and abandoned Arab villages mutely testify, the most endangered, quasi-absent presence is the one that persists most stubbornly. Granted: the trees, like the people who care for them, are vulnerable in their exposure to violence and the possibility of being felled or uprooted. But, with time, the trace, like a ghost into which Derrida transfigured it in his later work,[4] comes to haunt those who think they have erased it.

Although they both work with limit concepts, deconstruction and weak thought are not satisfied with "sitting on the fence" (or, in this case, on the Wall). Far from purely academic exercises, their forays are practical and political interventions, responding to the singular demands of justice. Derrida once said that deconstruction is the possibility of justice. He had in mind deconstruction's extreme sensitivity to the context of its engagements, as much as to the subtle forms which violence can assume, for instance, in the name of universality. To deconstruct Zionism is, therefore, to demand justice for its victims—not only for the Palestinians, who are suffering from it, but also for the anti-Zionist Jews, "erased" from the officially consecrated account of Zionist history. By deconstructing this ideology, we shed light on the context it strives to repress and on the violence it legitimizes with a mix of theological-metaphysical reasoning and affective appeals to historical guilt for the undeniably horrific persecution of Jewish people in Europe and elsewhere.

It is, of course, possible to appeal to justice without evoking deconstruction, which is not, in formal philosophical terms, the necessary condition of possibility for this demand. Why, then, deconstruct Zionism? Why now? And, in the first place, what does such a deconstruction entail?

Let us begin with the meaning of deconstruction as it bears on Zionism. There are two interrelated ways of hearing the injunction to deconstruct Zionism, both of them at play in the essays that comprise this volume. The first, and the more colloquial, sense is that of a radical ideology critique with its careful examination of all the presuppositions hidden in an "-ism." History matters: like other ideologies, Zionism was a historical construction, a more or less coherent project that assumed a vast array of forms, running the gamut from the religious to the secular. Deconstruction replays the history of Zionism backwards, teasing out its motivations, strategies, and above all the unstated preconditions for what is included in its doctrine (for instance, the dismissal, pre-1948, of the already existing non-Jewish inhabitants of Palestine in the slogan, "A land without a people for a people without a land").

The second, technical, meaning of deconstruction has to do with its specifically Derridian (and Heideggerian) connotations. Taken in this sense, deconstruction is something more than a good old ideology critique: it is a critique of "the metaphysics of presence." We can succinctly explain the metaphysics of presence starting from the philosophy of Heidegger, according to whom every epoch in the history of Western thought named (and misnamed) Being as Ideas, the unmoved mover, substance, God, subject, the thing-in-itself, Spirit, and so forth. Every single item on this brief philosophical list is endowed with a presumably eternal, immutable, originary, and unitary character, even when, like Hegel's Spirit, it makes itself known in and through actual history. These same characteristics become the targets of deconstruction that insists on irreducible transience and dispersion, from which even the most entrenched metaphysical certainties do not escape. Derrida, in his turn, goes a step further than Heidegger: rather than "rectify" the sins of previous philosophers and call metaphysical constructs by their name (Being), he draws attention to the porous boundaries between Being and non-Being, presence and absence, most emblematically in the figures of the trace and the specter.

Zionism is a relatively recent political variation on the theme of metaphysics. In all its forms it takes the concept of the Jewish people and its connection to the "Land of Israel" to be transhistorical and unitary, temporary exiles notwithstanding. Proclaiming Jerusalem to be the "eternal and indivisible" capital of the State of Israel, it willfully neglects the city's historicity, its changing architectural, demographic, and political realities along the centuries. Zionism further presupposes the return of the Jewish people to their "historical Homeland" and, thus, a recovery—political and otherwise—of the lost unity of the exiled.

Deconstruction, on the other hand, highlights the diasporic condition of all beings, which it encodes in the term "dissemination."[5] It embraces spatial scatter as much as temporal dispersion. Both diaspora and dissemination name, according to their Greek and Latin provenances, the splitting and spreading of the seed, a primordial multiplicity not gatherable into the totality of the one State, People, History, Tradition, and so on. Nothing and no one is left untouched by the diasporic condition of dispersion, inherent in places, events, things, collective and individual subjects, and texts. Even when not openly anti-Zionist, deconstruction, insofar as it is a critique of the metaphysics of presence, rejects the assumptions Zionism takes to be untouchable. Just as deconstruction is the possibility of justice, so it is the necessity of a diaspora, without return to the fictitious sameness of the origin.

To be sure, the so-called progressive strands of Zionism acknowledge the need for an evolution in the Jewish relation to the "Holy Land," as they realize that, without reinventing itself and adjusting to the changing historical and geo-political realities, their ideology runs the risk of quickly becoming outdated and irrelevant. What they never call into question is the belonging of the Jewish people to Israel, and of Israel—with or without the areas that have now been formally recognized by the UN as the State of Palestine—to the Jewish people. The Being, as much as the destiny, of the Jewish people and that of the State of Israel are assumed to be one and the same.

To deconstruct Zionism in this second sense of deconstruction is to interrogate, at once with rigor and with intense personal and political commitment, the myths of national-religious-ethnic origins, of an Odysseus-like return to the place from which ancestors were exiled, and of the unshatterable unity of a people underlying the diversity of its exilic identities. It is, also, to scrutinize the modes of representation that, in lieu of the impossible full presence (especially that of "all" the Jews within the physical boundaries of the State of Israel that are purposefully kept indeterminate through Jewish settlement activity), deign to speak in the name of world Jewry as though it were a monolithic construct, wedded, whether it wants this or not, to a small Middle Eastern state.

Deconstructing Zioninsm entails—let us not forget—unearthing the traces of self-critique, if not an auto-deconstruction, in the Zionist movement itself, which is not and has never been a homogeneous ideology, just as the Jewish theological, intellectual, and political traditions have not been uniform, univocal, or unambiguous. (Suffice it to recall, in this context, a biblical story of ancient political disagreements. The last of the Judges, Samuel, vehemently disapproved plans for the creation of a kingdom put forth by the Israelites who wanted to be like all the other nations, with a king of their own. Samuel took these proposals to be heretical: they stood for failures to recognize the true Lordship of God. Unable to resist the monarchists, he prophesied that they would get a human king who would plunder their houses, rape their women, and make their lives utterly miserable.[6] How is it possible to avoid the temptation to see in the institution of a Jewish kingship a precursor to the nineteenth- and twentieth-century Zionist plea for a Jewish State?) Finally, to deconstruct Zionism is to demand justice for the Palestinian victims of the metaphysical, onto-theological, and neoliberal state machinery, invested in keeping *its* despised, destitute, denigrated Others stateless and hence traceless.

We can already anticipate some of the criticisms that will be addressed to any attempt to deconstruct Zionism. These are likely to fall into three broad categories:

1. *A focus on Zionism but not on Palestinian ideologies is one-sided and therefore asymmetrical. It lacks the neutrality that marks scholarly research.* – But how can one champion a neutral and symmetrical scholarly approach in situations where conditions on the ground are decidedly asymmetrical and become ever more so day-by-day? What is symmetrical about a confrontation between a powerful state and a stateless people? More often than not, scholarly neutrality is but a subterfuge, a cover of neutralization and depoliticization (as Carl Schmitt

would have it[7]) that creates the desired "every story has at least two sides" effect, allowing injustice to proceed with impunity. This is a textbook case of such a stratagem. The plea for neutrality is itself a part of the metaphysical narrative to be deconstructed.

2. *Scrutinizing Israeli Zionism, instead of discussing the oppression prevalent in other states in the region, is unfair. Israel is singled out for no apparent reason from among Middle Eastern regimes, many of them much worse than it.* – Curiously, the proponents of this argument would not have a problem endorsing Israel's exceptionalism: for instance, when it becomes the first country in the world to refuse the request to appear before the UN Human Rights review.[8] At once a state among other states and a unique state above international law, it is ideally rendered immune to criticism. Our task is to single it out precisely because it is a state that is quite exceptional, though not in the same sense as those making this claim have in mind. Israel's exceptionalism hinges on the fact that it was a state created thanks to a massive displacement of Arab populations that inhabited the area under the British Mandate and an equally massive influx of immigrants from war-torn Europe and the Middle East. A state that was constituted, presumably, to atone for one of the biggest tragedies of the twentieth century and that, without delay, perpetrated countless crimes against its Palestinian neighbors. A state that, to this day, re-founds and legitimizes itself based on a mix of millennia-old theodicy and a frozen mold of nineteenth-century European-type nationalism, which has not survived in this form anywhere in Europe. A state that proclaims itself to be the only democracy in the Middle East, while systematically treating its Arab members as third-class citizens and keeping the imprisonment of some of its Jewish citizens secret. We should add that all metaphysically inspired ideologies deserve to be deconstructed; the deconstruction of Zionism does not stand in the way of deconstructing other types of nationalism, racism, etc. No one dreams of objecting to a critical analysis of Italian fascism, taken to be an example of twentieth-century totalitarianism, as an unfair "singling out" of Mussolini's Italy, when Nazi Germany was far more lethal.

3. *Critique of Zionism is rooted in contemporary anti-Semitism, practiced by dissident Jews and non-Jews alike. To criticize Israel is to hate the Jewish people and to prepare the grounds for a new Shoah.* – First, the biggest threat to the well-being and security of Israeli Jews (and, often, by implication of Jews who live elsewhere in the world and are assumed to be the supporters of Israeli policies) is neither Iran nor Syria; it is the State of Israel itself. Aside from Israel's belligerent behavior on the regional and international arenas, its Occupation of Palestine not only makes the lives of people who live under this regime impossible, but is also unsustainable as it drains public resources for the purpose of providing "security" to fanatical settlers. It is imperative to deconstruct Zionism not out of hatred but out of intense concern for the Jewish Israelis, who are set on a path of self-destruction in oppressing and decimating a neighboring Palestinian population. Second, the conflation of Zionism and Judaism is a gross mistake: many Jews, in Israel and outside its boundaries, are non- or anti-Zionist, while

many Zionists are not practicing Jews. Even a conflation of Zionism and the current State of Israel is unjustifiable, as many in the history of the Zionist movement considered the possibility of creating a Jewish state elsewhere—for instance, in East Africa. Third, the project of deconstructing Zionism is not just critique; it is, as the subtitle of our collection suggests, an exercise in unraveling a political metaphysics. Zionism is a metaphysically inflected ideological and political worldview, not a religion and, most definitely, not an ethnicity. To criticize it is no different from criticizing, say, Portuguese imperialism in the period between the fifteenth century and the end of the Salazarist New State in 1974 (except that Portuguese imperialism is already a thing of the past, while Zionist Occupation is still ongoing). A deconstruction of Portuguese imperialism, with its own metaphysical and Messianic penchant, is certainly not rooted in anyone's hatred of the Portuguese people. Why, then, would a philosophical critique of Zionism be associated with the deplorable ideology of anti-Semitism?

Finally, why now? The question echoes that of a Jewish sage, Rabbi Hillel, who famously asked: "If I am not for myself, then who will be for me? And if I am only for myself, then what am I? And if not now, when?"[9] A question of ethical commitment, "Why now?" receives a response in the form of another question: "If not now, when?" Deconstructing Zionism is a matter of urgency, because the past, present, and future victims of Zionist oppression demand justice. We must—ontologically as much as ethically—*be for them*. Only then can we hope to be anything at all.

Notes

1 Jacques Derrida, *Demeure: Fiction and Testimony*, trans. Elizabeth Rottenberg (Stanford, CA: Stanford University Press, 2000).
2 Santiago Zabala, *The Remains of Being: Hermeneutic Ontology After Metaphysics* (New York: Columbia University Press, 2009).
3 Jacques Derrida, *Of Grammatology*, trans. Gayatri C. Spivak (Baltimore, MD: Johns Hopkins University Press, 1997).
4 Jacques Derrida, *Specters of Marx: The State of the Debt, the Work of Mourning, and the New International*, trans. Peggy Kamuf (New York: Routledge, 1994).
5 Jacques Derrida, *Dissemination*, trans. Barbara Johnson (Chicago, IL and London: University of Chicago Press, 1981).
6 See I Samuel 8.10–18: "Samuel told all the words of the Lord to the people who were asking him for a king. He said, 'This is what the king who will reign over you will claim as his rights: He will take your sons and make them serve with his chariots and horses, and they will run in front of his chariots. Some he will assign to be commanders of thousands and commanders of fifties, and others to plow his ground and reap his harvest, and still others to make weapons of war and equipment for his chariots. He will take your daughters to be perfumers and cooks and bakers. He will take the best of your fields and vineyards and olive groves and give them to his attendants. He will take a tenth of your grain and of your vintage and give it to his

officials and attendants. Your male and female servants and the best of your cattle and donkeys he will take for his own use. He will take a tenth of your flocks, and you yourselves will become his slaves. When that day comes, you will cry out for relief from the king you have chosen, but the Lord will not answer you in that day.'"

7 Cf. Carl Schmitt, "The Age of Neutralizations and Depoliticizations," in *The Concept of the Political*, Expanded Edition, trans. G. Schwab (Chicago, IL and London: The University of Chicago Press, 2007).

8 Phoebe Greenwood, "Israel Refuses to Appear Before UN Human Rights Review," the *Telegraph*, January 29, 2013. http://www.telegraph.co.uk/news/worldnews/middleeast/israel/9834336/Israel-refuses-to-appear-before-UN-human-rights-review.html [date accessed August 28, 2013]

9 Ronald L. Eisenberg, *Essential Figures in the Talmud* (Plymouth: Jason Aronson, 2013), p. 91.

1

Anti-Semitism and its Transformations

Slavoj Žižek

Back in the 1930s, Hitler offered anti-Semitism as a narrative explanation of the troubles experienced by ordinary Germans: unemployment, moral decay, social unrest—behind all this stands the Jew, i.e. the "Jewish plot" made everything clear by way of providing a simple "cognitive mapping." Does today's hatred of multiculturalism and of the immigrant threat not function in a homologous way? Strange things are happening, financial meltdowns occur, which affect our daily lives, but are experienced as totally opaque. The rejection of multiculturalism introduces a false clarity into the situation: it is the foreign intruders who are disturbing our way of life. There is thus an interconnection between the rising anti-immigrant tide in Western countries (which reached a peak in Anders Behring Breivik's killing spree) and the ongoing financial crisis. Clinging to ethnic identity serves as a protective shield against the traumatic fact of being caught in the whirlpool of non-transparent financial abstraction. The true "foreign body," which cannot be assimilated, is ultimately the infernal self-propelling machine of the Capital itself.

There are good reasons to think of Breivik's ideological self-justification as well as of reactions to his murderous act. The manifesto of this Christian "Marxist hunter" who killed more than 70 people in Oslo is precisely *not* a case of a madman's rambling; it is simply a consequent exposition of "Europe's crisis," which serves as the (more or less) implicit foundation of the rising anti-immigrant populism, the very inconsistencies of which are symptomatic of the inner contradictions of this view. The first thing that cannot but strike the eye is how Breivik constructs his enemy out of the combination of three elements (Marxism, multiculturalism, Islamism), each of which belongs to a different political space (Marxist radical Left, multiculturalist liberalism, Islamic religious fundamentalism). The old fascist habit of attributing to the enemy mutually exclusive features ("Bolshevik-plutocratic Jewish plot" translates into the Bolshevik radical Left, plutocratic capitalism, and ethnic-religious identity) returns here in a new guise. Even more indicative is the way Breivik's self-designation shuffles the cards of the radical right-wing ideology. Breivik advocates Christianity, but remains a secular agnostic. Christianity is for him merely a cultural construct to oppose Islam. He is anti-feminist and thinks women should be discouraged from pursuing higher education, but he favors a "secular" society, supports abortion, and declares himself pro-gay. Furthermore, Breivik combines Nazi features (also in part—for example, his sympathy for Saga, the Swedish pro-Nazi folk-singer) with the hatred for Hitler: one of his heroes is Max Manus, the leader of the Norwegian anti-Nazi resistance. Breivik is not so much racist as anti-Muslim: all his hatred is focused on the Muslim threat. And, last but not least, Breivik is anti-Semitic, but pro-Israel, since the State of Israel is the first defense line against the Muslim expansion. He even wants to see the Jerusalem Temple rebuilt. His view is that Jews are OK as long as there aren't too many of them, or, as he wrote in his "Manifesto":

> There is no Jewish problem in Western Europe (with the exception of the UK and France) as we only have 1 million in Western Europe, whereas 800,000 out of these 1 million live in France and the UK. The US, on the other hand, with more than 6 million Jews (600% more than Europe) actually has a considerable Jewish problem.

His figure thus embodies the ultimate paradox of a Zionist Nazi. But how is this possible?

A key is provided by the reactions of the European Right to Breivik's attack. Its mantra was that, in condemning his murderous act, we should not forget that he addressed "legitimate concerns about genuine problems" which mainstream politics is failing to address, such as the corrosion of Europe by Islamicization and multiculturalism. Or, to quote *The Jerusalem Post*, we should use the Oslo tragedy "as an opportunity to seriously re-evaluate policies for immigrant integration in Norway and elsewhere."[1] (Incidentally, it would be nice to hear a similar appreciation of the Palestinian acts of terror, going along the lines of "these acts of terror should serve as an opportunity to re-evaluate the Israeli politics.") A reference to Israel is, of course, implicit in this evaluation: a "multicultural" Israel has no chance to survive, and apartheid is the only realistic option. The price for this properly perverse Zionist–rightist pact is that, in order to justify the claim to Palestine, one has to acknowledge retroactively the line of argumentation, which was previously, in earlier European history, used against the Jews. The implicit deal is that "we are ready to acknowledge your intolerance towards other cultures in your midst if you acknowledge our right not to tolerate Palestinians in our midst." The tragic irony of this implicit deal is that, in the European history of the last centuries, Jews themselves were the first "multiculturalists": their problem was how to survive with their culture intact in places where another culture was predominant. (Actually, one should note here that, in the 1930s, in direct response to Nazi anti-Semitism, Ernest Jones, the main agent of the conformist gentrification of psychoanalysis, engaged in weird reflections on the percentage of foreign population a national body can tolerate in its midst without putting in danger its own identity, and thereby accepting the Nazi problematic.) At the end of this road lies the extreme possibility which should in no way be discarded—that of a "historic compromise" between Zionists and Muslim fundamentalists.

But what if we are entering a new era where this new reasoning will impose itself? What if Europe should accept the paradox that its democratic openness is based on exclusion, since there is "no freedom for the enemies of freedom," as Robespierre put it long ago? In principle this is, of course, true, but it is here that one has to be very specific. In a way, Breivik was right in his choice of target: he didn't attack the foreigners but those within his own community who were too tolerant towards the intruding foreigners. The problem is not the foreigners; it is our own (European) identity. Although the ongoing crisis of the European Union appears as a crisis of economy and finances, it is in its fundamental dimension an *ideologico-political* crisis. The failure of referendums about the EU constitution a couple of years ago gave a clear signal that voters perceived the EU as a "technocratic" economic union, lacking any vision which could mobilize people (until the recent protests, the only ideology able to mobilize people was the anti-immigrant defense of Europe).

Recent outbursts of homophobia in East European post-communist states should also give us a pause to think. In early 2011 there was a gay parade in Istanbul where thousands paraded in peace, with no violence or other disturbances. In gay parades that took place at the same time in Serbia and Croatia (Belgrade, Split), police were not able to protect the participants who were ferociously attacked by thousands of violent Christian fundamentalists. *These* fundamentalists, not Turkey, stand for the true threat to European legacy. So, when the EU basically blocked Turkey's entry, we should have raised the obvious question: What about applying the same rules to Eastern Europe? (Not to mention the weird fact that the main force behind the anti-gay movement in Croatia is the Catholic Church, well known for numerous paedophiliac scandals.)

It is crucial to locate anti-Semitism in this series, as one of the elements alongside other forms of racism, sexism, homophobia, etc. In order to ground its Zionist politics, the State of Israel is here making a catastrophic mistake: it decided to downplay, if not outright ignore, the so-called "old" (traditional European) anti-Semitism, focusing instead on the "new" and allegedly "progressive" anti-Semitism masked as the critique of the Zionist politics of the State of Israel. Along these lines, Bernard Henri-Levy (in his *The Left in Dark Times*) recently claimed that the anti-Semitism of the twenty-first century will be "progressive" or there will be none. Brought to its logical conclusion, this thesis compels us to turn around the old Marxist interpretation of anti-Semitism as a mystified/displaced anti-capitalism, where, instead of blaming the capitalist system, the rage is focused on a specific ethnic group accused of corrupting the system. For Henri-Levy and his partisans, today's anti-capitalism is a disguised form of anti-Semitism.

This unspoken but no less efficient prohibition against attacking the "old" anti-Semitism is taking place at the very moment when the "old" anti-Semitism is returning all around Europe, especially in post-communist East European countries. We can observe a similar weird alliance in the US: how can the US Christian fundamentalists, who are, as it were, by nature anti-Semitic, now passionately support the Zionist policy of the State of Israel? There is only one solution to this enigma. It is not that the US fundamentalists changed, it is that Zionism itself, in its hatred of the Jews who do not fully identify with the politics of the State of Israel, paradoxically became anti-Semitic, i.e., constructed the figure of the Jew who doubts the Zionist project along anti-Semitic lines. Israel is playing a dangerous game here: Fox News, the main US voice of the radical Right and a staunch supporter of Israeli expansionism, recently had to demote Glen Beck, its most popular host, whose comments were becoming openly anti-Semitic.[2]

The standard Zionist argument against the critics of the policies of the State of Israel is that, of course, like every other state, the State of Israel can and should be judged and eventually criticized, but that the critics of Israel misuse the justified critique of Israeli policy for anti-Semitic purposes. When the unconditional Christian fundamentalist supporters of the Israeli politics reject leftist critiques of Israeli policies, their implicit line of argumentation is best rendered by a wonderful cartoon published in July 2008 in the Viennese daily *Die Presse*. It shows two stocky Nazi-looking Austrians, one of them holding in his hands a newspaper and commenting to his friend: "Here you can see again how a totally justified anti-Semitism is being misused for a cheap critique of Israel!" *These* are today's allies of the State of Israel. Jewish critics of the State of Israel are regularly dismissed as self-hating Jews; however, are the true self-hating Jews, those who secretly hate the true greatness of the Jewish nation, not precisely the Zionists making a pact with anti-Semites? How did we end up in such a weird situation?

The fantasmatic status of anti-Semitism is clearly designated by the statement attributed to Hitler: "We have to kill the Jew within us." A. B. Yehoshua provided an adequate comment to this statement:

> This devastating portrayal of the Jew as a kind of amorphous entity that can invade the identity of a non-Jew without his being able to detect or control it stems from the feeling that Jewish identity is extremely flexible, precisely because it is structured like a sort of atom whose core is surrounded by virtual electrons in a changing orbit.[3]

In this sense, Jews are effectively the *objet petit a* of the Gentiles. They are what is "in Gentiles more than Gentiles themselves"—not another subject that I encounter in front of me but an alien, a foreign intruder, *within* me, what Lacan called *lamella*, the amorphous intruder of infinite plasticity, an undead "alien" monster who can never be pinned down to a determinate form. In this sense, Hitler's statement tells more than it wants to say: against its intention, it confirms that the Gentiles need the anti-Semitic figure of the "Jew" in order to maintain their identity.[4] It is thus not only that "the Jew is within us"; what Hitler fatefully forgot to add is that *he, the anti-Semite, his identity, is also in the Jew*.[5] What does this paradoxical entwinement mean for the destiny of anti-Semitism?

One of the supreme ironies of the history of anti-Semitism is that Jews can stand for both poles of an opposition: they are stigmatized as upper class (rich merchants) and low class (filthy), as too intellectual and too earthly (sexual predators), as lazy and workaholics. Sometimes they stand for the stubborn attachment to their particular life-form which prevents them from becoming full citizens of the state they live in; sometimes they stand for a "homeless" and uprooted universal cosmopolitanism, indifferent towards all particular ethnic form. The focus changes with different historical epochs. In the era of the French Revolution, the Jews were condemned as too particularist, as they continued to stick to their identity, rejecting the need to become abstract citizens like everyone else. In late nineteenth century, with the rise of imperialist patriotism, the accusation is turned around, and Jews become all too "cosmopolitan," lacking all roots.

The key change in the history of Western anti-Semitism occurred with their political emancipation (the granting of civil rights), which followed the French Revolution. In the early modernity, the pressure on them was to convert to Christianity, and the problem was: Can one trust them? Did they really convert, or do they secretly continue to practice their rituals? However, in the later nineteenth century, a shift occurs which culminates in the Nazi anti-Semitism. Conversion is now out of the question, meaningless. Why? For the Nazis, the guilt of the Jews is directly rooted in their biological constitution. One does not have to prove that they are guilty, as they are guilty solely by being Jews. The question remains: Why?

The key is provided by the sudden rise, in the Western ideological imaginary, of the figure of the wandering eternal Jew in the age of Romanticism, i.e., precisely when, in real life, with the explosion of capitalism, features attributed to Jews expanded to the whole of society (since commodity exchange became hegemonic). It was thus at the very moment when Jews were deprived of their specific properties, which made it easy to distinguish them from the rest of the population, and when the "Jewish question" was "resolved" at the political level by the formal emancipation of the Jews (i.e. by granting to Jews the same rights as to all other "normal" Christian citizens) that their "curse" was inscribed into their very being. They were no longer ridiculous misers and usurers but demoniac heroes of eternal damnation, haunted by an unspecified and unspeakable guilt, condemned to wander around, and longing to find redemption in death. So it was precisely when the specific figure of the Jew disappeared that the *absolute* Jew emerged, and this transformation conditioned the shift of anti-Semitism from theology to race. Their damnation was their race; they were not guilty for what they did (exploit Christians, murder their children, rape their women, or, ultimately, betray and murder Christ), but for what they were. Is it necessary to add that this shift laid the foundations for the Holocaust, for the physical annihilation of the Jews as the only appropriate final solution of their "problem"? Insofar as Jews were identified by a series of their properties, the goal was to convert them, to turn them into Christians, but, from the moment that Jewishness concerns their very being, only annihilation can resolve the "Jewish question."

The true mystery of anti-Semitism, however, is why it is such a constant. Why does it persist through all historical mutations? Perhaps this is somewhat similar to what Marx said about Homer: the true mystery to be explained is not its origins, its original form (how Homer's poetry is rooted in early Greek society) but why it persists in its supreme artistic charm today, long after the social conditions that gave birth to it disappeared. It is easy to date the original moment of European anti-Semitism. It all started not in Ancient Rome but in eleventh- and twelfth-century Europe, which was awakening from the inertia of the "Dark Ages" and experiencing a fast growth in market exchange and the greater prominence of money. At that precise point, "the Jew" emerged as the enemy: the usurper, the parasitic intruder who disturbs the harmonious social edifice. Theologically, this moment is also the moment of what

Jacques le Goff called the "birth of the *Purgatorium*," the idea that the choice is not only between Heaven and Hell but that there has to be a third, mediating, place, where one can make a deal, pay for one's sins (if they are not too great) with a determined amount of repentance—money again!

So where are we today? Asked about his anti-Semitism, the Croat nationalist rock-singer Marko Perkovic Thompson said in an interview: "I have nothing against them and I did nothing to them. I know that Jesus Christ also did nothing against them, but still they hanged him on the cross." This is how anti-Semitism works today: it is not we who have anything against the Jews; rather, it is how the Jews themselves are. On top of it all, we are witnessing the final version of anti-Semitism, which reached the extreme point of self-relatedness. The privileged role of Jews in the establishment of the sphere of the "public use of reason" hinges on their subtraction from every state power. Theirs is the position of the "part of no-part" in every organic nation-state community, and it is this position, not the abstract-universal nature of their monotheism, that makes them the immediate embodiment of universality. No wonder, then, that, with the establishment of the Jewish nation-state, a new figure of the Jew emerged: a Jew resisting identification with the State of Israel, refusing to accept the State of Israel as his true home, a Jew who "subtracts" himself from this State, and who includes the State of Israel among the states towards which he insists on maintaining a distance, to live in their interstices. And it is *this* uncanny Jew who is the object of what one cannot but designate as "Zionist anti-Semitism," the foreign excess disturbing the community of the nation-state. These Jews, the "Jews of the Jews themselves," worthy successors of Spinoza, are today the only Jews who continue to insist on the "public use of reason," refusing to submit their reasoning to the "private" domain of the nation-state.

This brings us to the political stakes and consequences of Zionist anti-Semitism. On August 2, 2009, after cordoning off a part of the Arab neighborhood of Sheikh Jarrah in East Jerusalem, Israeli police evicted two Palestinian families (more than 50 people) from their homes and allowed Jewish settlers to move immediately into the empty houses. Although Israeli police cited a ruling by the country's Supreme Court, the evicted Arab families had been living there for more than 50 years. The event, which, rather exceptionally, did attract the attention of the world media, is part of a much larger and mostly ignored ongoing process. Five months earlier, on March 1, 2009, it was reported[6] that the Israeli government had drafted plans to build more than 70,000 new housing units in Jewish settlements in the occupied West Bank. If implemented, the plans could increase the number of settlers in the Palestinian territories by about 300,000—a move that would not only severely undermine the chances of a viable Palestinian state, but also hamper the everyday life of Palestinians. A government spokesman dismissed the report, arguing that the plans were of limited relevance: the actual construction of new homes in the settlements required the approval of the Defense Minister and the Prime Minister. However, 15,000 of the planned units have already been fully approved, with an additional 20,000 of the planned units lying in settlements that are far from the "green line" that separates

Israel from the West Bank, i.e., in the areas Israel cannot expect to retain in any future peace deal with the Palestinians. The conclusion is obvious: while paying lip-service to the two-state solution, Israel is busy creating the situation on the ground which will render a two-state solution *de facto* impossible. The dream that underlies this politics is best rendered by the wall that separates a settler's town from the Palestinian town on a nearby hill somewhere in the West Bank. The Israeli side of the wall is painted with the image of the countryside beyond the wall, but without the Palestinian town, depicting just nature, grass, trees and so on. Is this not ethnic cleansing at its purest, imagining the outside beyond the wall as it should be, namely empty, virginal, waiting to be settled?

This process is sometimes covered in the guise of cultural gentrification. On October 28, 2008, the Israeli Supreme Court ruled that the Simon Wiesenthal Center could build its long-planned Center for Human Dignity, the Museum of Tolerance, on a contested site in the middle of Jerusalem. (Who but) Frank Gehry will design the vast complex consisting of a general museum, a children's museum, a theater, conference center, library, gallery and lecture halls, cafeterias, etc. The museum's declared mission will be to promote civility and respect among different segments of the Jewish community and among people of all faiths—the only obstacle (overrun by the Supreme Court's ruling) being that the museum site served as Jerusalem's main Muslim cemetery until 1948 (the Muslim community appealed to the Supreme Court that museum construction would desecrate the cemetery, which allegedly contained the bones of Muslims killed during the Crusades of the twelfth and thirteenth centuries).[7] This dark spot wonderfully enacts the hidden truth of this multi-confessional project: it is a place celebrating tolerance, open to all, but protected by the Israeli cupola, which ignores the subterranean victims of intolerance, as if one needs a little bit of intolerance to create the space for true tolerance.

And as if this were not enough, as if one should repeat a gesture to make its message clear, there is another, even vaster, similar project going on in Jerusalem. Israel is quietly carrying out a $100 million, multi-year development plan in the so-called "holy basin," the place of some of the most significant religious and national heritage sites just outside the walled Old City, as part of an effort to strengthen the status of Jerusalem as its capital. "The plan, parts of which have been outsourced to a private group that is simultaneously buying up Palestinian property for Jewish settlement in East Jerusalem, has drawn almost no public or international scrutiny."[8] As part of the plan, garbage dumps and wastelands are being cleared and turned into lush gardens and parks, now already accessible to visitors who can walk along new footpaths and take in the majestic views, along with new signs and displays that point out significant points of Jewish history. Conveniently, many of the "unauthorized" Palestinian houses had to be demolished to create the space for the redevelopment of the area.

The "holy basin" is an infinitely complicated landscape, dotted with shrines and still hidden treasures of the three major monotheistic religions, so the official argument is that its improvement is for everyone's benefit—Jews, Muslims, and Christians—since it involves restoration that will draw more visitors to an area of exceptional global interest that has long suffered neglect. However, as Hagit Ofran of Peace Now noted, the plan aimed to create "an ideological tourist park that will determine Jewish dominance in the area." Raphael Greenberg of Tel Aviv University put it even more bluntly: "The sanctity of the City of David is newly manufactured and is a crude amalgam of history, nationalism and quasi-religious pilgrimage ... the past is used to disenfranchise and displace people in the present." Another big religious venue, a "public" inter-faith space under the clear domination and protective cupola of Israel.

What does all this mean? To get at the true dimension of the news, it is sometimes enough to read two disparate news items together. Meaning emerges from their very link, like a spark, exploding from an electric short-circuit. On October 13, 2007, the Vatican's press representative Federico Lombardi confirmed that the Vatican had suspended a priest occupying a high place in Vatican hierarchy who, in an interview for Italian TV, publicly admitted his homosexuality, insisting that he doesn't feel in any sense guilty for practicing homosexuality. He was suspended because he broke the Church law. The obscenity of this message becomes clear the moment one juxtaposes it with the fact that hundreds of pedophiliac priests are not suspended, but a priest is suspended if he publicly admits his orientation. The message is unmistakable here: what matters is appearance, not reality.

On the very same day these reports hit the media (March 2), Hilary Clinton criticized the rocket fire from Gaza as "cynical," claiming: "There is no doubt that any nation, including Israel, cannot stand idly by while its territory and people are subjected to rocket attacks." But should the Palestinians stand idly by while land in the West Bank is taken from them day by day? When Israeli peace-loving liberals present their conflict with Palestinians in neutral "symmetrical" terms, admitting that there are extremists on both sides who reject peace, etc., one should ask a simple question: What goes on in the Middle East when *nothing goes on there* at the direct politico-military level (i.e. when there are no tensions, attacks, negotiations)? What goes on is the incessant slow work of taking the land from the Palestinians on the West Bank, the gradual strangling of the Palestinian economy, the parceling of their land, the building of new settlements, the pressure on Palestinian farmers to make them abandon their land (which goes from crop burning and religious desecration up to individual killings)—all this supported by a Kafkaesque network of legal regulations. Saree Makdisi, in *Palestine Inside Out: An Everyday Occupation*,[9] described how, although the Israeli Occupation of the West Bank is ultimately enforced by the armed forces, it is an "occupation by bureaucracy": its primary forms are application forms, title deeds, residency papers, and other permits. It is this micro-management of daily life that does the job of securing the slow but steadfast Israeli expansion. One has to ask for a permit in order to leave with one's family, to farm one's own land, to dig a well, to go to work, to school, to a hospital. One by one, Palestinians born in Jerusalem are thus stripped of the right to live there, prevented from earning a living, denied housing permits, etc.[10] Palestinians often use the problematic cliché of the Gaza Strip as "the greatest concentration camp in the world"; however, in the past year, this designation has come dangerously close to truth. This is the fundamental reality which makes all abstract "prayers for peace" obscene and hypocritical. The State of Israel is clearly engaged in a slow process, invisible, ignored by the media, a kind of underground digging of the mole, so that, one day, the world will awaken and realize that there is no more Palestinian West Bank, that the land is Palestinian-*frei*, and that we can only accept that fact. The map of the Palestinian West Bank already resembles a fragmented archipelago.

In the last months of 2008, when the attacks by illegal West Bank settlers on Palestinian farmers became a regular daily occurrence, the State of Israel tried to contain these excesses (the Supreme Court ordered the evacuation of some settlements, etc.); but, as many observers noted, these measures cannot but appear half-hearted, counteracting a politics which, at a deeper level, *is* the long-term politics of the State of Israel which massively violates the international treaties signed by Israel itself. The reply of the illegal settlers to the Israeli authorities is basically: we are doing the same thing as you, just more openly, so what right do you have to condemn us? And the answer of the State is basically: be patient, don't rush too much, we are doing what you want, just in a more moderate and acceptable way.

The same story seems to go on from 1948: while Israel accepts the peace conditions proposed by the international community, it bets that the peace plan will not work. The wild settlers sometimes sound like Brunhilde from the last act of Wagner's *Walkuere*, reproaching Wotan that, by counteracting his explicit order and protecting Siegmund, she was only realizing Wotan's own true desire which he was forced to renounce under external pressure, in the same way that the illegal settlers only realize the State's true desire it was forced to renounce because of the pressure of the international community. While condemning the open violent excesses of "illegal" settlements, the State of Israel promotes new "legal" West Bank settlements, continues to strangle the Palestinian economy, etc. A look at the continuous changes of the map of East Jerusalem, where the Palestinians are gradually encircled and their space sliced, tells it all. The condemnation of extra-statist anti-Palestinian violence obfuscates the true problem of *state* violence; the condemnation of "illegal" settlements obfuscates the illegality of the "legal" ones. Therein resides the two-facedness of the much-praised non-biased "honesty" of the Israeli Supreme Court. By way of occasionally passing a judgment in favor of the dispossessed Palestinians, proclaiming their eviction illegal, it guarantees the legality of the remaining majority of cases.

Consequently, in the Israel–Palestinian conflict also, *soyons realistes, demandons l'impossible!* If there is a lesson to be learned from the endlessly protracted negotiations, it is that the main obstacle to peace is precisely what is offered as a realistic solution, i.e. the two separate states. Although none of the two sides really wants it (Israel would probably prefer a little bit of West Bank that it is ready to cede to become a part of Jordan, and the Palestinians consider also the pre-1967 Israel as a part of their land), it is somehow accepted by both sides as the only feasible solution. What both sides exclude as an impossible dream is the simplest and most obvious solution—a bi-national secular state comprising all of Israel plus the occupied territories and Gaza. To those who dismiss the bi-national state as a utopian dream disqualified by the long history of hatred and violence, one should reply that, far from being utopian, *the bi-national state already is a fact*. The reality of today's Israel and West Bank is that it is one state (i.e. the entire territory is *de facto* controlled by one sovereign power, the

State of Israel), divided by internal borders, so that the task should rather be to abolish the apartheid and transform it into a secular democratic state.[11]

Furthermore, this entire topic is to be seen against the background of a long-term rearrangement of the political space in Western and Eastern Europe. Until recently, the political space of European countries was dominated by two main parties that addressed the entire electoral body: a Right-of-center party (Christian-Democrat, liberal-conservative, the people's party) and a Left-of-center party (socialist, social-democratic), with smaller parties addressing a narrower electorate (ecologists, communists, and so on). The latest electoral results in the West as well as in the East signal the gradual emergence of a different polarity. There is one predominant centerist party which stands for global capitalism as such, usually with a liberal cultural agenda, including tolerance towards abortions, gay rights, and religious and ethnic minorities. Opposing this party is an increasingly stronger anti-immigrant populist party, which, on its fringes, is accompanied by directly racist neofascist groups. The exemplary case here is Poland: after the disappearance of the ex-communists, the main parties are the "anti-ideological" centerist liberal party of the Prime Minister Donald Dusk and the conservative Christian party of the Kaczynski brothers. Similar tendencies are discernible in the Netherlands, Norway, Sweden, Hungary. How did we come to this?

After decades of the (promise of) a welfare state, when financial cuts were limited to short periods and sustained by a promise that things would soon return to normal, we are entering a new epoch in which the crisis—or, rather, a kind of economic state of emergency—with the need for all sorts of austerity measures (cutting benefits, diminishing free health and education services, making jobs more and more temporary, etc.) is permanent, turning into a constant, becoming simply a way of life. After the disintegration of the communist regimes in 1990, we entered a new era in which the predominant form of the exercise of state power became a depoliticized expert administration and coordination of interests. The only way to introduce passion into this field, to actively mobilize people, is through fear—fear of immigrants, fear of crime, fear of godless sexual depravity, fear of the excessive state (with its burden of high taxation and control), fear of ecological catastrophe, but also fear of harassment (political correctness is the exemplary liberal form of the politics of fear). Such a politics always relies on the manipulation of a paranoid *ochlos*, the frightening rallying of frightened men and women. This is why the big event of the first decade of the new millennium was that anti-immigration politics went mainstream and finally cut the umbilical cord that had connected them to far Right fringe parties. From France to Germany, from Austria to Holland, in the new spirit of pride at one's cultural and historical identity, the main parties now found it acceptable to stress that immigrants are guests who have to accommodate themselves to the cultural values that define the host society: "it is our country, love it or leave it."

Progressive liberals are, of course, horrified by such populist racism. But a closer look reveals how their multicultural tolerance and respect of (ethnic, religious, sexual) differences share with the anti-immigration advocates the need to keep others at a proper distance. The others are OK, I respect them, but they should not intrude too much into my own space. The moment they do it, they harass me with their smell, their dirty talk, their vulgar manners, their music, their cuisine, and so on. I fully support affirmative action for the blacks, but I am in no way ready to listen to loud rap music. What is increasingly emerging as the central human right in late capitalist societies is *the right not to be harassed*, which is the right to be kept at a safe distance from others. A terrorist whose deadly plans should be prevented and who belongs in Guantanamo, the empty zone exempted from the rule of law; a fundamentalist ideologist who should be silenced because he is spreading hatred; a parent, teacher, or priest who abuses and corrupts children—all these are toxic subjects who disturb my peace.

In today's market we find a whole series of products deprived of their malignant property: coffee without caffeine, cream without fat, beer without alcohol. And the list goes on: what about virtual sex as sex without sex, the Colin Powell doctrine of warfare with no casualties (on our side, of course) and warfare without warfare, the contemporary redefinition of politics as the art of expert administration, or politics without politics, up to today's tolerant liberal multiculturalism as an experience of the Other deprived of its Otherness—the decaffeinated Other who dances fascinating dances and has an ecologically sound holistic approach to reality, while features like wife-beating remain out of sight?

The mechanism of such neutralization was best formulated back in 1938 by Robert Brasillach, the French fascist intellectual condemned and shot in 1945, who saw himself as a "moderate" anti-Semite and invented the formula of "reasonable anti-Semitism":

> We grant ourselves permission to applaud Charlie Chaplin, a half Jew, at the movies; to admire Proust, a half Jew; to applaud Yehudi Menuhin, a Jew; and the voice of Hitler is carried over radio waves named after the Jew Hertz. ... We don't want to kill anyone, we don't want to organize any pogrom. But we also think that the best way to hinder the always unpredictable actions of instinctual anti-Semitism is to organize a reasonable anti-Semitism.[12]

Is this same attitude not at work in the way our governments are dealing with the "immigrant threat"? After righteously rejecting direct populist racism as "unreasonable" and unacceptable for our democratic standards, they endorse "reasonably" racist protective measures, or, as today's Brasillachs, some of them even Social Democrats, are telling us:

> We grant ourselves permission to applaud African and East European sportsmen, Asian doctors, Indian software programmers. We don't want to kill anyone, we don't want to organize any pogrom. But we also think that the best way to hinder the always unpredictable violent anti-immigrant defensive measures is to organize a reasonable anti-immigrant protection.

This vision of the detoxification of the Neighbor presents a clear passage from direct barbarism to barbarism with a human face. It practices the regression from the

Christian love of the Neighbor back to the pagan privileging of our tribe (Greeks, Romans, etc.) versus the barbarian Other. Even if it is cloaked as a defense of Christian values, it is itself the greatest threat to Christian legacy.

Notes

1 Editorial on "Norway's Challenge," July 24, 2011.
2 Another figure in this series of anti-Semitic Zionists is John Hagee, the founder and National Chairman of the Christian-Zionist organization Christians United for Israel. At the top of the standard Christian conservative agenda (Hagee sees the Kyoto Protocol as a conspiracy aimed at manipulating the US economy; in his bestselling novel *Jerusalem Countdown*, the Antichrist is the head of the European Union), Hagee has been to Israel 22 times and has met with every prime minister since Begin. However, despite his professed "Christian Zionist" beliefs and public support for the State of Israel, Hagee has made statements that definitely sound anti-Semitic: he has blamed the Holocaust on the Jews themselves; he has stated that Hitler's persecution was a "divine plan" to lead the Jews to form the modern state of Israel; he calls liberal Jews "poisoned" and "spiritually blind"; he admits that a pre-emptive nuclear attack on Iran that he favors will lead to the deaths of most Jews in Israel. (As a curiosity, he claims in *Jerusalem Countdown* that Hitler was born from "a lineage of accursed, genocidally murderous half-breed Jews.")
3 A. B. Yehoshua, "An Attempt to Identify the Root Cause of Antisemitism," *Azure* no. 32 (spring 2008), available online at http://azure.org.il/article.php?id=18 [date accessed August 7, 2013].
4 A taboo question should be raised: what does the fixation of Arab countries and worldwide Muslim communities on the State of Israel mean? It cannot be accounted for in terms of the real threat to the Arab nation (after all, Israel occupies a tiny piece of land), so its role is obviously symptomatic. When regimes as different as the utterly corrupt Saudi monarchy and the anti-establishment populist movement focus on the same enemy, an external intruder, does this not bear witness to a strategy of avoiding the true internal antagonism?
5 I am here, of course, paraphrasing Lacan's famous statement: "The picture is in my eye, but me, I am in the picture."
6 See Tobias Duck, "Israel Drafts West Bank Expansion Plans," *Financial Times*, March 2, 2009.
7 See Tom Tugend, "Israel's Supreme Court OKs Museum of Tolerance Jerusalem Project," *Observer*, October 29, 2008.
8 See Ethan Bronner and Isabel Kershner, "Parks Fortify Israel's Claim to Jerusalem," *New York Times*, May 9, 2009.
9 See Saree Makdisi, in *Palestine Inside Out: An Everyday Occupation* (New York: Norton, 2008).
10 We witnessed a similar oppression without (too much) open brutality in post-1968 Czechoslovakia. In his dissident classic *Normalization*, Milan Simecka described how, after 1968, the hardline communists enforced the "normalization" of the Czech population, their awakening from the dream of 1968 to crude socialist reality. There was little direct brutal pressure, since most of the job was done through the

gentle art of low-level everyday corruption and blackmail, in the style of: "You want your children to go to university? Then just sign a statement which will not even be published, saying that you were seduced in participating in 1968 events and that you now see it was a mistake." Is not something similar going on in our late capitalist liberal societies, where there is no open brutal pressure, just small everyday clear signals that it is better for your career not to overstep certain limits? There is nonetheless a key difference between late socialist corruption and our late capitalist corruption, a difference which concerns the status of appearance. What mattered in socialist regimes was maintaining the appearance—just recall the (deservedly) famous example of the vegetable store seller from Vaclav Havel's "Power of the Powerless," who obediently displays in the window of his store official propaganda slogans, although neither he nor his customers take them seriously. What matters is the gesture of obedience. In liberal capitalism, however, not only does nobody care (within certain limits, of course) what slogans one puts in the window, but also provocative ones are welcomed, if they help the sales. The market is the greatest ironizer. Recall how big companies sometimes use for publicity purposes ironic paraphrases of communist topics. One cannot imagine the authorities in state socialism doing the same with capitalist topics.

11 I owe this line of thought to Udi Aloni.
12 See Slavoj Žižek, *First as Tragedy, Then as Farce* (London and New York: Verso, 2009), 48.

2

How to Become an Anti-Zionist

Gianni Vattimo
Translated by Robert T. Valgenti

Despite what the President of the Italian Republic, Giorgio Napolitano, often repeats, one can be an anti-Zionist without being anti-Semitic. This is so not only because there are plenty of Jews in the world who take their tradition seriously without identifying it with the state of Israel, from which they continually dissociate themselves, but also because, as the non-Zionist Jews themselves teach, the richness of Jewish culture and its distinct presence in the spirit of the West and the modern world in general did not establish itself with the creation of the State of Israel, and in fact is seriously threatened by it. Today, it makes far more sense to repeat what one Jewish intellectual had the courage to say—that among all the harms produced by Hitler's politics and by the Holocaust, one can also list the creation of Israel as a Jewish state in 1948.

For many European intellectuals who came of age in the middle of the twentieth century, a reflection on Zionism appears in terms rather similar to those that shape the biography of Ilan Pappe.[1] It presents itself as the history of a sharing that turns into a progressive dissolution of a "constitutive" mythology—the very thing that today continues to be valued in the self-awareness of many Jews who remain tied to this mythology. We, namely Europeans who were born around the time of the Second World War, were raised—save for rare exceptions, as rare as those who remained fascists at the end of the 1940s—on the myth of the antifascist resistance and on the painful memory of the Holocaust. At the time immediately after the war in Italy, but I think generally in Europe, to be antifascists, democrats, and to stand behind the Jews and their struggle to return to their homeland, Palestine, was one and the same thing. Whoever knows Italian history in the second half of the twentieth century knows that only in recent years have the parties that refer back to the inheritance of fascism been "cleared," or in other words, readmitted to a place of honor by a political system that wanted to rebuild itself, including its right-wing components. In principle, this was done so that no one was excluded from the democratic dialogue, and yet more immediately for reasons of electoral advantage. It is also noteworthy that the re-emergence of "democratic" parties that no longer demonize the fascist legacy (a famous claim comes from Gianfranco Fini, then leader of the Italian Social Movement, and today President of the House of Deputies, who described Mussolini as the greatest statesman of the twentieth century) has not in a similar manner diminished the love for Israel in the opinion of the Italian public. Still today, even though Fini is the third in charge of the State and ex-fascists have for some time held government positions (along with the Northern League and Silvio Berlusconi), every once in a while the authoritative voices of politicians of every orientation clamour to propose laws that punish the denial of historical crimes, on the basis that even with the acceptance of fascism, the pro-Zionist sentiment remains largely dominant in Italian public consciousness. Moreover, with the help of many American films that have told the story of the return of the Jews to Palestine before and after 1948, the Zionist epic has for some time stood in the imagination of the Italian public as analogous to the epic of the antifascist resistance and, in its more spectacular aspects, something akin to the conquering of the West by nineteenth-century Yankees. This last "cinematographic" reference appears somewhat forced, but it comes to mind for good reason, since no viewer of Westerns, except in recent years, has ever been concerned with the fate of the Native Americans exterminated by the advance of the white settlers and their cowboys—in a way completely analogous to the absolute forgetting endured by the Palestinians in the epic of the birth of Israel.

It was precisely the discovery of the Nakba in his second year of high school—that is, of the "disaster" represented for the Palestinians by the ethnic cleansing exercised by Israel from 1948 onward (and up until today, I must add)—that pushed Ilan Pappe from his initial leftist Zionism to his current, and radical, polemic stance against Israel—against the leaders of Israel, but also against the Jewish State itself, the State, for which he would like to substitute, if he could, a secular, democratic and egalitarian state. It is here, with all of its differences, that the history of Western, often also decidedly "Atlantic" democratic intellectuals (or even convinced that the communist danger might still threaten Europe and therefore likely to approve without or with little reservation the imperialist politics of the United States), approximates that of Pappe. We started with a "Zionist" mythology—the right of Israel to have its own state, legitimized by the horror of the Shoah and by the apparent lack of democracy in the entire Middle East—and we have over time abandoned it precisely when we discovered the Nakba; that is, when we opened our eyes, or when they were opened, to the colonialist and nationalist (even racist) sin that remains like an original sin upon the foundation of the State of Israel.

As with all mythologies, this one too is not dissolved by simply taking note of the "true" nature of things. It was, and it is now for many of us, a complex process that involved the whole of our socio-political, and in the end also our ethical and religious, conceptions, such that even our long friendships are put into crisis, along with other aspects of our private lives (starting from a certain ostracism by the most official and mainstream mass media). Meanwhile, it is no coincidence that I recalled the Atlanticism that accompanies, well beyond the antifascist commitment, our spontaneous "Zionism" in the years after the war. The right of Israel to establish a state appeared to be directly tied to the destiny of Western democracy, or what the Voice of America was apt to call "the free world." As I am not writing a documentary autobiography of an ex-Zionist, but only searching to reconstruct the meaning and the motives behind my (and not only mine, as I think it is widely shared) present anti-Zionism, I will not try to stick to precise chronological terms. In addition, this anti-Zionism matured in me alongside the dissolution of my faith in the West and the "free world." On the one side, the end of the "American myth" was certainly decisive, which was by then totally accomplished in 1968, but that became crystal clear in 1989 with the fall of the Berlin Wall and the dissolution of the Soviet Union. In 1968 many of us held the conviction that Israeli Jews were constructing an authentic rather than a Stalinist form of socialism—that same conviction which led many Italian families on the Left (but not only) to send their own children to work on kibbutzes so that they might learn what democratic socialism is. What did we know or think then of the Palestinians who were driven out of their homes and their land? We more or less believed the slogan: a land without people for a people without a land. The Palestinians, literally, did not exist, as Pappe explains well in his autobiographical book. In the years that followed, we began to know the Palestinians as terrorists and suicide bombers: a desperate few turned fanatics by religious hatred, animated by blind anti-Semitic rage (I seem to remember that in recent years a French-Jewish intellectual—I believe it was André Glucksmann—had even spoken about them as an example of lived nihilism, a sort of pure and simple incarnation of Evil).

For a long time there was a story that in Nasser's Egypt ex-Nazi officers were all the rage as instructors determined to export the *Shoah* to the Middle East as well. Therefore, once again, one had to be a Zionist in order to be an antifascist. But with the fall of the Berlin Wall and the dissolution of the Soviet Union, things began to change, even for the general picture of the "democratic" West. The "unipolar" world, freed from the Soviet threat, showed that the escalation of "international terrorism" before and after September 11 (with all of the mythology shrouding this date, beginning with the unbelievable official version of the facts provided by the US government) was more dangerous than the Cold War, and involved an intensification of every type of control along with the multiplication of "peripheral" wars in every part of the world where the "terroristic beast" was being pursued (preferably, if located in an oil-producing region). The fight against terrorism brought with it, perhaps naturally or more likely due to a deliberate choice by the Israeli government, an intensification of tensions in the Middle East: for example, the idea that Iran's "atomic race" could be broken with ever stronger sanctions, more rigorous controls, and even a pre-emptive war if necessary. And alongside this there was "Operation Cast Lead" against Gaza at the end of 2008 to 2009, destined to interrupt the launching of the almost totally harmless missiles into Israeli territory. Better still: the entire Gaza affair contributed in a decisive way, more than any other aspect of Israeli politics, to the idea (I believe with great likelihood) that against the risk of a return of refugees, which would entail the end of the "Jewishness" of the State of Israel, this situation might see no other solution than the progressive extermination of Palestinian Arabs. All of this comes with ever-renewed settlement construction, promised in every way with a racially oriented politics of accommodation that, as we all know, is also creating tensions within Israel between two grades of immigrants—fundamentally a class conflict.

From Israel we hear ever more frequently the voices of the many Israelis who, beginning with the movement of Peace Now, condemn the politics of their government against Palestinians. Usually, even these movements of opposition still tend to take seriously the project of "two people, two states," which by now has been revealed as a means to prolong infinitely (after the past 20 years or so) the pseudo-attempts to solve the problem. In the meantime, the settlements multiply, the construction of new residences in East Jerusalem intensifies, and above all the wall that divides Palestine in two and makes the lives of Palestinians, including the citizens of Israel, ever more unbearable continues to grow. The myth of "two states for two peoples," another aspect of the Zionist mythology, is all too clearly a way of protracting matters so that it does not appear to be an ongoing excuse by Western democracies to avoid their responsibilities, a way to give Israel the time to continue the genocide, in Gaza and elsewhere, and also to reinforce themselves militarily in every way, including the possession of atomic weapons.

Let us—we anti-Zionist supporters of Palestinians—not hide the fact that one of the reasons behind our attitude is also and above all the increasing awareness of the link between Israeli politics and the politics of American interests. Without following theories about the Jewish-Masonic conspiracy that have the sole effect of ridiculing opinions which are often not unfounded, we are in recent years—above all, since the USA began its war against "international terrorism," and namely against all countries and political powers that did not submit to their command—more aware that the Palestinian cause is also the cause of the people who rebel against imperialism. That Brazil's president Lula was among the first "Western" leaders to welcome Iran and Ahmadinejad has an emblematic value that goes far beyond the particular significance of his visit. One must also add all of the old (Cuba) and new progressive governments of Latin America that took a stand. Never before was it so evident (at least it seems so to us) that what is up for grabs in Palestine is the destiny of oppressed peoples who try to avoid the rule of the new colonialism—economic, but often also military—of global capital concentrated in the United States (even if it is distributed among many countries, all of them "Atlantic"). So by now anti-Zionism is synonymous with leftist world politics, no matter what the attitudes of individuals and movements that believe—as I recalled at the beginning in citing the positions of President Giorgio Napolitano—Israel can still be included among the states that are democratic, progressive, etc. It is also not worth recalling the usual excuse of those who invite us to distinguish the State of Israel—whose legitimacy should never be placed in doubt—from the leaders of Israel who are responsible for the racist and anti-democratic politics that scandalize us, as it is a laughable excuse. But when was there ever a government in Israel that did not pursue this sort of politics of expansion and thus the diminishing of the rights of Palestinians? The Nakba was the archetype for all Israeli politics since 1948; moreover, it was understandable given the proposal to preserve the Jewishness of the state and therefore to close off every possibility of return for the refugees and also to foreclose every demographic or social expansion of the Arab population. Doesn't this mean that what makes Israel "unacceptable" as a state is its racist-colonialist-anti-egalitarian original sin?

For good reasons of international stability, one never dares—or almost never, except in the case of Islamic heads of state like Ahmadinejad—to question the very legitimacy of Israel's existence. Let us start from the fact that if a war breaks out for a brief time, it will be the "pre-emptory" type that Israel wants to fight and that makes the West fight due to the Iranian threat—a threat that is exactly what is contained in the bellicose speeches of the heads of states who do not have any real possibility of making it happen. Israel presses continually because the West might embark upon a preventive war against Iran, a war that surely would have the character of the self-destructive nihilism that Glucksmann (or someone in his place) attributed to the Islamic terrorists who have fallen prey to a desperate cult of death. As to the idea of making the state of Israel "disappear" from the map—one of the usual themes of the Iranian "threat"—its sense may not be completely unreasonable: it could, and ought, according to us, mean that the State of Israel becomes a secular, democratic, non-racist state, without walls and without discrimination among its citizens. We know well that this seems like the destruction of the State of Israel, but, it would mean only a transformation of the sort that Ilan Pappe would also view favorably. Neither destruction nor bombing nor violent change of geographical boundaries, but finally a modernization of the sort which has occurred in many other states that supported the birth of Israel and yet feel a certain embarrassment about its politics. When Ahmedinejad invokes the end of the State of Israel, he merely expresses a demand that should be more explicitly shared by the democratic countries that instead consider him an enemy.

The democratic anti-Zionism about which I speak and write—in short, an autobiography—does not really consider the destruction of Israel (but who really thinks like this? not even Ahmedinejad, for sure), neither with Iran's atomic bombs (today about as threatening as the rockets fired from Gaza, which have done hardly any damage, even though the Palestinians have paid for them with operation "Operation Cast Lead"), nor even with that secular and democratic transformation which could make Palestine a modern and ultimately livable country. And then what? We should carry Israel with us, in us, as a weight from which we will not free ourselves any time soon, almost like the inerasable memory of the Holocaust that is imposed like a penalty, and for which we have yet to atone. Only Israel itself—its politicians, its citizens—could set itself free with a radical change in politics. This is unlikely, let us be clear, because it would also be unbearable for the American power that supports Israel, even as it serves it as its very own Middle-Eastern policeman. To speak of Israel as an "irredeemable sin" is therefore not so excessive: whether one thinks about how, since its birth, the Jewish state has utilized the Holocaust as a permanent weapon against anyone who might question its politics (just look at Finkelstein); or if one considers how the Holocaust has been experienced by much of contemporary philosophy—a sort of parameter by which the acceptability of philosophies is measured, a type of Nuremburg tribunal before which all thinkers are brought in order to be judged.

First of all, of course, we are dealing with the philosophy of Heidegger, who surely was wrong to side for a time with Hitler's regime and paid rather heavily for his sin after the war's end (above all, by being forbidden to teach, and so on). But, for all its shamefulness, the episode remains the subject of analysis by many Nazi hunters who never seem to get enough of justice-vengeance. Many recent studies, which are helped by new documents brought to light after the publication of Farias' famous book in 1983—and I am thinking above all of Emmanuel Faye—continue to pile guilt not only on the Heidegger of 1933 and after, but on all of his philosophy, which has been depicted as a philosophical tradition of Hitlerism. The many who have read, interpreted, and at times followed Heidegger, even on the left, are called to order: if by now they are unaware that they are following a Nazi thinker, they had better take note. With this, a great deal of contemporary thought that had defined the culture of recent decades—I am thinking above all of Derrida and of hermeneutics—has been, so to speak, "cleansed." No more deconstruction, no more hermeneutic ontology—only the mainstream thinking of the Atlantic, North American, and Anglo-Saxon sort! Moreover, one can add that the same Farias, in writings that followed his first text, has also pointed out a dangerous proximity between Heideggerianism and Iranian Islamic thought.

When they are not explicitly called to demonstrate that the only philosophy one can practice today is the apologetic-realistic form found in Anglo-Saxon universities (Searle and company), the works by those like Faye recall Zionism in its substantially vindictive significance. It remains a matter of making someone pay for their sins against the people of Israel, even those who are no longer able to constitute a real threat. The use of the *Shoah* as an all-encompassing justification for all the illegitimate actions of Israel (from the continual violation of the UN resolutions to the systematic decimation of the Palestinian population) is also revealed here to be a form of radical and vindictive executionism, much more than a form of simple and cynical political expediency. All of this is done to evoke the suspicion, from those who always believed they belonged to the Judeo-Christian tradition, that the God of Israel who was believed to be the father of Jesus Christ is instead only and properly the God of the hosts of nomadic people who from their own mythology (divine election, the Covenant, the purity of the race) draw their legitimacy and their claim to exceptionality.

When I confront the question of Israel today, particularly with the bad conscience of the Christian world for the persecution the Jews have suffered over the centuries, more and more I have the impression that this history has nothing to do with me. For example, when I continue to recite, in the Latin breviary, certain psalms like the 12th, (*Cum reduceret Dominus captivos Sion ...*), I increasingly feel its literal more than its allegorical sense: this is not a song of liberation from sin, but a song of jubilation for the military victory by one people over another. And the psalms against the Babylonians who were guilty of enslaving the Jews, with the curse on the newborns of Babylon who should be smashed against the walls and massacred in the name (of the justice) of God.... All in all, even the archetype of the return—from *regiones dissimilitudinis* (an expression from St. Augustine) to the house of the father, an archetype that I also feel in my spiritual life I cannot do without—is perhaps none other than the feeling of a nomadic people with whom, in the end, I have nothing in common... And Kafka, Rosenzweig, Walter Benjamin, Bloch... I certainly do not want to do without all of these essential components of my and our culture. I will not do to them what the Zionist Nazi hunters have done to Heidegger, when they think of liquidating him because he sided with Hitler. Once again I cannot free myself from the problem of Israel; it is ultimately like the original sin spoken of in the Old Testament, the Hebrew Bible. Here I will take up, to conclude this unconcludable reflection, a summary of my article that has never appeared—not by my choice—in an Italian newspaper, but that crystalizes much of what I have in mind when I speak of Zionism and anti-Zionism. It begins with the viewing of the Cohen brothers' film *A Serious Man*, released some years ago and perhaps one that has not been discussed and understood enough.

So is it true, as Deleuze once said, that Kafka's *The Trial* (and perhaps also *The Castle*) is a grand comedic novel? This idea returned to me after having viewed the last film of the Cohen brothers, *A Serious Man*. The hypothesis, in its entirety, would be this: *just as* the corruption and the thirst for money and the power of the Church (not only that of Ratzinger, alas) has allowed us (ex-)Catholics to discover not only all of the inquisitorial and colonial depravities of the past, but also the absurdity today (from the banning of condoms in the age of AIDS, to survival at any cost through tubes and wires, and finally to the Pope not relinquishing the "rights" of the embryo, obviously always represented by the Holy Roman Church), so too perhaps the bloody racist politics of the State of Israel have begun to push the American Jewish community—its better parts, certainly, starting with Chomsky—to take note that the very praiseworthy richness and profundity of the Jewish tradition is only so much putrid, hot air from which one must free oneself in order to avoid spilling blood on account of the Tomb of Rachel, of the Temple grounds, or of the sacred rights of the Jews to the Promised Land. The empty and sententious rabbis of the Cohen brothers and Woody Allen are just like our bishops and cardinals. They are nothing but giant balloons filled with "mystic" rhetoric that sweeps us up for the love of God—the God who torments Job, his family, and the animals due to an absurd bet with that other comic character, the devil (will anyone publish this elementary reflection?).

Note

1   Ilan Pappe, *Out of the Frame; The Struggle for Academic Freedom in Israel* (New York: Pluto Press, 2010).

3

Is Judaism Zionism?

Or, Arendt and the Critique of the Nation-State

Judith Butler

Clearly, Zionism is one way that religion has entered public life, although there are ways of thinking about Zionism that are obviously antireligious, including ways of defining Jewishness for the purpose of Israeli citizenship that are shorn of explicit religious references. Indeed, the category of "Jewish" proves complex in these debates, since rabbinic law defines Jewishness for an apparently secular state law in Israel that in other respects distinguishes itself emphatically from rabbinic law. How does this ambiguity affect the more general discussions of religion and public life that seem to be so much with us during these times?

Doubtless, we have to be very careful when we refer to "religion" in public life, since it may not be possible finally to talk about religion as a category in this sense. Depending on which religion we have in mind, its relation to the public will be different. Indeed, there are a variety of religious positions on public life and a variety of ways of conceiving public life within religious terms. If we begin by asking about "religion" in "public life" we run the risk of simply filling in the category "religion" with a variety of specific religions; and the sphere of "public life" somehow remains stable, enclosed, and outside of religion. If the entry of religion into public life is a problem, then it would seem we are presupposing a framework in which religion has been outside public life, and we are asking about how it enters and whether it enters in a justifiable or warranted way. But, if this is the operative assumption, it seems we have to ask first how religion became private and whether the effort to make religion private ever really succeeded. If one implicit question of this inquiry presupposes that religion belongs to a private sphere, we have first to ask, "which religion" has been relegated to the private, and which, if any, circulates without question in the public sphere. Perhaps then we might have another inquiry to pursue, namely one that differentiates between legitimate and illegitimate religions; that is, those that are considered to implicitly support a secular public sphere and those that are considered to threaten the secular public, or, equivalently, those that, like Christianity, are understood to provide the cultural preconditions of the public, whose symbols circulate freely within the public, and those that are considered to threaten the foundation of secular life, whose symbols circulating within the public are considered ostentatious or threatening to democracy itself. If the public sphere is a protestant accomplishment, as several scholars have argued, then public life presupposes and reaffirms a dominant religious tradition as the secular. And if there are many reasons to doubt whether secularism is as liberated from its religious makings as it purports to be, we might ask whether these insights into secularism also apply, in some degree, to our claims regarding public life in general. In other words, some religions are not only already "inside" the public sphere, but they help to establish a set of criteria that distinguish the public from the private. This happens when some religions are relegated to the "outside"—either as "the private" or as the threat to the public as such—while others function to support and delimit the public sphere itself. If we could not have the distinction between public and private were it not for the protestant injunction to privatize religion, then religion—or one dominant religious tradition—underwrites the very framework within which we are operating. This would indeed constitute quite a different point of departure for a critical inquiry into religion in public life, since both public and private would form a disjunctive relation that would be, in some important sense, "in" religion from the start.

My point is not to rehearse the questions about secularism, which have been ably expounded by Talal Asad, Saba Mahmood, Michael Warner, William Connolly, Charles Taylor, Janet Jakobsen and Ann Pellegrini, and Charles Hirschkind. On the basis of this new scholarship, it is clear that secularization may be a fugitive way for religion to survive; we always have to ask, which form and path of secularization do we mean? My point is to suggest, first, that any generalizations we make about "religion" in "public life" are suspect from the start if we do not think about which religions are being presupposed in the conceptual apparatus itself, especially if that conceptual apparatus, including the notion of the public, is not understood in light of its own genealogy and secularization projects. It makes a different kind of sense to refer to a secular Jew than to a secular Catholic; whereas both may be presumed to have departed from religious belief, there may be other forms of belonging that do not presume or require belief; secularization may well be one way that Jewish life continues as Jewish.[1] We also make a mistake if religion becomes equated with belief, and belief is then tied to certain kinds of speculative claims about God—a theological presumption that does not always work to describe religious practice. That effort to distinguish the cognitive status of religious and nonreligious belief misses the fact that very often religion functions as a matrix of subject formation, an embedded framework for valuations, and a mode of belonging and embodied social practice. Of course, the legal principle of the separation of state and religion haunts any and all of our discourses here, but there are many reasons to think that the juridical conception is insufficient to serve as the framework for understanding the larger questions of religion in public life. Also insufficient are the debates about religious symbols and icons that have produced widespread disagreement about first amendment rights, on the one hand, and the protection of religious minorities against discrimination and persecution, on the other hand.[2]

I enter this fray with another problem, namely the tension that emerges between religion and public life when public criticism of Israeli state violence is taken to be anti-Semitic or anti-Jewish, as it so often is. For the record, I would like to make clear that some of those criticisms do employ anti-Semitic rhetoric and argument and so must be opposed absolutely and unequivocally. But the legitimate criticisms, and there are many, do not. Included among them are criticisms of Israeli state violence that emerge from within Jewish struggles for social justice (which are not the same as struggles for social justice only for Jews). Jewish opposition to Zionism accompanied the founding proposals made by Herzl at the International Zionist Congress in 1897 in Basel, and it has never ceased since that time.[3] It is not anti-Semitic or, indeed, self-hating to criticize the state violence exemplified by Zionism. If it were, then Jewishness would be defined, in part, by its failure to generate a critique of state violence, and that is surely not the case. My question is whether the public criticism of state violence—and I know that term is yet to be explained—is warranted by Jewish values, understood in noncommunitarian terms.

One asks this question because if one openly and publicly criticizes Israeli state violence, then one is sometimes, and in certain circumstances almost always, considered anti-Semitic or anti-Jewish. And yet to openly and publicly criticize such violence is in some ways an obligatory ethical demand from within Jewish frameworks, both religious and nonreligious, that sustain necessary ties to broader movements against state violence of this kind—thus Jewish and departing from Jewishness at once. Of course, you will already see a second set of quandaries introduced by this formulation. As Hannah Arendt made clear in her early writings, Jewishness is not always the same as Judaism.[4] And, as she made clear in her evolving political position on the State of Israel, neither Judaism nor Jewishness necessarily leads to the embrace of Zionism.

My aim is not to repeat the claim that Jews differ among themselves on the value of Zionism, on the injustice of the occupation, or on the military destructiveness of the Israeli state. These are complex matters, and there are vast disagreements on all of them. Nor is my point to say simply that Jews are obligated to criticize Israel, although in fact I think they are or, rather, we are; given that Israel acts in the name of the Jewish people, casts itself as the legitimate representative of the Jewish people, there is a struggle over what is done in the name of the Jewish people and so all the more reason to reclaim that tradition and ethics in favor of a politics that prizes social and political justice above a nationalism that depends fundamentally on military violence to sustain itself. The effort to establish the presence of progressive Jews runs the risk of remaining within certain identitarian and communitarian presumptions; one opposes any and all expressions of anti-Jewish anti-Semitism and one reclaims Jewishness for a project that seeks to dismantle Israeli state violence and the institutionalization of racism. This particular form of the solution is challenged, however, if we consider that there are several ethical and political frameworks in which such a critique is obligatory.

Moreover, as I have sought to suggest, Jewishness can and must be understood as an anti-identitarian project insofar as we might even say that being a Jew implies taking up an ethical relation to the non-Jew, and this follows from the diasporic condition of Jewishness where living in a socially plural world under conditions of equality remains an ethical and political ideal. Indeed, if the relevant Jewish tradition for waging the public criticism of Israeli state violence is one that draws upon cohabitation as a norm of sociality, then what follows is the need not only to establish an alternative Jewish public presence (distinct from AIPAC, to be sure, but also from J. Street) or an alternative Jewish movement (such as Jewish Voice for Peace, Independent Jewish Voices in the UK, Jews for Justice for Palestinians, to name but a few), but to affirm the displacement of identity that Jewishness requires, as paradoxical as that may first sound. Only then can we come to understand the mode of ethical relationality that informs some key historical and religious understandings of what it is to "be" a Jew. In the end, it is not about specifying the ontology of the Jew over and against some other cultural or religious group—we have every reason to be suspicious of any effort to do such a thing. It is rather a question of understanding the very relation to the non-Jew as the way of configuring religion in public life within Judaism. The point is not simply to scatter geographically, but to derive a set of principles from scattered existence that can serve a new conception of political justice. That conception would entail a fair doctrine on the rights of refugees and a critique of nationalist modes of state violence that sustain the occupation, land confiscation, and the political imprisonment and exile of Palestinians. It would also imply a notion of cohabitation whose condition of emergence would be the end of settler colonialism. More generally formulated, it is on the basis of this conception of cohabitation that the critique of illegitimate nation-state violence can and must be waged—with no exceptions.

There are, of course, both risks and obligations of public criticism. It remains true that the criticism of Israeli state violence, for instance, can be construed as a critique of the Jewish state on the same grounds as those one would use to base criticism of any other state that engaged in the practices of occupation, invasion, and the destruction of a livable infrastructure for a subjugated or minority population. Or it can be construed as a critique of the Jewish state, emphasizing the Jewishness of that state and thus prompting the fear that it is because the state is Jewish that it is criticized. What is usually feared then is that an anti-Jewish impetus drives the criticism. But such a fear often deflects from the legitimate concern articulated here, namely that it would be unjust for any state to insist on one religious and ethnic group maintaining a demographic majority to create differential levels of citizenship for majority and minority populations (even internally valorizing Ashkenazi origins and narrative accounts of the nation over Sephardic and Mizrahi cultural origins within its mandated educational curriculum and public discourse). If, then, the problem is this last one, it is still difficult to enunciate this in public, since there will be those who suspect that really something else is being said or that anyone who calls into question the demand for Jewish demographic majority in particular is motivated by insensitivity to the sufferings of the Jewish people, including the contemporary threat they experience, or by anti-Semitism, or both.

And of course, it makes a difference whether one is criticizing the principles of Jewish sovereignty that have characterized political Zionism since 1948 or whether one's criticism is restricted to the occupation as illegal and destructive (and so situating itself in a history that starts with 1967) or whether one is more restrictively criticizing certain military actions in isolation from both Zionism and the occupation, such as the assault on Gaza in 2008 to 2009, which included clear war crimes, or the growth of settlements, continuing forms of land confiscation of other kinds, or the policies of the current right-wing regime in Israel. But in each and every case, there is a question of whether the criticism can be registered publicly as something other than an attack on the Jews or on Jewishness. Depending where we are and to whom we speak, some of these positions can be heard more easily than others. And yet, as we know, there are contexts in which none of these criticisms can be heard without an immediate suspicion that the person who articulates them has something against the Jews or, if Jewish herself, has something against herself. Moreover, in every case we are confronted with the limits on audibility by which the contemporary public sphere is constituted. There is always a question: should I listen to this or not? Am I being heard or misconstrued? The public sphere is constituted time and again through certain kinds of exclusions: images that cannot be seen, words that cannot be heard. And this means that the regulation of the visual and audible field—the regulation of the senses more generally—is crucial to the constitution of what can become a debatable issue within any version of the "legitimate" sphere of politics.[5]

If one says that one would be opposed to any state that restricted full citizenship to any religious or ethnic group at the expense of indigenous populations and all other coinhabitants, then one might well be charged with not understanding the exceptional and singular character of the State of Israel and, more importantly, the historical reasons for claiming that exception. But if the state is "excepted" from international standards of justice, or if it clearly abrogates principles of equality and nondiscrimination—to draw attention at this moment only to its infractions against liberalism—then its existence is bound to a contradiction that it can "resolve" only through violence or radical transformation. For Arendt, the call to rethink federal authority or binationalism for the region to politically embody principles of cohabitation envisages a way out of violence rather than a path that would lead to the destruction of any of the populations on that land. The political point is that one cannot defend the Jewish people against destruction without defending the Palestinian people against destruction. If one fails to universalize the interdiction against destruction, then one pursues the destruction of the "Other" with the assumption that only through that destruction can one oneself survive. But the truth remains that the destruction of Palestinian lives and livelihoods can only increase the threat of destruction against those who have perpetrated it, since it gives ongoing grounds for a resistance movement that has its violent and nonviolent versions. One does not need to be an advanced student of Hegel to grasp this point. And if someone counters with the claim that I fail to consider the faults of the Palestinian in this scenario, my reply is that there are surely better and worse ways of waging a resistance movement to colonial occupation. But any evaluation of Palestinian strategies would have to take place within the framework of political resistance. The positions have never been equal, and so it makes no sense to treat the relations between Israel and Palestine as "two sides" of a conflict. Those models that assume equal contributions of Israel and Palestine build equality into their explanatory model and so efface the inequality on the ground. Once political conditions of equality are established, we can then perhaps begin to talk within terms of equality, but only then.

In this spirit I propose thinking about Hannah Arendt, whose political views made many people doubt the authenticity of her Jewishness. Indeed, as a result of her salient criticisms of political Zionism and the State of Israel in 1944, 1948, and 1962, her claim to belong to the Jewish people was severely doubted, most famously by Scholem.[6] As I indicated elsewhere, Scholem more quickly embraced a conception of political Zionism, whereas Buber in the teens and twenties actively and publicly defended a spiritual and cultural Zionism that, in his early view, would become "perverted" if it assumed the form of a political state. By the 1940s, Arendt, Buber, and Magnes argued in favor of a binational state, proposing a federation in which Jews and Arabs would maintain their respective cultural autonomy. It is worth noting as well that Franz Rosenzweig also elaborated a diasporic opposition to Zionism in his *The Star of Redemption*, where he wrote that Judaism is fundamentally bound up with waiting and wandering, but neither with the claim of territory nor the aspirations of a state.

[As I indicated in Chapter 1,] Edward Said proposed that Palestinians and Jews have an overlapping history of displacement, exile, living as refugees in diaspora among those who are not the same. This is a mode of living in which alterity is constitutive of who one is. Said did not clarify in what way these traditions of exile might be overlapping, but he was careful not to draw strict analogies. Does this suggest that one history might inform or interrupt another in ways that call for something other than comparison, parallelism, and analogy? Were Buber and Arendt thinking about a similar problem when, for instance, mindful of the massive numbers of refugees after World War II, they expressed their concerns about the establishment of a Jewish state in 1948 that would be based on the dis-enfranchisement and expulsion of Arabs as a national minority—one that turned out to expel more than seven hundred thousand Palestinians from their rightful homes—now more often estimated as nine hundred thousand? Arendt refused any strict historical analogy between the displacement of the Jews from Europe and those of the Palestinians from a newly established Israel; she surveyed a number of historically distinct situations of statelessness to develop the general critique of the nation-state in *The Origins of Totalitarianism* in 1951. There she attempted to show how, for structural reasons, the nation-state produces mass numbers of refugees and must produce them in order to maintain the homogeneity of the nation it seeks to represent, in other words, to support the nationalism of the nation-state. This led her to oppose any state formation that sought to reduce or refuse the heterogeneity of its population, including the founding of Israel on principles of Jewish sovereignty, and it is clearly one reason she reflected on the postsovereign and postnational promise of federalism. She thought that any state that failed to have the popular support of all its inhabitants, and that defined citizenship on the basis of religious or national belonging, would be forced to produce a permanent class of refugees; the critique extended to Israel, which, she thought, would find itself in endless conflict (and heighten the danger to itself) and would perpetually lack legitimacy as a democracy grounded in a popular will, especially in light of its continued reliance on "superpowers" to maintain its political power in the region. That

Arendt moved from an analysis of a series of stateless conditions to a consideration of Palestine as a stateless condition is significant. The centrality of the European refugee situation both under fascist Germany and after its demise informs her politics here. But this is certainly not to say that Zionism is Nazism. She would have refused such an equation, and we should, too. The point is that there are principles of social justice that can be derived from the Nazi genocide that can and must inform our contemporary struggles, even though the contexts are different, and the forms of subjugating power clearly distinct.

If cohabitation may be understood as a form of convergent exiles, it will be important not to take this convergence as a form of strict analogy between separate terms. Edward Said made that claim about the exilic condition of both Palestinian and Jewish people, and Arendt made it differently when she wrote that the conditions of statelessness under the Nazi regime require a larger critique of how the nation-state perpetually produces the problem of mass refugees. She did not say that the historical situation under Nazi Germany was the same as the situation in Israel. Not at all. But the former was part, not all, of what led her to develop a historical account of statelessness in the twentieth century and to derive general principles that oppose the reproduction of stateless persons and persons without rights. In some ways she invoked the repetition of statelessness as the condition from which a critique of the nation-state had to take place, in the name of heterogeneous populations, political plurality, and a certain conception of cohabitation. It is clear that Jewish history comes to bear on Palestinian history through the impositions and exploitations of a project of settler colonialism. But is there yet another mode in which these histories come to bear upon one another, one that sheds another kind of light?

One persistent question is, what is finally Jewish about Arendt's thought, if anything? Although I think there are some religious sources for Arendt's political thought, I am in a minority in this regard.[7] It is clear that her early work on Augustine, for instance, focuses on neighborly love.[8] And, in the early writings on Zionism, she seeks recourse to the famous formulation of Hillel, "If I am not for myself, who will be for me? If I am not for others, what am I? And if not now, when?" In 1948 she wrote an essay, "Jewish History, Revised," in which she assesses the importance of Scholem's *Major Trends in Jewish Mysticism*, published two years before. There she considers the importance of the messianic tradition for establishing the notion of God as "impersonal" and "infinite" and as linked less with stories of creation than with accounts of emanation.[9] Commenting on the "esoteric character" of such mystical ideas, Arendt underscores a more important legacy of mysticism in the notion that humans participate in the powers that shape the "drama of the world," thus delineating a sphere of action for humans who saw themselves as obligated to a broader purpose. As messianic hopes proved less credible and legal exegesis less efficacious, this resolution of the mystical tradition into a form of action became more important. But this idea of action depended on the exilic existence of the Jewish people, a point explicitly made by Isaac Luria, which Arendt cites: "Formerly [the Diaspora] had been regarded either as a punishment for Israel's sins or as a test of Israel's faith. Now it still is all this, but intrinsically it is a mission; its purpose is to uplift the fallen sparks from all their various locations" (309). To uplift the fallen sparks is not necessarily to gather them again or to return them to their origin. What interests Arendt is not only the irreversibility of "emanation" or dispersal, but the revalorization of exile that it implies. Is there perhaps also a way to understand that the embrace of heterogeneity is itself a certain diasporic position, one conceptualized in part through the notion of a scattered population? The kabbalistic tradition of scattered light, of the sephirot, articulated this notion of a divine scattering that presupposes the dwelling of Jews among non-Jews.

Although Arendt scorned explicitly political forms of messianism, the exilic tradition from which and about which she wrote was also bound up with a certain version of the messianic, one that interested her, for instance, in Benjamin's reading of Kafka. Over and against the messianic version of history Scholem later adopted, which provided a redemptive historical narrative for the establishment of the State of Israel, Arendt was clearly closer to Benjamin's countermessianic view (or alternative form of the messianic, depending on how one reads it). In his view, the history of the suffering of the oppressed flashes up during moments of emergency, which interrupts both homogeneous and teleological time. Here I agree with Gabriel Piterberg's argument that Benjamin's "Theses on the Philosophy of History" constituted "an ethical and political drive to redeem humanity's oppressed,"[10] over and against Scholem, who finally understood the messianic as implying a return of the Jews to the land of Israel, a return from exile to history. As an effort to reverse the devalorization of "exile" (and galut) within Zionist historiography, several scholars, including, prominently, Amnon Raz-Krakotzkin,[11] focus their reading of Benjamin on the recognition and remembrance of the dispossessed. No one people could claim a monopoly on dispossession. The exilic framework for understanding the messianic provides a way to understand one historical condition of dispossession in light of another. Forms of national historiography that presuppose an internal history of the Jews are able to understand neither the exilic condition of the Jews nor the exilic consequences for the Palestinians under contemporary Zionism.[12] Redemption itself is to be rethought as the exilic, without return, a disruption of teleological history and an opening to a convergent and interruptive set of temporalities. This is a messianism, perhaps secularized, that affirms the scattering of light, the exilic condition, as the nonteleological form that redemption now takes. This is a redemption from teleological history. But how, we might surely ask, does the remembrance of one exile prompt an attunement or opening to the dispossession of another? What is this transposition? If it is something other than historical analogy, how is to be described? And does it take us to another notion of cohabitation?

Raz-Krakotzkin writes that the tradition of Benjamin's "Theses" does not mobilize the memory of the oppression of the Jews in order to legitimate the particularist claims of the present, but serves as a catalyst for building a more general history of oppression; the generalizability and transposability of that history of oppression is what leads to a politics that broadens the commitment to alleviating oppression across various cultural and religious differences.[13]

Although Arendt rejected all messianic versions of history, it is clear that her own resistance to the progressive narrative of political Zionism was formed in part within terms offered by Benjamin. In her introduction to Benjamin's *Illuminations*, Arendt remarks that, in the early 1920s, Benjamin's turn to baroque tragic drama in the Trauerspiel seemed to parallel, if not draw upon, Scholem's turn to the Kabbalah. Arendt suggests that throughout the Trauerspiel Benjamin affirms that there is no "return" either to German, European, or Jewish traditions in their former condition. And yet, something from Judaism, namely the exilic tradition, articulates this impossibility of return. Instead, something of another time flashes up in our own. Arendt writes that there was in his work of this time "an implicit admission that the past spoke directly only through things that had been handed down, whose seeming closeness to the present was thus due precisely to their exotic [perhaps esoteric?] character, which ruled out all claims to a binding authority." She understood as "theologically inspired" Benjamin's conclusion that the truth could not be directly recovered and so could not be "an unveiling which destroys the secret, but the revelation that does it justice."

The revelation that does the secret justice does not seek to recover an original meaning or to return to a lost past, but rather to grasp and work with the fragments of the past that break through into a present marked by oblivion, where they become episodically available. This view seems to find resonance in that remark in the "Theses on the Philosophy of History" that "the true picture of the past flits by. The past can be seized only as an image which flashes up at the instant when it can be recognized and is never seen again" (TPH, 255). If [as I argued in the last chapter] what flashes up is a memory of suffering from another time, then it interrupts and reorients the politics of this time. This would not be rightly described as a transgenerational memory, since the generational line is traversed by a memory that crosses over from one population to another, thus assuming a break in both filial linearity and the temporal continuity of national belonging. In fact, Benjamin makes clear in the seventeenth thesis that this flashing up makes possible an interruption of established forms of historical development; it constitutes a "cessation of happening" (TPH, 263) and so a calling into question of progressive historiography itself. Only such a cessation of happening, he tells us, can produce "a revolutionary chance in the fight for the oppressed past" (TPH, 263). Modes of progressive history, including those that assume the progressive realization of political ideals (Zionism among them), reinstitute amnesia with every step "forward." Thus, stepping forward has to be stopped if the history of the oppressed is to come to the fore. The point is not for that history to lead to revenge (which would be a cyclical form of history that Benjamin would reject), but rather to an active battle against those forms of political amnesia that "found" progress. [14] If one temporality emerges within another, then the temporal horizon is no longer singular; what is "contemporary" are forms of convergence that are not always readily legible.

Arendt agreed with the necessity to criticize certain forms of historical progress. Whereas Benjamin seemed to have the progressive claims of capitalism in mind when he sought to redefine historical materialism and describe the increasing quantification of value, Arendt was clearly thinking of more teleological forms of historical materialism when she contested the notion of progress as an inevitable unfolding of political ideals. For Arendt, politics would be a matter of action, and action could only be understood on the basis of political plurality. Although her ideas of plurality and cohabitation are formulated in many published texts, there is one formulation that emerges in her book on Eichmann, published in 1962, that has special relevance to this discussion.

According to Arendt, Eichmann thought that he and his superiors might choose with whom to cohabit the earth and failed to realize that the heterogeneity of the earth's population is an irreversible condition of social and political life itself.[15] This accusation against him bespeaks a firm conviction that none of us should be in the position of making such a choice. Those with whom we cohabit the earth are given to us, prior to choice and so prior to any social or political contracts we might enter through deliberate volition. In fact, if we seek to make a choice where there is no choice, we are trying to destroy the conditions of our own social and political life. In Eichmann's case, the effort to choose with whom to cohabit the earth was an explicit effort to annihilate some part of that population—Jews, gypsies, homosexuals, communists, the disabled and the ill, among others—and so the exercise of freedom upon which he insisted was genocide. If Arendt is right, then it is not only that we may not choose with whom to cohabit, but that we must actively preserve and affirm the unchosen character of inclusive and plural cohabitation: we not only live with those we never chose and to whom we may feel no social sense of belonging, but we are also obligated to preserve those lives and the plurality of which they form a part. In this sense, concrete political norms and ethical prescriptions emerge from the unchosen character of these modes of cohabitation. To cohabit the earth is prior to any possible community or nation or neighborhood. We might sometimes choose where to live, and who to live by or with, but we cannot choose with whom to cohabit the earth.

In *Eichmann in Jerusalem*, she clearly speaks not only for the Jews, but for any other minority who would be expelled from habitation on the earth by another group. The one implies the other, and the "speaking for" universalizes the principle even as it does not override the plurality for which it speaks. Arendt refuses to separate the Jews from the other so-called nations persecuted by the Nazis in the name of a plurality that is coextensive with human life in any and all its cultural forms. Is she subscribing here to a universal principle, or does plurality form a substantial alternative to the universal? And is her procedure, in some ways, related to the problem of convergent and interrupting histories mentioned by Said and Benjamin in different ways?

Perhaps we can say there is a universalization at work in her formulation that seeks to establish inclusiveness for all human society, but posits no single defining principle for the humanity it assembles. This notion of plurality cannot be only internally differentiated, since that would raise the question of what bounds this plurality; since plurality cannot be exclusionary without losing its plural character, the idea of a given or established form for plurality would pose a problem for the claims of plurality. For Arendt, nonhuman life already constitutes part of that outside, thus denying from the start the animality of the human. Any present notion of the human will have to be differentiated on some basis from a future one. If plurality does not exclusively characterize a given and actual condition, but also always a potential one, then it has to be understood as a process, and we will need to shift from a static to a dynamic conception.

Following William Connolly, we could then speak of pluralization.[16] Only then can the differentiation that characterizes a given plurality also mark those sets of differences that exceed its givenness. The task of affirming or even safeguarding plurality would then also imply making new modes of pluralization possible. When Arendt universalizes her claim (no one has the right to decide with whom to cohabit the earth; everyone has the right to cohabit the earth with equal degrees of protection), she does not assume that "everyone" is the same—at least not in the context of her discussion of plurality. One can surely see why there would be a Kantian reading of Arendt, one that concludes that plurality is a regulative ideal, that everyone has such rights, regardless of the cultural and linguistic differences by which anyone is characterized. And Arendt herself moves in this Kantian direction, though mainly through the extrapolation of Kant's notion of aesthetic judgment rather than his moral philosophy.

The distinction between pluralization and universalization is important for thinking about unchosen cohabitation. Equal protection or, indeed, equality is not a principle that homogenizes those to whom it applies; rather, the commitment to equality is a commitment to the process of differentiation itself. One can surely see why there can be a communitarian reading of Arendt, since she herself elaborates the right to belong and rights of belonging. But there is always a redoubling here that dislocates the claim from any specific community: everyone has the right of belonging. And this means there is a universalizing and a differentiating that takes place at once and without contradiction—and that this is the structure of pluralization. In other words, political rights are separated from the social ontology upon which they depend; political rights universalize, although they do so always in the context of a differentiated (and continually differentiating) population. And though Arendt refers to "nations" or sometimes communities of belonging as the component parts of this plurality, it is clear that the principle of pluralization applies as well to these parts, since they are not only internally differentiated (and differentiating), but they are themselves defined in relation to variable and shifting relations to the outside.

Indeed, this is one point I have been underscoring about the problem of Jewishness. It may be that the sense of belonging to this group entails taking up a relation to the non-Jew that requires departing from a communitarian basis for political judgment and responsibility alike. It is not that "one" (over here) approaches the "other" (over there), but that these two modes of existence are radically implicated in one another, for good and bad reasons.[17] "Here" and "there" as well as "then" and "now" become internally complicated modalities of space and time that correspond to this notion of cohabitation.[18] Moreover, if Jewishness mandates this departure from communitarian belonging, then "to belong" is to undergo a dispossession from the category of Jewishness, a formulation as promising as it is paradoxical. It also obligates the development of a politics that exceeds the claims of communitarian belonging. Although Arendt herself values the way exile can lead to action in the service of broader purposes, here we might read dispossession as an exilic moment, one that disposes us ethically. Paradoxically, it is only possible to struggle to alleviate the suffering of others if I am both motivated and dispossessed by my own suffering. It is this relation to the other that dispossesses me from any enclosed and self-referential notion of belonging;

otherwise, we cannot understand those obligations that bind us when there is no obvious mode of belonging and where the convergence of temporalities becomes the condition for the memory of political dispossession as well as the resolve to bring such dispossession to a halt.

Can we now think about the transposition that happens from the past to the future? Precisely because there is no common denominator among the plural members of this stipulated humanity, except perhaps the ungrounded right to have rights, which includes a certain right to belonging and to place, we might only begin to understand this plurality by testing a set of analogies that will invariably fail. In fact, precisely because one historical experience of dispossession is not the same as another, the right to have rights invariably emerges in different forms and through different vernaculars. If we start with the presumption that one group's suffering is like another group's, we have not only assembled the groups into provisional monoliths—and so falsified them—but we have launched into a form of analogy building that invariably fails. The specificity of the group is established at the expense of its temporal and spatial instability, its constitutive heterogeneity, and for the purpose of making it suitable for analogical reasoning. But analogy fails because specificities prove obdurate. The suffering of one people is not exactly like the suffering of another, and this is the condition of the specificity of the suffering for both. Indeed, we would have no analogy between them if the grounds for analogy were not already destroyed. If specificity qualifies each group for analogy, it also defeats the analogy from the start. And this means that another sort of relation must be formulated for the problem at hand, one that traverses the inevitable difficulties of translation.

The obstruction that thwarts analogy makes that specificity plain and becomes the condition for the process of pluralization. Through elaborating a series of such broken or exhausted analogies, the communitarian presumption that we might start with "groups" as our point of departure meets its limit, and then the internally and externally differentiating action of pluralization emerges as a clear alternative. We might try to overcome such "failures" by devising more perfect analogies, hoping that a common ground can be achieved in that way ("multicultural dialogue" with an aim of perfect consensus or intersectional analysis in which every factor is included in the final picture). But such procedures miss the point that plurality implies differentiations that cannot be (and should not be) overcome through ever more robust epistemological accounts or ever more refined analogies. At the same time, the elaboration of rights, especially the right of cohabitation on the earth, emerges as a universal that governs a social ontology that cannot be homogenized. Such a universalizing right has to break up into its nonuniversal conditions; otherwise it fails to be grounded in plurality.

Arendt seeks something other than principles to unify this plurality, and she clearly objects to any effort to divide this plurality, although it is, by definition, internally differentiated. The difference between division and differentiation is clear: it is one thing to repudiate some part of this plurality, to bar admission of that part into the plurality of the human, and to deny place to that portion of humanity. And it is another to recognize the failed analogies by which we have to make our way politically.

One suffering is never the same as another. At the same time, any and all suffering by virtue of forcible displacement and statelessness is equally unacceptable.

If, following Benjamin, we are to allow the memory of dispossession to crack the surface of historical amnesia and reorient us toward the unacceptable conditions of refugees across time and context, there must be transposition without analogy, the interruption of one time by another, which is the counternationalist impetus of the messianic in Benjamin's terms, what some would call a messianic secularism that relates clearly to his work on translation: how does another time break into this time, through what vessel, and through what transposition? One time breaks into another precisely when that former time is a history of oppression at risk of falling into oblivion. This is not the same as the operation of analogy, but neither is it precisely the same as the temporality of trauma. In trauma the past is never over; in historical amnesia the past never was, and that "never was" becomes the condition of the present. One can, of course, claim that unacknowledged histories of oppression can never be part of the past, but continue as spectral dimensions of present time. Of course, that is right. But though there are historical traumas that have this character, what is lost and what is gained by reducing a history of oppression to the discourse of trauma? Although the struggle for the history of the oppressed is surely assisted by the acknowledgment and working through of trauma, sometimes the history of the oppressed continues in the present forms of oppression—one need only consider the recurrent history of land confiscation by the State of Israel. In those cases, it is not just the trauma of the catastrophic displacement of Palestinians from their homes in 1948 that must be documented, but the ongoing practices of land confiscation that make it wrong to relegate such a practice to the past alone.

I have been arguing that the very possibility of ethical relation depends upon a certain condition of dispossession from national modes of belonging. We are outside ourselves, before ourselves, and only in such a mode is there a chance of being for another. In *Frames of War* I suggested that we are already in the hands of the other before we make any decision about with whom we choose to live. This way of being bound to one another is precisely not a social bond that is entered into through volition and deliberation; it precedes contract, is mired in interdependency, and is often effaced by those forms of social contract that presume and instate an ontology of volitional individuals. Thus, it is even from the start to those who are not readily identifiable as part of "one's community" that we are bound, the one, or the ones, we never knew, and never chose, whose names may be difficult to remember or pronounce, who live in different lexicons of the everyday. If we accept this sort of ontological condition, then to destroy the other is to destroy my life, that sense of my life that is invariably social life. And this does not mean that, if I destroy the other, the chances are increased that I myself will be destroyed (although this makes good sense as a calculation). The point is rather that this very selfhood is bound up with what we call the Other in ways that do not allow me to differentiate the value of my persistence from the value of the persistence of any others.[19] This may be less our common condition, conceived existentially, than our convergent condition—one of proximity, adjacency, up-againstness, being interrupted and constituted by the memory of someone else's longing and suffering, in spite of oneself—ways of being bound by spatial and temporal relations that articulate the present moment. The co of cohabitation cannot be thought simply as spatial neighborliness: there is no home without adjacency, without a line that demarcates and binds one territory to another and so no way to reside anywhere delimited without the outside defining the space of inhabitation. The co of cohabitation is also the nexus where convergent temporalities articulate present time, not a time in which one history of suffering negates another, but when it remains possible that one history of suffering provides the conditions of attunement to another such history and that whatever connections are made proceed through the difficulty of translation. In sum, cohabitation implies an affirmation that one finds the condition of one's own life in the life of another where there is dependency and differentiation, proximity and violence; this is what we find in some explicit ways in the relation between territories, such as Israel and Palestine, since they are joined inextricably, without binding contract, without reciprocal agreement, and yet ineluctably. So the question emerges: what obligations are to be derived from this dependency, contiguity, and proximity that now defines each population, which exposes each to the fear of destruction, which, as we know, sometimes incites destructiveness? How are we to understand such bonds, without which neither population can live and survive, and to what postnational obligations do they lead?

Practically, I think none of these views can be dissociated from the critique of the ongoing and violent project of settler colonialism that constitutes political Zionism. To practice remembrance in the Benjaminian sense might lead to a new concept of citizenship, a new constitutional basis for that region, a rethinking of binationalism in light of the racial and religious complexity of both Jewish and Palestinian populations, a radical reorganization of land partitions and illegal property allocations, and even minimally a concept of cultural heterogeneity that extends to the entire population and is protected rather than denied by rights of citizenship. Now one might argue against all these propositions that they are unsuitable to be spoken in public, that they carry too much risk, that equality would be bad for the Jews, that democracy would stoke anti-Semitism, and that cohabitation would threaten Jewish life with destruction. But perhaps such responses are only utterable on the condition that we fail to remember what Jewish means or that we have not thought carefully enough about all the possible permutations of "never again"; after all, remembrance does not restrict itself to my suffering or the suffering of my people alone. The limit on what can be remembered is enforced in the present through what can be said and what can be heard, the limits on the audible and the sensible that contingently constitute any public sphere. For remembrance to break through into that public sphere would be one way for religion, perhaps, to enter into public life. A politics, Jewish and not Jewish and, indeed, not restricted to that binary, indeed extending, as it must, to a field of open differentiation uncontained by the universalization that it supports. This politics might then emerge in the name of remembrance, both from and against dispossession, and in the direction of what may yet be called justice.

Hannah Arendt and the end of the nation-state?

Hannah Arendt has never been easy to categorize and that probably has to do in part with her rather insistent critique of settled categories within her political writings of the 1930s and 1940s. There are a series of divisions that she sought to evade and reconceptualize in her early political thinking. They include, for instance, the ostensible differences between Zionism and assimilationism, Zionism and anti-Semitism, the nation-state and the rights of man, and even the polar positions of left and right within the political spectrum. She was engaged in a very particular kind of critical practice, one that sought to underscore the political paradoxes of the nation-state. For instance: if the nation-state secures the rights of citizens, then surely the nation-state is a necessity; but if the nation-state relies on nationalism and invariably produces massive numbers of stateless people, it clearly needs to be opposed. And: if the nation-state is opposed, then what, if anything, serves as its alternative? Arendt refers variously to modes of "belonging" and to conceptions of the "polity" that are not reducible to the idea of the nation-state. She even refers, in her early writings, to the idea of a "nation" that might be delinked from both statehood and territory. As such we might ask: does she settle on an answer to the question of whether there is an end to the nation-state? Or does she only unsettle a number of assumptions about political life as she tries to approach and evade this problem?

Let us consider two quotations that bring us into a critical encounter with a certain kind of equivocation that marks her political thinking in this domain. She was once asked, are you a conservative? Are you a liberal? And she replied this way:

> I don't know. I really don't know and I've never known. And I suppose I never had such a position. You know the left think that I am conservative, and the conservatives think I am left or I am a maverick or God knows what. And I must say that I couldn't care less. I don't think the real questions of this century will get any kind of illumination by this kind of thing.[20]

The second quotation makes clearer what is at stake in her refusal of a certain kind of positioning of political place and, indeed, with the spectrum of right and left that it is up against. It emerges in the course of a correspondence in 1963 with Gershom Scholem [that I cited in Chapter 1]. It is fairly well known, but in my view not extremely well understood. The background is that Arendt had taken at least two public positions that irked Scholem. One of them had to do with her critique of the founding of the State of Israel in the late forties and early fifties. But the other was the publication and defense of her book *Eichmann in Jerusalem* in 1963. Her phrase "the banality of evil" enraged many members of the Jewish community who thought that the description refused the exceptional evil at work in the camps and worried that her formulation risked banalizing our understanding of the catastrophic extermination of over six million Jews by the Nazi genocidal regime.

Scholem calls Arendt "heartless" for criticizing the Jewish politics at the time, suggesting that the criticism she leveled had to be read as evidence of a failure of love. Arendt's text was controversial, of course, on a number of accounts. There were those who thought she misdescribed the relevant history for the trials, including the history of the Jewish resistance under fascism, and those who wanted her to name and analyze Eichmann himself as an emblem of evil. Her account of those trials, however, tries to debunk speculations on psychological motives as relevant to judgments that are in the service of justice. And, though she agreed with the final decision of the Israeli court that Eichmann was guilty and deserved the death penalty, she took issue with the proceedings and with the grounds on which that judgment was finally based. Some objected to her public criticism of the Israeli court, arguing that it was untimely or unseemly to criticize Israeli political institutions. Others wanted her to take the occasion of the trial to level a stronger indictment of anti-Semitism. That she finds Eichmann careerist, confused, and unpredictably "elated" by various renditions of his own infamy failed to satisfy those who sought to find in his motivations the logical culmination of centuries of anti-Semitism reflected in the policies of the Final Solution that sought the full extermination of the Jews.

Arendt refused all these interpretations (including other psychological constructs like "collective guilt") in order to establish (a) that "one cannot extract any diabolical or demonic profundity from Eichmann," and if he is in this sense "banal," he is not for that reason "commonplace"; and (b) that accounts of his action on the basis of "deeper explanations" are debatable, but that "what is not debatable is that no judicial procedure would be possible on the basis of them" (EJ, 290).

[As mentioned in Chapter 1,] Scholem continued his criticism by famously impugning Arendt's own motives, accusing her of coming from the German left and not loving the Jewish people. She responded by remarking that her love was for persons, not people.

Arendt is notably devoid of a certain pathos in her reply, but why? Do we know what it means to say she was a Jew as a matter of course, beyond dispute or argument? Was she saying that she was only nominally a Jew: a matter of genetic inheritance or historical legacy or a mixture of the two? Was she saying that she was sociologically in the position of the Jew? In response to Scholem calling her a "daughter of the Jewish people," Arendt writes, "I have never pretended to be anything else or to be in any way other than I am, and I have never felt tempted in that direction. It would have been like saying that I was a man and not a woman—that is to say, kind of insane" (JW, 466). She goes on to term "being Jewish" an "indisputable fact of my life" and adds: "there is such a thing as a basic gratitude for everything that is as it is; for what has been given and not made; for what is physei and not nomos" (JW, 466). What is remarkable here is that being a woman and a Jew are part of physei and, so, naturally constituted rather than part of any cultural order or cultural practice. But does she overstate the case?

In other words, are such categories given or made, and is there a "making" of what is "given" that complicates the apparent distinction between physei and nomos? One can, after all, refuse those categories, disown Jewishness or change gender, or one can affirm them in a mode of gratitude, as Arendt claims she does. But the very fact that one could be ungrateful or unhappy with either of those particular assigned categories suggests that how one comes to approach the category becomes central to its significance. As a result, an equivocation emerges between physei and nomos, suggesting that it is not always possible to stabilize the distinction between the two. It matters that we understand she is defending herself not in a court of law but in a letter addressed to Scholem, who has, with his own accusation, appointed himself to represent "the Jewish people." In elaborating the sense in which she is Jewish, Arendt invariably declares and constitutes her Jewishness in a specific way. We can read the letter as one such instance of discursive self-constitution, if you will. In this way, it seems important to consider that in the writing of this letter, as in her publications throughout the thirties and forties, Arendt is presenting herself as a Jew who can take such a stand. It would be difficult to read her response to Scholem as something other than an effort to make sense of, or give a particular construction to, the physei that she is. And if she is doing that, physei is subject to a cultural crafting.

Indeed, one can see in her *Jewish Writings* that, from the 1930s through the 1960s, Arendt is struggling with what it means to be Jewish without strong religious faith and why it might be important to distinguish, as she does, between the secular and the assimilated Jew. After all, she marks herself as a Jew, even expresses gratitude for that fact of her life and so takes distance from an assimilationist view. Not all forms of secular Jewishness are assimilationist. In an unfinished early piece on "Anti-Semitism" dated around 1939, Arendt argues that both Zionism and assimilationism emerge from a common dogmatism. Whereas assimilationists think that Jews belong to the nations that host them, Zionists think that the Jews must have a nation because every other nation is defined independently of its Jewish minorities. Arendt rebukes them both: "these are both the same shortcoming, and both arise out of a shared Jewish fear of admitting that there are and always have been divergent interests between Jews and segments of the people with whom they live" (JW, 51). For Arendt, the persistence of "divergent interests" does not constitute grounds for either absorption or separation. Both Zionists and assimilationists "retain the charge of foreignness" leveled against the Jews: the assimilationists point to this foreign status and seek to rectify it through gaining entrance into the host nation as full citizens, whereas the Zionists assume that there can be no permanent foreign host for the Jewish people, that anti-Semitism will visit them in any such arrangement, and that only the establishment of a specifically Jewish nation could provide protection and place. Both positions subscribe to a certain logic of the nation that Arendt starts to take apart, first in the 1930s in her investigations into anti-Semitism and the history of the Jews in Europe and then throughout the forties in her published writings in *Aufbau*, the German Jewish newspaper, on Palestine and Israel, and in her trenchant critique of the nation-state and the production of stateless persons in *The Origins of Totalitarianism* in the early fifties.

Obviously, it would be an error to read her response to Scholem as an espousal of assimilationism. She was a secular Jew, but that secularity did not eclipse the Jewishness; secularism functioned, rather, as a way of historically specifying that Jewishness and even resisting assimilation. The Jewish form of secularism to which she subscribed is accordingly specific; in her own words, she lived in the wake of a certain lost faith (although in 1935 she praised Martin Buber for renewing Judaism's religious values). Her experience of German fascism, her own forced emigration to France in the thirties, her escape from the internment camp at Gurs and subsequent emigration to the US in 1941 formed a historically specific perspective on refugees, the stateless, and the transfer and displacement of large numbers of peoples, a position that made her critical of nationalism and its pathos and gave rise to a set of vexed reflections on the status of the nation-state.

That she was not a nationalist does not mean that she was not a Jew: on the contrary, hers was a specific critique of nationalism that emerged, in part, from the historical situation of exile and displacement. For her, this was not exclusively a "Jewish" problem, but we can see that this conclusion emerges from the ability—even the political obligation—to analyze and oppose deportations, population transfers, and statelessness—in ways that refuse a nationalist ethos. On this basis, then, one can make sense of her critique of certain forms of both Zionism and assimilationism. With these considerations on the historical parameters of her Jewishness in mind, let me return to the apparent nominalism of her final remark to Scholem, that she neither "loves" the Jews nor "believes" in them, but merely "belongs" to them "as a matter of course and beyond dispute or argument." In this sentence, both "love" and "belief" are housed in quotation marks, but I wonder whether it is not also the generality, "the Jews," to which she objects. After all, she has said she can love no people, only persons (though she once wrote of "the love of the world" as both possible and obligatory). What is wrong with the notion of loving a people? In the late 1930s, Arendt argued that the efforts to "emancipate" the Jews in nineteenth-century Europe were invested less in the fate of "the Jews" than in a certain principle of progress, one requiring that the Jews be thought of as an abstraction: "liberation was to be extended not to Jews one might know or not know, not to the humble peddler or to the lender of large sums of money, but to 'the Jew in general'" (JW, 62).

Just as there were Jews considered to be exceptional, such as Moses Mendelsohn, who came to stand for "the Jews in general," so the "Jew" came to stand for the progress of human rights. The abstract Jew required that a distinction be drawn and secured between the exceptional and ordinary Jew. This distinction, in turn, formed the basis of an anti-Semitism that would consistently cast the ordinary Jew as noxious. We might see here a certain formulation in which a progressive enlightenment opposition to anti-Semitism severed the principle from the persons, providing a certain schizoid formation of the anti-Semitic opposition to anti-Semitism. Arendt argued that "the classic form in which the Jewish question was posed in the Enlightenment provides classic anti-Semitism its theoretical basis" (JW, 64).

When Arendt refuses to love "the Jewish people," she is refusing to form an attachment to an abstraction that has served questionable purposes. Generated by a historical logic that insistently separates the abstract principle, "the Jewish people," from the living plurality of beings it claims to represent, this version of the Jewish people can only reinforce both anti-Semitism and its wrong-minded opponents. Presumably "the Jewish people" includes those who are lovable and those who are not, most of whom are not known well enough to decide the matter of their lovability. In any case, the idea that love could be sustained for an abstraction called "the Jewish people" presumes a logic that, for Arendt, belongs to the history of anti-Semitism, which is reason enough to refuse the formulation. It is this principle of abstraction that she refuses in refusing Scholem's language, as well as his nationalism. Scholem's rebuke is especially problematic here since he is writing from Israel in 1963 and objecting to Arendt's quite merciless account of the Israeli court procedures at the Eichmann trial. So he is not only accusing her of not loving the Jewish people, but presuming as well that Israel and its courts—and perhaps also its strategies of demonization—legitimately "represent" those people. Effectively, he is excluding the diasporic or non-Zionist Jew—a rather large population that happens to include Arendt herself—from "the Jewish people" in whose name he writes.

Arendt herself is no less complicated. Although she claims in 1963 that being Jewish is simply something given and indisputable, she has earlier opposed those who "loftily declare themselves above ties to nations." So is Jewishness a fact of existence or a national mode of belonging? She argued as well that if one is attacked as a Jew, one must fight back as a Jew (though she rejected the Sartrean formulation that held that anti-Semitism has produced the Jew). As a result, even if to be a Jew is a matter of physei, it does not sanction assimilation or individualism. But can it imply national belonging? Indeed, she describes the Jews as a nation throughout her writings in the 1930s and 1940s. For Arendt, the key was to think this mode of belonging in a way that refuses nationalism and escapes the bad dialectical logic that spawns abstract idealization, on the one hand, and particularist denigration, on the other, both of which support classical formulations of anti-Semitism. Could Arendt be speaking for the Jews as a nation even when she opposes certain forms of Zionism and nationalism and, eventually, even when she opposes the idea of a Jewish nation-state?

As for Jewish nationalism founded on secular presumptions, she is clearly opposed. This doesn't mean she wants a polity based on religious grounds either. Any polity considered to be just will have to extend equality to all citizens and to all nationalities: that is in many ways the lesson she learns from opposing German fascism and tracing the recurrent patterns of statelessness in the twentieth century. She worries openly about the devolution of Judaism from a set of religious beliefs into a national political identity. She writes,

> those Jews who no longer believe in their God in a traditional way but continue to think of themselves as "chosen" in some fashion or other, can mean by it nothing other than that by nature they are wiser or more rebellious or more salt of the earth. And that would be, twist and turn it as you like, nothing other than a version of racist superstition. (JW, 162)

She claims at one point that "our national misery" followed from the "collapse of the Shabbetai Tzevi movement. Ever since then we have proclaimed our existence per se—without any national or usually any religious content—as a thing of value" (JW, 137).[21] Although she clearly understands the struggle to survive as indispensable to the twentieth-century fate of the Jews, she finds unacceptable the notion that "survival itself" has trumped ideals of justice, equality, or freedom. A politics committed to these latter norms undercuts those national ties whose realization depends upon and exceeds the matter of survival.

If Arendt opposes assimilation and individualism alike, and voices skepticism toward those who understand themselves to be aloof from all notions of nation, how are we to understand, in her terms, in what sense the Jews are a nation and whether they can be a nation without nationalism and without a nation-state? In the late thirties and early forties Arendt thought that the Jews might become a nation among nations, part of a federated Europe; she imagined that all the European nations who were struggling against fascism could ally with one another and that the Jews might have their own army that would struggle against fascism in alliance with other European armies. She argued then for a nation without territory (typical of early cultural Zionist views) that only makes sense in a federated form, a nation that would be defined by its constitutive plurality. This position would lead her to prefer the proposal of a federated Jewish-Arab state in the place of Israel as a state grounded in Jewish sovereignty. In her view of 1943, "Palestine can be saved as the national homeland of Jews only if it is integrated into a federation" (JW, 19s).

In the struggle against German fascism, however, she thought that equality was to be found among the nations struggling for freedom and against fascism. Although this is a secular political solution, she states the rationale for such a political organization through recourse to a religious parable within Judaism. "As Jews," she writes, "we want to fight for the freedom of the Jewish people because 'if I am not for me—who is for me?' As Europeans we want to fight for the freedom of Europe, because 'If I am only for me—who am I?'" (JW, 142). This last question is, as I mentioned earlier, the famous question of Hillel, the Jewish commentator from the first century AD. Interestingly, she does not use that citation when she writes to Scholem, but is it perhaps there, haunting the response ? In countering Scholem, she refuses to offer a religious formulation of her own identity. But here and elsewhere, for instance in her discussion of forgiveness in *The Human Condition*, she draws upon the Jewish religious tradition to formulate political principles that organize the secular field of politics (this is something other than grounding a secular politics on religious principles). We can perhaps discern the ethical disposition that she finds in Hillel in the words she does use: this "love of the Jews" would appear to me, since I am myself Jewish, as something rather suspect. I cannot love myself or anything which I know is part and parcel of my own person. And then again, in "and now this people believes only in itself? What good can come out of that?" She cannot be only for herself, for then who would she be? But if she is not for herself, who will be? However important survival may be, it is not the end of an ethical life. One must be for something other than one's own persistence, even though, we may assume, one cannot continue to be for anything (and so live ethically) without also persisting. And as a constitutive feature of that persistence, that which she cannot, or will not, deny, is her Jewishness. Hence, we might argue, as Jewish, she must be for something that is not the same as herself.

Arendt's way of negotiating this site of belonging and obligation to others does not escape a paradoxical formulation. Her response to Scholem does not exactly establish her status as an assimilated Jew, but rather as one whose critical task is to oppose the abstraction of the Jewish people that has supported assimilationism, Zionist nationalism, and anti-Semitism alike. Moreover, she seeks recourse to a sense of belonging to the world of the non-Jew, a belonging that is neither radical identification nor radical differentiation and so at once preserves Jewish difference and resists Jewish identitarianism. The preferred non-Jew she has in mind is, of course, the European, and though she will later make some efforts to think about what "belonging" might mean for Jews and Arabs who inhabit the same land, her views throughout this period are emphatically Eurocentric. "We enter this war as a European people" she insisted in the late 1930s. But this is, of course, to skew the history of Judaism, to marginalize the Sephardim, the Jews from Spain and North Africa, and to write out, once again, Mizrachim, the Jews from Arab countries, or Arab Jews, those who receive brief mention as "Oriental Jews" in *Eichmann in Jerusalem*.[22] Indeed, this presumption about the cultural superiority of Europe pervades much of her later writings and becomes most clear in her intemperate criticisms of Fanon, her debunking of the teaching of Swahili at Berkeley, and her dismissal of the black power movement in the 1960s.[23] But perhaps the most dramatic example of her European arrogance is found in a letter she wrote to Karl Jaspers in 1961 during the Eichmann trial; she developed a racist typology of what she saw:

> My first impression. On top, the judges, the best of German Jewry. Below them, the persecuting attorneys, Galicians, but still Europeans. Everything is organized by a police force that gives me the creeps, speaks only Hebrew and looks Arabic. Some downright brutal types among them. They would follow any order. And outside, the oriental mob, as if one were in Istanbul or some other half-Asiatic country. In addition, and very visible in Jerusalem, the peies and caftan Jews, who make Me impossible for all the reasonable people here.[24]

Clearly, the "reasonable people" are neither religious nor Arab, and her reference to "the oriental mob" makes clear that some part of her objection to Israel has to do with the offensive thought that European Jews would be situated in the Middle East, intermixed with Arab and Sephardic jews. Arendt's sense of Jewishness was pervasively European, and though she argued that she could only love persons, not "people" of any kind, it would be interesting to know whether she could nevertheless hate "people"— collectivizing them as she did into "oriental mobs" and the like.[25] If European Jews had a purchase on "reasonableness" and those from Arab cultures would "follow any order," then she unwittingly draws a parallel between Eichmann, whom she also accuses of following any order, and the non-European Jews she encounters at a distance at the Jerusalem trial. Both are outside the presumptive culture of reason, and yet Eichmann is very clearly both German and European.

This possibly unconscious linking of the Arab Jew with Eichmann reveals a serious fault line in Arendt's thinking. There is a certain kind of Jew she does not like (Arab) and a certain kind of German she does not like (Nazi). If both fall outside the domain of reason and would follow any order out of blind obedience, then neither are properly thinking. Proper thinking appears to belong to that subset of Jew and European who is German Jewish, although probably not exclusively. Arendt's pervasive Eurocentrism (one that could, following Toqueville, make room for the exemplary character of the American Revolution) can be seen as a continuation of a German Jewish connection articulated most dramatically by Hermann Cohen. His essay, "Deutschtum and Judentum," published in 1915, made the case that Jews did not really need a homeland, since they belonged essentially to the definition of Europe.[26] Cohen's argument was directed against early versions of Zionism (the First Zionist Congress took place in Basel in 1897). But it also affirmed a faith he had in Europe as the proper, even the safest, place for Jews. Of course, Cohen's article has become increasingly painful to read over time, since he believed that Germany would protect Jews against anti-Semitism. His essay maintains a tenacious belief that Jewishness and Germanness are interlinked, and that it is not possible to think the one mode of belonging without the other. Obviously, Cohen denied the historical evidence for German anti-Semitism available at the time. But, for him, Europe was not the name for all the sociological phenomena that existed within its territories, but for an ideal, mainly Kantian, that he associated with German ethical philosophy. In fact, his ethical philosophy, associated with the Marburg school of neo-Kantianism, tried to reconcile certain notions of social justice, derived from Jewish theological resources, with principles of universality derived from Kant. Cohen argued explicitly for a marriage of German humanism and Jewish messianism, a coupling that he understood to yield "a religion of reason." Although he saw Germany close its doors to eastern European Jews during the First World War, and publicly opposed it, he continued to pledge allegiance to a culture that showed increasing signs that it would not only fail to protect the Jews but endanger them fundamentally. Cohen died in 1918, so what he actually witnessed was rising anti-Semitism in public discourse and increasingly strict immigration quotas. But it remains painful to consider the pledge he made and thought others should make as well.

Of course, it seems like Zionism wins the day, if we consider Cohen's tragic embrace of Germany as fatherland as the only alternative. Although that is not the path Arendt finally takes, these two thinkers remain cognate. They both maintain a faith in Europe, indeed a strange sort of Eurocentrism, and an identification of what is best in German culture with Kant's philosophy. In this context, it is interesting to note that during Hitler's regime, when Arendt was contributing war journalism in Germany and France (where she lived briefly before leaving for New York City and the New School in 1940), she argued in favor of a Jewish army. She called for a Jewish army that would join the fight against National Socialism, and she imagined that it would work in concert with other European armies—as part of a federated collective. Conceived as a nation, the Jews would fight alongside the noncollaborationist French, Dutch, and the antifascist Italians. On the one hand, it was remarkable that Arendt understood the Jewish people as a nation and, especially, a European nation. And on the other hand, it is interesting to note that even here, or perhaps beginning here, she is trying to elaborate a notion of international resistance and cooperation that was neither Marxist nor based on classically liberal notions of individualism.

One can clearly see how both Arendt and Cohen seek to restrict the idea of Jewishness to what is European, which becomes a way of denying the existence and importance of non-European Jewish traditions. But, most important, both look to Kant as a way of securing the European intellectual connection for a "reasonable" Jewish culture. This will turn out to be important in Arendt's *Eichmann in Jerusalem* when she objects to Eichmann allying himself with Kant's moral philosophy [a topic we will consider in the following chapter].

Scholem's difficulties with Arendt seem to have nothing to do, however, with her racist views about Jewish demographics in Israel. He is implicitly raising the question of whether her apparent lack of love for the Jewish people could account for her criticisms of the founding of Israel and her refusal to back its claims of Jewish sovereignty in the period 1944 to 1948. The efforts to place her on "the left" may seem understandable in this regard, but whatever resonance there may be with the left is surely only a partial one. We would misunderstand the line she seeks to walk if we accepted that placement too easily. For instance, in the criticism of the nation-state that she supplied in *The Origins of Totalitarianism*, she is clear that the modern nation-state is bound up, by a kind of necessity, with the production of massive numbers of refugees or stateless persons. On the other hand, she is quick to criticize as useless and impotent those existing forms of international alliance that seek to secure human rights for the stateless. She offers a long catalog of foiled international efforts to articulate, secure, and enforce human rights outside the framework of the nation-state (OT, 267–302). This has led many readers of Arendt to conclude that the nation-state is inevitable and that, if we care about rights, we will seek to establish, build, and protect nation-states that will articulate and secure the basic human rights of all their inhabitants.

Such views, however, fail to take seriously her proposals regarding federated polities, ones that she developed in relation to Europe and Palestine. Accordingly, one can see a highly ambivalent relationship to Zionism as a result. In the 1930s she maintains a significant paradox within her political thinking: she asserts that national belonging is an important value and she maintains that nationalism is a noxious and fatal political formation. In the early forties she supported the Jewish emigration from Europe to Palestine, but only on the condition that Jews also fought for recognition as a "nation" within Europe. In 1935 she praised Martin Buber and the socialist project of the kibbutzim, and another year later she warned against thinking that the Jewish occupation of Palestine could ever work as a permanent protection against anti-Semitism. In the early 1940s she wrote several editorials in which she asked that the idea of nation be separated from that of territory. It was on the basis of this view that she defended the proposal for a Jewish army and leveled a strong criticism of the British government's "equivocal" relation to the Jews, as evidenced by the famous White Paper of 1939 that limited the number of Jewish refugees permitted into Palestine.[27] In the late 1930s, though, she also wrote that "the bankruptcy of the Zionist movement caused by the reality of Palestine is at the same time the bankruptcy of autonomous, isolated Jewish politics" (JW, 59). In 1943 she worried that the proposal for a binational state in Palestine could only be maintained by enhancing the reliance of Palestine on Britain and other major powers, including the United States. She sometimes actively worried as well that binationalism could only work to the advantage of the Arab population and to the disadvantage of the Jews. In 1944, in "Zionism Reconsidered," she argued forcefully that the risks of founding a state on principles of Jewish sovereignty could only augment the problem of statelessness that had become increasingly acute in the wake of the First and Second World Wars (JW, 343–74). By the early 1950s Arendt openly argued that Israel was founded through colonial occupation and with the assistance of superpowers and on the basis of citizenship requirements that were pervasively antidemocratic. If, in the 1930s, she worried about the Jews becoming increasingly stateless, in the late 1940s and early 1950s she was attuned to the displacement of Palestinians and developed a more comprehensive account of statelessness.

In "Zionism Reconsidered" Arendt offers an interesting historical account of the inception of Zionism and its changes in the mid-twentieth century. There she remarks that it is absurd that a Jewish state should be erected in what she calls a "sphere of interest" of the superpowers. Such a state suffers under the "delusion of nationhood," and, she concludes, "only folly could dictate a policy which trusts a distant imperial power for protection, while alienating the good will of its neighbors" (JW, 372). On the one hand, she is clearly anxious to find ways for Israel/Palestine to survive and actively worries that the foundations for the polity can only lead to ruin. She writes, "if a Jewish commonwealth is obtained in the near future" (with the assistance of American Jews) and

> proclaimed against the will of the Arabs and without the support of the Mediterranean peoples, not only financial help but political support will be necessary for a long time to come. And that may turn out to be very troublesome for Jews in this country, who after all have no power to direct the political destinies of the Near East. (JW, 373)

What Arendt objects to in the nation-state is nationalism and its consequence: the forced exile of those nationalities that are not recognized as the one nation expressed by the state. Given that modern states house increasing numbers of nationalities, the conceit of the nation-state can only be a dangerous one, since it seeks to align nation with state through the expulsion of those nationalities that do not conform to the idea of the nation that sanctions the state. In "The Decline of the Rights of Man and the End of the Nation-State" (1951), Arendt argues that the power of totalitarian denationalization could not be countered by a doctrine of human rights and that that doctrine finally functions as a weak instrument. As in her early writings, she finds most of these international accords to be useless. If there is to be a safeguard for rights, it will have to be found within the context of a polity. This polity would have to be something other than the nation-state. If the nation-state is built upon national assumptions that require the expulsion of national minorities, then it produces the acute vulnerability of stateless persons— understood as disenfranchised minorities—to exploitation and violence. Indeed, Arendt gives as the reason for the rise of European fascism the massive increase in stateless peoples after World War I. Nationalism overwhelms the rule of law, and minority populations become subject to denationalization, expulsion, and extermination.[28] The rule of law, understood as something that should apply to all people equally, became less important than the will of the nation; at the same time, the nation, defined racially and ethnically, began to treat the stateless as a population to be managed and controlled. The state thus took on a function unregulated by the rule of law, and, in Arendt's terms, "denationalization became a powerful weapon of totalitarian politics" (OT, 269).

We might say that this is one of the rhetorical aims of denationalization, to show that depriving groups of their citizenship produces a picture of those deprived as essentially inhuman, and this picture of their inhumanness, their status as scum, conversely serves to justify the policy of denationalization. A stateless person is an "outlaw" by definition and so is not "deserving" of legal protection (OT, 283). Arendt is clear that statelessness was not an exclusively Jewish problem, and those who saw it this way failed to understand that the twentieth-century reduction of "German Jews to a nonrecognized minority in Germany," the subsequent expulsions of the Jews as "stateless people across the borders," and then the "gathering of them back from everywhere in order to ship them to extermination camps was an eloquent demonstration to the rest of the world how really to 'liquidate' all problems concerning minorities and the stateless" (OT, 290). Thus, she continues, bravely, I might add:

> After the war it turned out that the Jewish question, which was considered the only insoluble one, was indeed solved—namely by means of a colonized and then conquered territory—but this solved neither the problems of the minorities nor the stateless. On the contrary, like virtually all other events of our century, the solution of the Jewish question merely produced a new category of refugees, the Arabs, thereby increasing the number of stateless and rightless by another 700,000 to 800,000 people. And what happened in Palestine within the smallest territory and in terms of hundreds of thousands was then repeated in India on a large scale involving millions of people. (OT, 290)

Although at the time of the Nakba Arendt could not have known that the number of displaced Palestinians possibly exceeded 900,000 and that the population of displaced persons would increase to 3.5 million, she was clear that such expulsions were bound to happen when states were based on principles of national belonging. Thus Arendt controversially insisted that one has to think about this problem of refugees and the stateless as a repeated problem attached to states that are formed on the model of the nation-state. One might well ask what states are like that are not the same as nation-states, whether nation-states can exist without producing the horrendous consequence of massive numbers of stateless minorities, whether the problem is structural or historical, or both.[29] After she conducts her searing critique of the nation-state, we are left with no sign of what the state or a polity might be that would be disjoined from the nation and what a nation might be that would be separated off from territory. And yet she offers us a few comments on "federations" that suggest she thought something might come of them. In 1944 Arendt presciently warned that "even a Jewish majority in Palestine—nay, even a transfer of all Palestine Arabs—would not substantially change a situation in which Jews must either ask for protection from an outside power against their neighbors or come to a working agreement with their neighbors." The alternative, she writes, is that "Jewish interests will clash with those of all other

Mediterranean peoples; so that, instead of one 'tragic conflict' we shall face tomorrow as many insoluble conflicts as there are Mediterranean nations" (JW, 345).

In 1943 Arendt wrote against the proposal for a binational state then defended by Judah Magnes and Martin Buber. She thought then that their use of the term *federation* named the nation-state in a different way. She wrote: "The use of the term 'federation' kills its new and creative meaning in the germ; it kills the idea that a federation is—in contrast to a nation—made up of different peoples with equal rights" (JW, 336). If she worried in 1943 that the Jews would be outnumbered and unprotected by their Arab coinhabitants, she revises this view only a year later in "Zionism Reconsidered." There she offers an extended criticism of the forms of nationalism upon which Zionism draws and which it fortifies and extends. After acknowledging that Jews have little reason to be happy about the decline of the nation-state or of nationalism, she makes the following prediction: "The resurgent problem of how to organize politically will be solved by adopting either the forms of empire or the form of federations." She continues:

> only the latter [federations] would give the Jewish people, together with other small peoples, a reasonably fair chance for survival. The former may not be possible without arousing imperialist passions as a substitute for outdated nationalism, once the motor to set men into action. Heaven help us if that comes to pass. (JW, 371)

In 1948, after the UN sanctioning of the State of Israel, Arendt predicts,

> even if the Jews were to win the war, its end would find the ... achievements of Zionism destroyed.... The "victorious" Jews would live surrounded by an entirely hostile Arab population, secluded inside ever-threatened borders, absorbed with physical self-defense to a degree that would submerge all other interests and activities. (JW, 396)

And, during this same year, she returns to Magnes's position, remarking that partition cannot work, that the best solution is a "federated state." This trusteeship, she wrote, would be composed of "small local units composed of Jews and Arabs under the command of higher officers from countries that are members of the United Nations and could become an important school for future cooperative self-government" (JW, 400). Such a federation, in her view, "would have the advantage of preventing the establishment of sovereignty whose only sovereign right would be to commit suicide" (JW, 399).

The idea of federation is clearly an alternative to established ideas about sovereignty in relation to the nation-state. That latter concept relies upon a serious error when it yokes two concepts together: the state, which is supposed to preserve a rule of law that would protect anyone and everyone regardless of nationality, and the nation, understood as a mode of belonging that is based on nationality and so makes exclusions on the basis of those who belong and those who do not. For this reason, she opposed the idea that nation-states should have sovereignty, and she opposed as well those versions of federated power that would give each member nation its own sovereign power. The point was not to distribute sovereignty to multiple nations, but to undo sovereignty through a conception of a federated plurality in which law and policy would be made in common. Sovereignty was not to be distributed among smaller "nations" but dispersed into a plurality that would be irreducible to multiple nationalities. Such a federation undoes the notion of sovereignty as unified and ultimate power and requires a deindividualization of the nation, so that it becomes quite literally impossible to conceive of a nation or its actions outside the context of plural and concerted action. National interests are not the same, she claims, as common interests. A federation might constitute a plurality of nations, but no nation could have sovereignty within the context of that polity. In 1951 a nation is, for her, a sphere of belonging, but certainly not the legitimate basis of the state. As a result, Jews can be imagined as a "nation" within a federation (in Europe or in the Middle East), but they would be committed to a form of political life that would demand power sharing, concerted action, the dissolution of sovereignty into plural power, and a commitment to equality across national ties. In this way, Arendt could conceive of the Jews as a nation only as long as that national status did not give them sovereign power to decide with whom to govern the state, that is, a nation without a nation-state, a nation that could constitute a sphere of belonging within a polity structured as a federated plurality.

By the time she wrote *The Origins of Totalitarianism* in 1951, Arendt was still hammering away at the problem of statelessness, though both the European and the Palestinian version of the federation fell from her vocabulary. In its place emerges an assertion of "common interest," one that she formulates over and against a human rights framework that remains committed to an individualist ontology. She reviews a litany of failures that marked the history of international accords and human rights declarations, yet it seems clear that she is not altogether done with *The Declaration of the Rights of Man*. After all, such declarations were evidence of collective deliberations of humans, in the plural, who allocate to themselves these rights and so declare them, announce them, and, through the power of that declaration, institute them as human accomplishments. The idea was that to declare the rights of man was to establish some protection against despotic political regimes. Those declarations cannot be exercised effectively outside the context of a polity grounded in common interests, but are they, then, altogether useless? In the second part of "The Decline of the Nation-State and the Rights of Man," Arendt outlines what she takes to be essential preconditions for the exercise of any rights at all. And these preconditions include place and political belonging. She writes, "the fundamental deprivation of human rights is manifested first and above all in the deprivation of a place in the world which makes opinions significant and actions effective" (OT, 296). It would follow that in and through this writing Arendt is seeking to rectify the ineffective rhetoric of human rights by laying out the conditions under which political rhetoric can become and remain effective. She is not only presenting the conditions for the exercise of effective discourse, but wielding discourse effectively—or at least trying to. And though she never says how her own rhetoric is linked to the critique of human rights discourse she offers, she effectively displaces that discourse with her own.

What this means for Arendt's notion of the social meaning of the human is significant. After all, she is suggesting that our efficacy and the true exercise of our freedom does not follow from our individual personhood, but rather from social conditions such as place and political belonging. This is not a matter of finding the human dignity within each person, but of understanding the human as a social being, as one who requires place and community in order to be free, to exercise freedom of thought as opinion, to exercise political action that is efficacious. It also means understanding that the human becomes politically destitute when these conditions are not met. She certainly sounds like a partisan of a doctrine of human rights grounded in an emphatically social ontology (as well as a critic of the nation-state) when she writes, "the right to have rights, or the right of every individual to belong to humanity, should be guaranteed by humanity itself" (OT, 298). And yet, the question remains: by what means would humanity guarantee such rights? She gives us no answer, though she does seek to supply the norm with which any answer would have to comply.

For Arendt, freedom is not an attribute of individuals, but an exercise and concerted action that is performed by a "we" and which, in the exercise and performance, institutes that "we" as the social condition of rights themselves. Thus, she writes, "our political life rests on the assumption that we can produce equality through organization, because man can act in and change and build a common world, together with his equals and only with his equals" (OT, 301). We would be making a mistake if we were to imagine a group of individuals amassing together as a collection of individual actors. None of those individuals are human unless and until concerted and collective action becomes possible. Indeed, to be human is a function, a feature of acting on terms of equality with other humans. One can hear the echoes of Heidegger's mitsein, but also some faint resonance of a leftist collectivity that Scholem suspected in his caricature of her politics. If to be human is to be in a relation of equality with others, then no one can become human outside of relations of equality. Does Arendt not ask us to consider that "human being" is a function or effect of this egalitarianism? Indeed, if there is no equality, no one is human. If equality decides the human, then no human can be human alone, but only with others, and only under conditions that sustain a social plurality in equality.[30]

It is doubtless important to note that the idea of "belonging" that informs her writing on "the nation" in the thirties and forties seems to slip away by the time the Eichmann trial arrives and plays out on the public stage. The idea of plurality seems to replace the idea of a nation that belongs to no territory and no state and in its commitment to equality resists absorption into nationalism. The irreducible complexity of the Jews as a people makes it difficult to speak for very long about a "nation," and Arendt turns her attention to forms of living in contestation and difference. If a notion of belonging still worked for her in the forties and early fifties, it seems already to have been displaced by a more antisolidaristic notion of political organization in *On Revolution* (1962), where she praises the "communal council system" in the French Revolution, understood as a spontaneously organized embrace of the federal principle. Similarly, Madison's federalism, which retained but subordinated the power of constituent states, drew a legitimating power from the states, but undid their sovereignty through federated authority. In Arendt s view, "the federal system was the sole alternative to the nation-state principle" in the American Revolution.[31]

It is difficult to imagine the hopes that Arendt invested in federated power. It was a way to institutionalize an equality that not only undercut national sovereignty, but eventually led her to leave the idea of the "nation" behind. Equality underwrites not only the social ontology of the human, for Arendt, but the political possibility of a postnational federation or a new and more efficacious human rights framework. If the polity that would guarantee rights is not the nation-state, then it would either be a federation in which sovereignty is undone through a distribution of its power or a human rights framework that would be binding on those who collectively produced its terms. The federation is what she imagined, perhaps naively, for the Jews in Europe in the late 1930s—which is why a Jewish army could represent the "nation" of Jews without having either state or territory as the presupposition of nationhood. It was also what she came to imagine in 1948 for Jews and for Palestinians, in spite of the founding of the State of Israel on nationalist premises and claims of Jewish sovereignty. She might be faulted for her naïveté in both instances, but then we would have to account as well for the prescience of her predictions, dire as they were: the recurrence of statelessness and the persistence of violence. If she had no love for the Jewish people, as Scholem claimed, then perhaps it was because, as a Jewish refugee, she took seriously the history of displacement and exile, and it became the basis of her critical commitment to the difficult task of securing rights for the stateless without resurrecting the nation-state and its ritual expulsions. She writes as a Jew concerned with the claims of refuge, and, precisely because she is concerned with those claims, her analysis cannot be restricted to the Jew ("if I am not for myself, who will be? If I am only for myself, what am I?"). Rights and justice cannot be restricted to the Jew or to any particular religious or cultural mode of belonging—and this very argument is made on the basis of Jewish thought.

Her critique of German fascism and nationalism led her to a politics centered not on a Jewish homeland but on the rights of the stateless. If this is Jewish, it is diasporic, and though she does not articulate this position in relation to Scholem, perhaps we can nevertheless see it at work in what she wrote. If she argues for home and for belonging, it is not to build a polity on those established ties of fealty, since a polity, to be legitimate, would have to be based on equality. This last is the only safeguard she can see against recurrent statelessness and its sufferings. Although belonging is a requirement of human life, it can never serve as a legitimate basis for a polity. From this vexed paradox, Arendt develops a critical practice that enters and departs from the category of the "Jewish people" as she articulates the discordant and convergent demands of belonging and universality. If she is a Jewish thinker who comes to oppose the dispossessions that afflict any and every minority, then this is a different kind of Jewish pursuit of justice—different from the one that would of necessity find its representation in the Israeli courts. It would be a position that does not universalize the Jew, but makes use of the historical conditions of displacement to oppose the sufferings of statelessness in every circumstance.

Arendt offers a significantly different set of theoretical resources than those who begin their analysis of contemporary politics through recourse to the idea of sovereignty. Instead, Arendt takes statelessness as her point of departure, a condition that is not always formally or actually linked to the problem of sovereignty. Indeed, her federated vision for Palestine sought to overcome statelessness through a deconstitution of sovereign power. Although those proposals formulated in 1946 to 1947 predated her work on the rights of the stateless in *The Origins of Totalitarianism*, she had already grasped that the repeated and devastating expulsion of populations from the nation-state produces a crisis that requires the rethinking of nationalism and the nation-state. Her insight implied as well that the refugees from Nazi Germany were part of a larger set of historical expulsions that needed to be understood in their specificity and structural similarity. By insisting that statelessness is the recurrent political disaster of the twentieth century (which now takes on new forms in the twenty-first that she could not have predicted), Arendt refuses to give a metaphysical cast to "bare life." Those who have been dispossessed of rights are actively dispossessed: they are not jettisoned from the polis into an apolitical realm (that is to let the classical idea of the polis decide all political relations). The rightless and stateless are maintained in conditions of political destitution, especially by forms of military power. And, even when their lives are destroyed, those deaths remain political. Indeed, Arendt writes quite clearly in *The Origins of Totalitarianism* that the ostensible "state of nature" to which displaced and stateless people are reduced is not natural or metaphysical at all, but the name for a specifically political form of destitution.

Notes

This chapter was originally given at a symposium on Religion in the Public Sphere in October 2009, with Cornell West, Charles Taylor, and Jürgen Habermas. It was republished in Jonathan Antwerpen and Eduardo Mendietta (eds), *The Power of Religion in the Public Sphere* (New York: Columbia University Press, 2011). The chapter was first published in Judith Butler's *Parting Ways: Jewishness and the Critique of Zionism* (New York: Columbia University Press, 2012). It is here reproduced with the permission of copyright holders.

1. David Biale, *Not in the Heavens: The Tradition of Jewish Secular Thought* (Princeton, NJ: Princeton University Press, 2011).
2. See Talal Asad, Wendy Brown, Judith Butler, and Saba Mahmood, *Is Critique Secular? Blasphemy, Injury, and Free Speech* (Berkeley: University of California Press, 2009).
3. See Theodor Herzl, *The Jewish State* (Rockville, MD: Wildside, 2008), 63–72.
4. Hannah Arendt, *The Origins of Totalitarianism* (New York: Harcourt Brace Jovanovich, 1951), p. 66; *Rachel Varnhagen: The Life of a Jewish Woman* (New York: Harcourt Brace Jovanovich, 1974), 216–28.
5. See Jacques Rancière, *The Politics of Aesthetics: The Distribution of the Sensible* (London: Continuum, 2006).
6. She emerged from a complex tradition of German Jewish thought, and I do not

mean to engage in an idealization here, since there are many reasons *not* to idealize her. She wrote and spoke some clearly racist beliefs and she is no model for a broader politics of understanding across cultural difference. But she continues a German Jewish debate that began in the late nineteenth century about the value and meaning of Zionism. There was, for instance, a famous debate between Hermann Cohen— whose views I will return to—and Gershom Scholem on the value of Zionism in which Cohen criticized the nascent nationalism of Zionism and offered instead a vision of the Jewish people as cosmopolitan or "hyphenated." Cohen argued that Jews were best served by becoming part of the German nation—a view that could only prove most painful and impossible with the development of German fascism and its virulent anti-Semitism. Arendt shared Cohen's high valuation of German culture, though she explicitly rejected that nationalism.

7   See Susannah Young-ah Gottlieb, *Regions of Sorrow: Anxiety and Messianism in W. H. Auden* (Palo Alto: Stanford University Press, 2003).
8   Hannah Arendt, *Love and Saint Augustine,* ed. Joanna Vecchiarelli Scott and Judith Chelius Stark (Chicago, IL: University of Chicago Press, 2007).
9   Hannah Arendt, "Jewish History, Revised" in *The Jewish Writings,* ed. Jerome Kohn and Ron H. Feldman (New York: Schocken, 2007), 305.
10 Gabriel Piterberg, *The Returns of Zionism* (London: Verso, 2008), 179.
11 Amnon Raz-Krakotzkin, "Jewish Memory Between Exile and History," *JQR* 97, no. 4 (2007): 530–43, "Exile Within Sovereignty," *Theory and Criticism*, no. 4 (2007), *Exil et souveraineté* (Paris: Fabrique, 2007).
12 Of course, as Arendt herself points out, the need to establish an "internal" history of the Jewish people is one way to counter the position, held by Sartre and others, that the historical life of the Jews is determined mainly or exclusively by anti-Semitism.
13 Amnon Raz-Krakotzin, "'On the Right Side of the Barricades': Walter Benjamin, Gershom Scholem, and Zionism" (on file with the author).
14 This raises a complex question about the relation between the "cessation of happening" characteristic of the general strike and the end to a homogeneous form of history. At what point does the first cessation become the condition for the second, or are they at some point continuous with one another?
15 Hannah Arendt, *Eichmann in Jerusalem* (New York: Schocken, 1963), 277–78.
16 William Connolly, *The Ethos of Pluralization* (Minneapolis: University of Minnesota Press, 2005).
17 See Emmanuel Levinas, *Otherwise Than Being; or, Beyond Essence,* trans. Alphonso Lingis (Pittsburgh: Duquesne University Press, 1998).
18 Hala Khamis Nassar and Najat Rahman (eds), *Mahmoud Darwish, Exile's Poet: Critical Essays* (Northampton, MA: Olive Branch, 2008). For a discussion of "here" and "there" in Darwish, see Jeffrey Sacks, "Language Places," ibid., 253–61. Sacks makes the connection between Darwish's poetic references to the shifting sense of "here" in relation to Hegel's *Phenomenology of Spirit*. In Hegel's *Phenomenology of Spirit* the discussion of the shifting "here" takes place in the section on sense-certainty. G. W. F. Hegel, *Phenomenology of Spirit,* trans. A. V. Miller (New York: Oxford University Press, 1977) 60–1.
19 See the introduction in my *Frames of War: When Is Life Grievable?* (London: Verso, 2009).
20 "Hannah Arendt on Hannah Arendt" in Melvyn A. Hill, ed., *Hannah Arendt: The Recovery of the Public World* (New York: St. Martin's Press, 1979), 333–4.

21 See Jacqueline Rose, *The Question of Zion* (Princeton, NJ: Princeton University Press, 2005), for a contrary view. Rose links the messianic movement with the Zionist pursuit of recurrent military catastrophe. My question is whether the messianic can give rise to a countermilitary position.
22 See note 25 below. See Amnon Raz-Krakotzkin, "Binationalism and Jewish Identity: Hannah Arendt and the Question of Palestine," in Steven E. Aschheim, ed., *Hannah Arendt in Jerusalem* (Berkley: University of California Press, 2001), 165–80, "Jewish Peoplehood, 'Jewish Politics,' and Political Responsibility—Arendt on Zionism and Partitions" (on file with the author).
23 Hannah Arendt, *On Violence* (New York: Harcourt, Brace, 1969), 20, 67, 80, 18, 24, 65.
24 Arendt to Jaspers, April 13, 1961, letter 285, in Hannah Arendt and Karl Jaspers, *Correspondence, 1926–1969*, Lotte Kohler and Hans Saner (eds), trans. Robert Kimber and Rita Kimber (New York: Harcourt Brace Jovanovich, 1992), 434–6.
25 See Raz-Krakotzkin, "Jewish Peoplehood." See also Anne Norton, "Heart of Darkness: Africa and African Americans in the Writings of Hannah Arendt," in Bonnie Honig, ed., *Feminist Interpretations of Hannah Arendt* (University Park: Pennsylvania State University Press, 1995), 247–62.
26 A selective English translation of Hermann Cohen's *Deutschtum und Judentum* can be found in Eva Jospe, ed. and trans., *Reason and Hope: Selections from the Jewish Writings of Hermann Cohen* (New York: Hebrew Union College Press, 1997).
27 The White Paper was a British document published in May of 1939 that sought to establish a "Jewish National Home" in Palestine, but refused to grant the notion of Jewish self-rule. It imposed restrictions on Jewish immigration and land acquisition in the territory and was regarded as a strike against Zionist nationalist aspirations. See Rashid Khalidi, *The Iron Cage: The Story of the Palestinian Struggle for Statehood* (Boston: Beacon, 2006), 31–64.
28 Arendt is clearly opposing any efforts on the part of a human rights discourse to seek its legitimacy in nature or natural rights. But it would be wrong to say she has no affinity with such positions. In "The Decline of the Rights of Man and the End of the Nation-State" it would appear that she is writing against those who claim that the state and its provisions of citizenship constitute the problem of modernity. But can we say the same for the nation-state? What is clear is that she has no particular sympathy with the idealization of nature one finds in certain Enlightenment texts and she disputes the notion that one might find in nature those principles of equality, justice, and freedom we might like to see in the context of political life. In her view, stateless people are returned violently to a state of nature where there are no protections and no entitlements and where it is impossible to maintain what she calls their "humanity." If there is to be a human subject, it must be made in the context of political life, made collectively; there can be no freedom outside a polis, a political community that is structured by equality and freedom. Of course, equality and freedom seem to have a status that does not fully depend on the contingent articulations performed by various states, and they seem to function as norms in her work, thus allying her with certain natural law theorists. Indeed, there seems to be something of an impulse of natural law that is void of the state of nature hypothesis, but this is a conjecture to pursue another time. What's clear here is that, in her view, the humanity of human beings only comes into being in the context of a political community and that those who are excluded, expelled, or, indeed, exterminated are

deprived of their humanity the moment their rights to citizenship are suspended or destroyed.

The massive expulsions of populations in the twentieth century have, in her view, brought this situation into relief. Arendt opens this essay by letting us know that it will be "almost impossible" to imagine what happened at the end of World War I. She describes the migrations of people who "were welcomed nowhere and could be assimilated nowhere." She describes as well a situation in which "hatred … began to play a role in public affairs everywhere," a "vague, pervasive hatred of everybody and everything, without a focus for its passionate attention, with nobody to make responsible for the state of affairs." She describes, within the context of Europe, the emergence of two victim groups, the stateless and the minorities (OT, 268). Both groups were deprived of rights of citizenship, settling uneasily with provisional legality in various countries where they were explicitly regarded as outsiders, as not belonging to the nation. The population thus divided into those with full legal entitlements and recognition as citizens and those who were disenfranchised but still under the jurisdiction of state authority.

29 It is interesting that at this point in "The Decline of the Rights of Man and the End of the Nation-State" she turns to a rather devastating critique of the "rights of man"—how useless and impotent the doctrine has turned out to be. What I'd like to suggest is that Arendt rebukes the discourse of the rights of man for being weak, but offers a certain reconceptualization of those rights and does this through her own kind of declaration, one that we might characterize as strong speech. This will come as no surprise to those who know what she has to say about words and deeds in *The Human Condition*, where persuasive speech is part of the very definition of the political realm. And yet there remains a question of who can exercise such rights and how the human is delimited in her view. Although one reads the essay as a defense, if not an enactment, of the rights of the stateless, she makes clear that the stateless are also a threat to the human. At the end of the essay, those who are stateless, including, presumptively, the Palestinians and the Pakistanis, threaten to become a "barbarous" force that attacks the "edifice of the human." At this point it seems that Israel and India are posited as national states that secure the "human" and so must be defended against the stateless that they themselves have produced. This runs counter to what seems to be the predominant argument of the essay, namely, that the stateless have the right to have rights.

30 Finally, then, I want to suggest that part of what Arendt is doing in this essay is defining these rights with assurance. In other words, she is providing, performing the rhetoric of definition in an assured fashion. Although she is no natural law theorist, Arendt lays out, even stipulates, the conditions of human life that precede and precondition any particular form of government and law. She does not base this view on prior principles, but elaborates it in the context of an address to her audience. Thus her rhetoric seeks to instantiate the social relation that she describes. Moreover, in laying out these conditions, she evacuates the first person "I." Arendt does not write this text as an "I," someone with an individual's perspective. When a pronoun appears, it is a "we," but who is this "we"? As whom and for whom is she speaking? Does she represent a "we" or does she invoke one when she claims, "We are not born equal: we become equal as members of a group on the strength of our decision to guarantee ourselves mutually equal rights" (OT, 301)?

31 Hannah Arendt, *On Revolution* (New York: Penguin, 1990), 166.

Abbreviations

EJ   Hannah Arendt, *Eichmann in Jerusalem* (New York: Schocken, 1963).

JW   *Hannah Arendt's Jewish Writings*, ed. Ronald Feldman and Jerome Kohn (New York: Schocken, 2008).

OT   Hannah Arendt, *The Origins of Totalitarianism* (New York: Harcourt Brace Jovanovich, 1951).

TPH   Walter Benjamin, "Theses on the Philosophy of History" in *Illuminations*, trans. Harry Zohn (New York: Schocken, 1969).

4

Decolonizing the Nation-State
Zionism in the Colonial Horizon of Modernity[1]

Walter D. Mignolo

The issues at hand[2]

Any conversation on Zionism leads generally to a polarization of positions, for Zionism and Judaism are conceived of as interchangeable: to be critical of Zionism is generally interpreted as being anti-Judaism. I am following here Marc Ellis's formula: "Judaism doesn't equal Israel."

I myself am not Jewish; I am a son of Italian immigrants, educated as a Catholic. What prevailed in the long run was my immigrant condition, which was replicated when I went to France to study and to the US to work, making me aware of the fact that secularism and modernity were only half of the story. The other half, coloniality, was hidden.[3] It was through coloniality, and the struggle for decolonization in Africa and Asia while I was a student in Paris, that I learned to see the emergence of the nation-state in nineteenth-century Europe as the solution for some (the bourgeoisie) and a problem for others. The form and the ideology of the nation-state established a clear-cut divide, in Europe, between national citizens and non-nationals (as well as non-citizens). But the consequences were more drastic in the colonies: the form nation-state was taken for granted, as much as in locales invaded by coloniality, such as China, Japan, Russia, Turkey, Persia/Iran, and so on.

My argument here is therefore that, while the State of Israel offered a solution for the Jewish people, it also became a problem for the Palestinians because the Zionist project was at the same time a movement of liberation mounted on the model of the modern European nation-state, which was already entrenched in European imperialism around the world. For this reason, to solve the conflict of Palestine/Israel would require more than peace agreements—it would require decolonizing the form of the modern European nation-state.

Since its coming into being and consolidation following the Glorious Revolution of 1688, the US Revolution of 1776, and the French Revolution of 1789, the nation-state was a solution for the emerging European bourgeoisie, desirous to establish its independence from the Church and the monarchical state. In the US, a solution was for the Anglo-Creoles to delink from the British monarchy. The processes that changed the world order over a century (1688–1789) were, however, good solutions for some (modernity) and disgraces for others (coloniality). The Glorious and the French Revolutions consolidated political control of the emerging ethno-class—the European bourgeoisie. The US Revolution consolidated the political and economic control of a new emerging class, namely the postcolonial elite. The postcolonial elite asserted itself in the name of Freedom, while at the same time depriving of freedom and dispossessing millions of Native Americans. That is, the postcolonial state reproduced coloniality in the hands of the revolutionaries.

In Europe, the story was different. There was not a lower social stratum of a different "race" to dispossess. The racial dispossessions took place in the colonies instead: as a matter of fact, since the sixteenth century Europe strengthened itself thanks to the benefits it had drawn from the colonies. Modernity and progress in Europe meant stagnation and misery (coloniality) in the rest of the world. Modernity and progress constituted, also, two key concepts in the rhetoric of salvation. Stagnation and misery were and still are phenomena about which the rhetoric of salvation is silent, hiding the logic of coloniality behind the rhetoric of modernity. Revolutions became signs of progressive changes. Their darker side, coloniality, was sacrificed for the benefit of its brighter side, modernity.[4]

The State of Israel itself is not, of course, an imperial state similar to England, France or the US. However, the discourses legitimizing its foundation, made possible by the dispossession of land, replicated previous imperial discourses, invoking the Bible. Irish Theologian Michael Prior argued convincingly that similar biblical arguments, based on the chosen people and their right, were invoked in the Spanish conquest of America, in the foundation of the US nation-state, in the European colonization of South Africa, and in the foundation of the State of Israel.[5] At the same time, the State of Israel is not a nation-state like the Republics of India (1947), Egypt (1953), or Algeria (1962). The last three were founded against the will of England and France, while Israel was founded with the support of both and the US. I thus propose to focus on the Zionist *state*, rather than on the *Zionist* state.

Judaism does not equal Israel

Let us start with the anti-Zionist arguments. One of the most radical voices here is the Jewish US citizen Marc Ellis, who also contributed a chapter to this collection.[6] "A Jew who takes side with the Palestinians" may sound like an anti-Semite. The accusation is common and logical within the form nation-state. During the Bush-Cheney era, every critique of the state was taken and chastised as critique of the nation: not, of course, as anti-Zionist, but as anti-patriotic. The content is different, but the logic is the same. As far as "Patria" is identified with the modern nation-state, in which one state corresponds to one nation, a citizen who is critical of his or her own state is accused of being anti-nationalist. Such a citizen presumably goes against his or her nation, the homogeneous community in the process of creating its own state identity; and such state critique was indeed un-American, since it went against the basic principles of the US as the leading democratic state in the world. In this complex scenario, Ellis is a citizen of the US. However, he assumes his Jewish identity, both ethnic and religious. His critique of Zionism addresses both Jews in Israel and in the diaspora, but it also addresses the role of United States foreign policy as it pertains to Israel.

The anchoring point of Ellis's argument is that "Judaism does not equal Israel." The first paragraph of Ellis's Preface to the book of the same title lays out the argument's framework with unmistakable transparency:

> The prophetic is the wild card of Jewish life and its primordial marker. Jewish life cannot be described without the prophetic, which always pushes Judaism to another dimension. In these pages I hold the prophetic marker of Judaism against its corrupting—and potentially fatal—identification with modern Israel. I also offer a prophetic, life giving way forward for Jewish life in the world. [7]

Although the expression "modern Israel" is not flagged in the paragraph, it is no doubt useful to flag it, since the creation of the State of Israel in 1948 was contemporary to the struggle for decolonization in Asia and Africa. This means that, while in Africa and Asia the struggle for decolonization was at its inception, the State of Israel emerged not as a decolonial state (like India or Algeria) but as a modern one. The problems of the state form are common to both insofar as the founding of Israel and the outcome of decolonizing struggles are concerned, even if the results and the consequences are quite different. I will come back to this issue below.

I want to stay a little longer with the issue "Judaism Does Not Equal Israel." Ellis's book has a short Preface by Bishop Desmond Tutu that begins with these words: "I thank God for my Hebrew antecedents and their Bible." Further in the Preface he notes:

> Jews are indispensable for a just and caring world. We need Jews faithful to their scriptures and to their prophetic vocation; these have meant so much for the world's morality—for our sense of what sets oppressed people free and of what is just.

Bishop Tutu acknowledges the relevance of Judaism and the contribution it makes to our (meaning "all of us" who work on the problem of injustice and work toward a just world that would supersede the foundations of injustice) current efforts at a poly-religious and poly-ethnic world. Bishop Tutu then goes into the central thesis advanced by Ellis:

> Equating the State of Israel with Judaism threatens with irrelevance the prophetic power and truth of the scriptures that have, for millennia, inspired and grounded Jews in their witness to God. Israel's treatment of the Palestinian people reminds me of Cape Town under apartheid: colored thrown out of their homes and relocated in distant ghetto townships, illegal walls, = encroaching on people's ancient lands, separated families, divided properties and the nightmare of running military checkpoint gauntlets. (vii–viii)

Bishop Tutu's efforts to downsize the State of Israel are very well known, beyond this Preface. A few years ago he urged the US pension fund of the Teachers Insurance and Annuity Association to cut their partnership with Israeli companies. Tutu campaigned to extend an arms embargo to Israel. In Cape Town, he started a periodic meeting of the "anti-Israeli Russell Tribunal," an international organization that had previously met in Barcelona and London. He has also contributed to stopping the cooperation of the University of Johannesburg in South Africa with Ben-Gurion University in Israel.[8] For all of that he has been strongly attacked as an anti-Semite.[9] Bishop Desmond Tutu is manifestly and openly anti-Zionist. From this, it does not follow that he is an anti-Semite.

In these debates, it seems impossible to escape from the "you are with us or against us" accusations, implying that if you are anti-Zionist you are an anti-Semite. To overcome the prison-house of religion, the nation, and the state is one of the most basic necessary conditions for resolving the Palestine/Israel conflict. The other is to understand the State of Israel in the global frame of modernity/coloniality. The difficulties of escaping this prison-house should not prevent us from conceptually disentangling the State of Israel from Judaism.

The difficulties of the entanglement come from the fact that religious Jews, who had criticized Zionism before the foundation of the State of Israel, have now lent it their clear and strong support, particularly after "The Six-Day War" in 1967.[10] Perhaps one of the reasons is that the focus has been on "Zionism" (religious or secular) rather than on the "State." It should be noted also that in 1948 the State of Israel came into being thanks to the support of Western imperial states, while the victories of the "Six-Day War" gave the State of Israel the necessary confidence to consolidate its territorial and national project. From the point of view of the Palestinians, both moments were detrimental: 1948, because the creation of the State forced Palestinian displacements; 1967, because the State of Israel implemented the very colonial strategies that had been previously enacted by Western imperial powers. Still, it would be hard to see Israel as an imperial power, although imperial/colonial strategies and arguments have been at work there since 1967.

In the following parts of the argument, I look at the State of Israel within the colonial horizon of modernity and, consequently, I focus on the prospect of decolonizing the state to which Zionism is indebted. Decolonizing the state means first and foremost unveiling the logic of coloniality implicit in the state form, along with its rhetoric of salvation and democracy. Decolonizing the state is, to be sure, a conceptual and philosophical issue. The modern form nation-state is supported by three centuries of Western political theory. Decolonizing the state means reducing the influence of the regional history and conceptual logic of Western political theory.[11]

Western racial configuration, the nation-state, and the idea of modernity

The State of Israel was established at the historical crossroads of race, religion, nationalism, secularism, and globalization. The modern and secular European nation-state (that is, post-enlightenment) displaced the theological formation of the communities of faith (Christian and Jews), regulated by the Church and the monarchy [12] and replaced them by communities of birth (*natio*), regulated by the secular state. "Secular Jews" who championed the Zionist project emerged roughly at this juncture in Central Europe. It is difficult to imagine that the political and now predominant branch of Zionism in Israel could have emerged in Australia, Argentina, South Africa, or even in the US, where many Jews were settled.[13] The splendor of the nation-state in Europe was to allow the emerging ethno-class, the bourgeoisie, to displace the joint alliance of the monarchy and the Christian Church, pegging one nation to one state.

If, in Europe, it was possible to attach one nation to a state, it was done mainly due to the relative homogeneity of the white, European, and Christian populations. The problems emerged later on, in Europe and in the colonies, since there aren't many places in the world outside of Europe where the state could be made to correspond to one nation. Even in Europe that was, but it is no longer the case. Immigration is moving Western Europe and the US to a future pluri-national state or some other form of governance we cannot yet imagine. The State of Israel has confronted from the beginning this insolvable problem of every modern nation-state: to look after the well-being of its citizens and to deem everyone else as suspicious or as a lesser human and dispensable in relation to a given nation-state. It is imperative to overcome the legalized violence of the nation-state form there and, of course, in every state in the world.

In Europe, the exacerbation of the ideology built around the equivalence of a nation and a state exploded under Nazism, when about sixteen million were killed, six million among them Jews, both German and non-German. The German state genocide and the bombing of Hiroshima and Nagasaki, that ended World War II, created the conditions for The Universal Declaration of Human Rights: the security of the nation ran parallel to the security of the Western civilization. That is to say, the discourse of human rights is a double-edged sword: they can be used to enforce the respect and protection of persons who defend certain values, and they could be violated in defense of these same values.[14]

Thus, while the German-engineered genocide [15] was the consequence of the internal limits of the form and the ideology that pegged one nation to one state, Hiroshima and Nagasaki were the consequences of this ideology in international relations that made them the representatives of the "yellow peril." [16] The model "one nation, one state" became the political pillar of Western civilization. The defeat of Hitler by the allies and the defeat of Japan's supreme ruler, Hirohito, consolidated the modern European nation-state political form both nationally, in Europe, and in international relations. Western European states and the US stopped the "yellow peril" posed by Japan to Western civilization since the bombing of Pearl Harbor in December 1941. However, while the form nation-state came into existence "naturally" in the history of Europe, it was a forced imposition or a forced adaptation in the non-European world. A great deal in the strengthening of the modern nation-state in South America (states grouped because of their French association as "Latin" America) in the nineteenth century and in Asia and Africa during the twentieth century is due, precisely, to the imposition (because it was offered as the only solution) of the modern nation-state onto histories and sensibilities alien to that form of governance. But, contrary to those experienced difficulties, and/or failure of state formation outside of Europe, Israel was successful.

Why was the State of Israel successful while nation-states in Africa and Asia went through all kind of difficulties, whose denouements we have been recently witnessing through the uprisings in North Africa and the Middle East? Even countries in "Latin" America, the republics formed in the first half of the nineteenth century, are still struggling with the form of the nation-state. One answer advanced by dependency theories in "Latin" America and embraced in Africa and Asia was the political and economic dependence of newly emerged states. The argument was economic dependency, though implicitly it referred to the reality of political dependency. Up until the present day, only in Bolivia following the election of Evo Morales was the modern form nation-state called into question: re-foundation or decolonization of this form are the questions at the core of current debates. Be that as it may, the State of Israel did not emerge from a struggle for independence that would overthrow imperial administrations and military forces (like in India, Algeria, or Egypt) but, instead, it enjoyed the support of imperial forces others were fighting to overthrow. However, it should be noted that, before the founding of the State of Israel, Zionists and Arabs in Palestine confronted the British who took over the area in the period between 1917 and 1948, subsequent to the collapse of the Ottoman Sultanate (I will come back to this point below).

The founding of the State of Israel was not only different from the newly created states that emerged from the effort of decolonization but it also offered similar justifications for territorial occupations to those prevalent in sixteenth-century Castile, Britain, France, and later the US. [17] The parallels are revealing. Dispossessions in the New World and in South Africa were argued for and enacted by actors of Western imperial states (Spain, England, Holland). In the case of Zionism, dispossession was argued for and enacted by people without state (e.g., those coming from the diaspora) in the process of building their own. However, the very founding of the State of Israel and its continuity is due in large part to the support of Western imperial states—England at the beginning of the process, and the US since 1967.

It is a telling paradox that the states which emerged from processes of decolonization either failed (Egypt, Tunisia, Libya, Yemen, Syria), or had great difficulties finding their way (Nigeria, India), or had to go through a second decolonization (Mandela's South Africa), while the State of Israel was established and consolidated. In the process Palestinians became, indeed, postmodern colonized people (like indigenous people who lived in the Americas and in South Africa before the European settlement and dispossession), dispossessed by the Israeli state's regulations with the support of England and the US. In addition to the first form of colonial dispossessions, the State of Israel inaugurated a second degree of dispossession.

European secularism and the emergence of political Zionism

Whatever the relations between Jews, Christians, and Muslims were before the end of the fifteenth century, those relationships were turned around *toward the end* of the fifteenth and *during* the sixteenth centuries. It is from this semantic mutation that Zionism emerges four centuries later. How come?

The expulsion of the Jews from the Iberian Peninsula is analogous but also dissimilar to the *Exodus* of the Jews from Egypt.[18] Even if in a non-Jewish account I/we interpret *Exodus* as an expulsion rather than voluntary exit, still the differences are significant and relevant to the present status of the story: Jews, guided by Moses, were not running away from Christians when leaving Egypt. Whether their departure was voluntary or forced, whether an exodus (from Egypt) or a forced expulsion (from the Iberian Peninsula), Jews were considered, both by those they left behind and by those who expelled them, undesirable. But in *Exodus*, Jews were undesirable mainly because of their belief in one God, and the attitude this belief engendered within Jewish communities, rather than in the enchanted world of many gods, in which Egyptians believed. Arabs were not yet in Egypt at the time of *Exodus* (around 1441 BC) and Christianity was still far from being born. On the other hand, when expelled from the Iberian Peninsula, Jews were interacting with Muslims and Christians, but Christians at that point had the upper hand and were able to expel both Jews and Muslims from Christian territories. Modern Western Christianity, during the European Renaissance, thus created the blueprint of the form nation-state: "purity of blood" was the principle upon which homogeneous communities of faith shall be built. Later on, the form nation-state replaced communities of faith by communities of birth and purity of blood by skin color.

The year 1492 witnessed, as we know, a series of decisive events, including the expulsions of Moors and Jews from the Iberian Peninsula. The Moors went to the South; the Jews to the North; and Columbus, sailing to the West, landed on a territory unknown to Europeans and which he named "Indias" and later on a European cartographer named "America" to honor Amerigo Vespucci. Soon after, the forced migration of enslaved Africans contributed to shaping the demography of the New World/America and created the preconditions for the modern/colonial racial matrix. Jews became part of a larger picture. Christians were in a position to classify and make their classifications valid for centuries to come: Jews, Muslims, "Indians," and "Blacks" formed the initial racial tetragon that has survived, with mutation and additions, to the present day.[19]

Muslims were expelled from Western Christendom, but at that point Muslims had behind them eight centuries of history from the Islamic Caliphate to the powerful Ottoman Sultanate. Aztec, Maya, and Inca civilizations were dismantled and their population degraded as "Indians." Enslaved Africans were detached from the Kingdom of Africa and identified as "Blacks." While Muslims became the external imperial enemy (e.g., the constant presence of the Ottomans in the North of Africa and the Southeast of Europe), and "Indians" and "Blacks" became the external colonial subject, Jews who remained in the lands of Western Christians (soon to become Europe), became the internal colonial subject. The reinscription of Zion within nineteenth-century Europe was a consequence of the life of the Jews as people without a state and as internal colonial subjects during the dissolution of European monarchy, the marginalization of the Christian Church, and the formation of the European form nation-state.

The State of Israel in the colonial horizon of imperial modernity

The creation of the State of Israel and its Western European support prompt questions about the historical nature of the modern nation-state in the transformation of the global order since the eighteenth century. Two issues are relevant for my argument: 1) the larger picture of inter-state relations under the hegemony of the *form* of the nation-state in the US, England, France, and Germany; 2) the *idea* of the "Nation" upon which the modern European state apparatus was established.

To elaborate on these issues, we need to revisit the events of the sixteenth and nineteenth centuries. I have already mentioned the expulsion, by Christians, of Jews and Muslims from the Iberian Peninsula. As is well known, in the sixteenth century, Muslims were not only in Spain and North Africa. They were also in the territories of the Islamic Caliphate—or, if you wish, the Islamic State that united the communities of believers (*ummah*) ruled by a single Caliph—that extended from Spain, to the Southeast through the North of Africa, across the Persian Shahanate,[20] all the way to today's South and Southeast Asia. The largest colony of the British Empire was in South Asia. The British invasion of India started by dismantling the Mughal Sultanate, based in Delhi extending from Kabul in the North to Calcutta and Madras in the South—almost the totality of India and today Afghanistan. By chance or design, the first large colony of the British Empire was a Sultanate.

Certainly, the first incursions were commercial, through the British East India Company, but the political control of "India" (1858) was set in place by overruling the Sultanate and implanting modern/colonial institutions. The second wave was British incursion into the Persian/Iranian Sultanate after oil was discovered in the region. Britain and the Soviet Union invaded Iran after World War II. Reza Shah was forced to abdicate and was replaced by his son, the pro-British Mohammad Reza Shah Pahlavi. Shah Pahlavi lasted until 1979, the year of the Iranian Revolution. Third, the Ottoman Sultanate fell under the British in 1922. From the debris of the Ottoman Sultanate emerged the republic (nation-state) led by Mustafa Kemel Ataturk, and another new state was formed in the territories occupied by the Ottomans: Iraq. Oil had been discovered in the area at the beginning of the twentieth century.

In 1917 the British entered and took hold of Jerusalem, until then under Ottoman rule. The city was in turmoil with constant confrontations between Muslims, Jews, and British. In 1947 the United Nations approved the partition of Palestine into two territories, one Arab and one Jewish—Israel and Jordan. To make a long story short, with the fall of the Ottoman Sultanate and the removal of Reza Shah in 1941, Britain managed to control a vast area from the Mughal Sultanate territories, contiguous with the Persian and the Ottoman Sultanate. The founding of the State of Israel was not only the Jews' return to the Promised Land, but also the securing of a key territory—the Eastern buffer zone of Europe. President Barack Obama's recent declaration of the "unbreakable alliance with Israel" means much more than maintaining the ties between the two countries with the larger Jewish population and the unity of the Judeo-Christian tradition. It also means geo-political alliances with important economic and military consequences: Iran and Syria on the other side of the border, and Russia and China toward the East.

The spread of the nation-state form carried with it the implicit idea of "one state, one nation." The fall of the Ottoman Sultanate brought about the modern republic of Turkey ruled by Ataturk. One of the shameful episodes in this transformation was the genocide against the Armenians in the name of national defense and unity. In "one state, one nation" there is no room for "non-nationals." The partition of India/Pakistan also derived implicitly from the assumption that one nation corresponded to one state. It was the same underlying assumption that prompted the mandates which created Iraq out of the ruins of the Ottoman Sultanate, although local histories were different. The British control of the Mughal Sultanate created the conditions for opium growth and, at the same time, for the Opium War with China. Oil was discovered in the region controlled by Safavid and Ottoman Sultanates at the end of the nineteenth and beginning of the twentieth century. Once it became a nation-state, Iraq did the same against the Kurds, and invaded Iran in 1980, to prevent potential uprisings of suppressed minorities in Iraq. All of that in the name of national unity: one nation, one state. Genocides and war have been fought in the name of national unity. The State of Israel did not escape the rule of nation-states in the modern/colonial world system.

The secular-religious state of Israel

That political Zionism originated in Europe during the nineteenth century is not a random event of universal history. It is a logical consequence of the modern/colonial world. It was the unfolding of European history, self-fashioned as "modernity," that needed and invented the form nation-state. At that junction, Jews were profiled as an ethnic rather than a religious community.

Statistically, today's world Jewish population is estimated at between 14 and 15 million. Of that total, 5.7 million live in Israel and 5.2 million in the US. Close to a million live in Europe (France, Belgium, The Netherlands, Britain, Germany, and Hungary), and about 300,000 in South America. South Africa, Australia, Ukraine, and Russia account for a further close to half a million.

But it was a Hungarian in the Austro-Hungarian Empire, Theodor Herzl (1860–1904), who during his short life accomplished so much in setting up the basic stone of Zionism in the search for the State of Israel. Herzl was doubly marginal, and he must have felt that: he was Jewish and he was in a marginal and decaying empire, the Austro-Hungarian, confronting the force of Western European and imperial nation-states. He was not the first to come up with the idea of Zionism, but he was the engine and engineer of the project. He was living in Europe at the time when the nation-state was being consolidated in the core Western European countries. The nation-state was a secular institution. And so was Herzl's Zionism.

A sign of modernity and progress, the European secular form of governance, which was the nation-state, was the model institution modeled for an emerging ethno-class, the bourgeoisie, associated with the Glorious Revolution and the Industrial Revolution in England, as well as the French Revolution in continental Europe. It was also the consequence of the Westphalia Treaty that ended the deadly Thirty Years War (1660–1715). In the US, it was not the bourgeois ethno-class who built the modern nation-state but the settler colonists. And it was not to solve religious conflicts between Christians, but to do away with British rule. Contrary to the European bourgeoisie who built the nation-state displacing the monarchy and the Church, the Founding Fathers in the US displaced and dispossessed Native Americans (Iroquois, Sioux, Osage, etc.). As in the case of Spanish colonization of the New World and the Boer and British colonization of South Africa, "Manifest Destiny" was claimed by the chosen people, encouraged by God to take possession of the land. Contrary to the Europe of the early nineteenth century where class superseded race issues, the Americas were from the very beginning marked by racial classifications and hierarchies: Native Americans ("Pueblos Originarios" in the South, First Nations in Canada) and enslaved Africans, transported to the New World, were the equivalents to the Moors and the Jews in sixteenth- and seventeenth-century Spain (when Europe was still known as Western Christendom). "Manifest Destiny" was clearly a racial doctrine that justified the appropriation of Native American lands. The parallels between the first nation-state gaining independence from imperial/colonial rules and the formation of the State of Israel, with the support of imperial/colonial states, are evident. Similar rhetoric with an emphasis on progress, modernity, salvation, and manifest destiny was employed to justify US control of Hawaii and the Philippines toward the end of the nineteenth century.[21]

Secularism in Europe established the separation of the state from the Church and put an end to monarchic-state form. However, neither the Church nor the monarchies vanished from sight. They kept their domain of influence behind the scenes, as we know by looking at all the so-called developed and industrialized countries in Europe. Still, nation-states, as the compound name indicates, were conceived as legal, administrative, and economic organizations based on communities of birth (nation) and not on hereditary family lineage or undemocratic elections in the Roman Papacy. The national subject was also united by the national language, national literature, and national culture (the concept of "culture" acquired a different meaning from the one it had in Latin-derived languages during the Middle Ages). National subjects then became "citizens" in the modern sense of the word, profiled in the Declaration of the Rights of Man and of Citizen.

Zionism in the vision and action of Theodor Herzl was basically a secular project. This meant that the Zionist vision of the state assumed that the Jews were an ethnic rather than a religious community. For that reason, the secular Zionist project had to confront the leaders of the Jewish religious communities opposing it. Michael Brenner described it in 2003 as a paradoxical international nationalism.[22] In this line of reasoning, another paradox is that a movement that at its inception was secular, and therefore emphasized ethno-Jewish nationality rather than theological legacies, was very much criticized by religious Jews who considered Zionism as an affront to Judaism. In no other part of the world, except Western Europe and the Americas, was a similar secular–sacred divide in state matters obtained.

The history of Zionism—its trajectory from its inception to the foundation of the State of Israel—has been told by Jews and non-Jews alike. In what follows I will start from the interpretation advanced by two controversial theologians I have already mentioned: one is Jewish and the other is Christian. The first is Marc Ellis, the second Michael Prior. Ellis is recognized for many insights, among them for insisting—as I have already mentioned—that Judaism does not equal Israel; and Prior—for framing the question of Palestine within the history of colonialism. My take, along the lines of the arguments advanced by both theologians, will be grounded on the coloniality of the modern European nation-state whence Zionism was derived. For Zionism, in other words, there was a logical-historical reason and not just a chance that explains why it emerged in Europe, in a decaying empire (the Austro-Hungarian), and not in any other place of the Jewish diaspora.

Global linear thinking, coloniality, and dispossession

If we follow the reasoning I have been pursuing, the Palestine/Israel question is not a local issue. It is entrenched in the global order. The global order I am talking about is the one that Carl Schmitt described as the "second *nomos* of the earth," regulated by global linear thinking. This is the European vision and it is one half of the story. The other half, the vision from the receiving end of global linear thinking, is the founding moment of the "colonial matrix of power" and the making of Western civilization.[23] International law regulating the "second *nomos*" is one aspect of the colonial matrix. Both narratives (that of the second *nomos* and that of the colonial matrix of power) have dispossession at the core. Global linear thinking is tantamount to international law: remapping the globe brought the second *nomos* into existence, and international law legalized dispossession from the inception of the second *nomos*, from the sixteenth century up until the partition of Africa following the Berlin Treatise of 1884. The foundation of the State of Israel benefited from one of the strategies of imperial expansion. In the vocabulary of the "colonial matrix of power," international law legalized the control and management of authority. Legal dispossession, linked to international law, was an affair of the state, monarchical or secular. And this is the constellation in which the State of Israel was founded: the return to the Promised Land was supported by the long-lasting trajectory of legalizing dispossession in the name of progress and civilization.[24]

But dispossession has tremendous implications beyond the law and can hardly be justified in the name of sacred texts: dispossession is both illegal and unsacred. There seems to be no law or sacred truth that can justify a human being's right to dispossess other human beings of what they have. *Sovereignty of the nation-state compromises the relations of sovereignty among human beings: no human being has the right to enslave, exploit, and dispose of other human beings.* The form nation-state has been compromising world peace by putting the security and well-being of nationals before the well-being of humanity and the planet. The continuity and complementarity in Western civilization between the law of the state and the truth of the sacred text have contributed to the ranking and racialization of lands, territories, and human beings. What Michael Prior shows are the biblical legitimations of dispossession that have become the legal principles of international law.[25]

Dispossession is, first and above all, dehumanizing and psychologically degrading. However, dehumanization is irrelevant in modern/colonial international relations: first comes state interest, second, the benefit of the citizens of the state who enact the dispossession and, third, the non-nationals being dispossessed. Here we touch upon one of the major drawbacks of the modern form nation-state: nationals have priorities over non-nationals, which means that non-nationals are the lesser humans. Second, nationals ethnically identified with the state have priorities over nationals (that is, legal citizens) who do not belong to the mono-ethnic nationality of the state. The Holocaust is one such instance: ethnic Germans had priority over German Jews who were endangering the homogeneity of the nation-state. And third, Palestinians are at once foreigners to the State of Israel and those who live in Israel do not belong to the ethnicity with which the State of Israel identifies.

Anti-Zionism or anti-nation-state?

I have been arguing that is not only necessary to uncouple Judaism from the State of Israel but also to uncouple Zionism from the State of Israel. If Judaism does not equal the State of Israel, then it is also important to uncouple Jewish Zionism from Judaism. The problem the international community has with Zionism is indeed a problem with the modern form nation-state and not with Judaism. There cannot be solutions to the Palestine/Israel conflict within this form, and in the network of international conflicts and struggles for natural resources and territorial control.

Jewish Zionism came into being—as I have already mentioned—in the nineteenth century. Jewish Zionism was the necessary response to, on the one hand, the long history of Jewish diaspora and, on the other hand, the transformation and subsequent persecution that Jews have endured in Europe. European enlightenment and secularization changed the status of the Jews. Religious Jews were included in the formation of national communities that prompted the emergence of secular Jews (*hiloni*, non-religious Jews). Therefore, if Zionism is a Jewish national movement claiming the right of Jews to return to their historical birthplace (*Zion*—the Land of Israel and Jerusalem), then it is consistent with the desire and the right of any community that has been dispossessed. In this regard, the formation of the Zionist project in nineteenth-century Europe responded to a predicament similar to that of the indigenous people of the planet who have been consistently dispossessed of their land since 1500: in the sixteenth century in America, in the nineteenth in New Zealand, Australia, and South Africa, and following the Berlin Conference in 1884, the entire African population was dispossessed by European imperial states. The paradox of the Zionist State is that the return to the land of their historical birth implied the dispossession of communities that have not conquered that land by dispossession.

It is at this crossroads that Herzl's project plays two cards: both the liberation of the Jewish people and the appropriation of discourses of dispossession. For where would the State of Israel be created in the mind of Herzl? One could purchase land in another country that Herzl discussed in ch. 3 ("Purchasing of Land"):

> Argentina is one of the most fertile countries in the world, extends over a vast area, has a sparse population and a mild climate. The Argentine Republic would derive considerable profit from the cession of a portion of its territory to us. The present infiltration of Jews has certainly produced some discontent, and it would be necessary to enlighten the Republic on the intrinsic difference of our new movement.

However, the situation changes when he considered Palestine. The implication is occupation (and dispossession) of the land (that he discussed in ch. 5) from the people who were already living in Palestine:

> Palestine is our ever-memorable historic home. The very name of Palestine would attract our people with a force of marvelous potency. If His Majesty the Sultan were to give us Palestine, we could in return undertake to regulate the whole finances of Turkey. We should there form a portion of a rampart of Europe against Asia, an outpost of civilization as opposed to barbarism. We should as a neutral State remain in contact with all Europe, which would have to guarantee our existence.

Argentina could not offer what Palestine offers, and not only because the latter alone was the "ever-memorable historic home." Imagining that the Ottoman Sultan would give Palestine to the Jews, the State of Israel would form "a rampart of Europe against Asia, an outpost of civilization against barbarism." Two cards are here played at the same time, and Jews would no longer be seen as "barbarians" but integrated into Western civilization in its struggle against barbarism.

The modern European form nation-state went hand in hand with the idea of the "nation" and "nationalism," offering a solution for nationals and difficulties for non-nationals. By creating the idea and the image of communities of birth (nationalism), it created also the opposite, namely xenophobia. In the process, the larger picture of "humanity" was, and continues to be, lost. The consequences have been disastrous in the history of the world since nationalism and the national state have been created. I have already mentioned the Armenian genocide when the Republic of Turkey was established; the genocide of the Jews and non-Germans under Hitler; the massive murders in Rwanda after Belgium left the country at the same time they left *in* the country those strong nationalist sentiments that ended up in the murderous clashes between Tutsi and Hutus. Beyond genocide, nationalist sentiments coupled with the state led to further dispossession, wars, and violence to maintain the purity of the nation-state being threatened by external forces. The State of Israel, once established, did not escape the logic of coloniality embedded in the form nation-state that has shaped and continues to shape the modern/colonial world since the end of the eighteenth century, an order that consolidated Western civilization's global designs.

Jewish Zionism before the creation of the State of Israel was a movement of liberation by and for the Jewish people, be they religious or secular ethnic Jews. To what extent Zionist Jews had a clear geo-political vision and ambition of what it would mean to create a Zionist State in the Middle East of the time, and to what extent that was a vision and ambition of the Western European imperial states supporting the Zionist project, are matters that deserve special attention. Here I am assuming that Zionism was a project of liberation seeking support from Western European imperial states (mainly England). However, risking redundancy, after the creation of the State of Israel, Zionism became a state ideology, with a legal and military apparatus to defend the interest of Israeli national citizens. The sense of the humanity of non-nationals was lost—and this is one of the points Marc Ellis is making—such that the State of Israel was not only un-Jewish but also, and because of that, un-human. Significantly, this is not an *ad hominem* charge against the State of Israel. It is a charge leveled against the modern, European, and imperial form nation-state.

It is notorious, for example, that in President Barack Obama's speech on the occasion of the ten-year anniversary of the invasion of Iraq, he spelled out in great detail the cost of human lives (and not only the dead but also personal psychological consequences for the soldiers and their families, physical wounds that will be with a person for the rest of his or her life, etc.). But he only mentioned the lives of US citizens and passed over in silence the hundred thousand-plus lives lost in Iraq, the dismantling of the country's infrastructure, and the disaggregation of the Iraqi state's social fabric.

The creation of the State of Israel was not only due to the actions of secular Jews who, in Europe, worked hard and advocated for the right of the Jewish people to return to their native and Promised Land. That idea could not have even emerged in the seventeenth century when the idea and the form nation-state was not in place; nor in nineteenth-century Australia, Argentina, or South Africa, all of them places with significant numbers of Jews, but where the form nation-state was either unknown or a distant form of government. The State of Israel came into being also due to the work of Western imperial interests playing a double card: solving a problem that Europe itself has created (the Jewish genocide under Hitler) while keeping an eye on the checkerboard of international politics and finding a solution for the mess the British have created in the Middle East. From the viewpoint of Jews themselves, at some point in the process, there were two different possibilities: *having* their own land (a secular solution) and *returning to* their own land (a religious solution). In the first case, the main issue was that the creation of a state could have been in other places; Argentina was one such place. On the other hand, the *return* implied the creation of a state in Zion. All this was due also to the particular circumstances in which England found itself after defeating the Ottoman Sultanate and taking control of Jerusalem (1922–48).

Closing remarks

In view of this narrative, the prospect of solving the conflict of Palestine/Israel does not look hopeful in the short term. The conflicts within the global order have intensified. The recent visit of President Barack Obama to Israel had several overlapping agendas and a clear message. One of the items on the agenda was to continue the talks toward a peaceful conflict resolution and to say that "a two-state solution is possible," a formula for delaying the solution that did not fool the Palestinians. In the meantime, there is more in Iran than meets the eye, and the State of Israel is a crucial anchor that advances the interests of the US in the Middle East. Third, there is Syria that, along with Iran, are territories being looked at, from Western perspectives and interests, as economically and geo-politically subdued, as was the case in Iraq. The "unknowns" in the equation are Russia to the North and China to the East of Syria and Iran. The State of Israel may very well be situated at the crossroads of global forces and conflicts, beyond the local tension between Israel and Palestine.

Being anti-Zionist is not being anti-Jewish; rather, it means being anti-nation-state, or, better yet, calling into question the idea that the nation-state is a universal form of governance. What are the options? I see three possible directions. That means no blueprint, but trajectories being worked out in the present toward possible futures and unknown outcomes. What is known as the form nation-state is nearing its exhaustion.

First, there is already the constitutional form pluri-national state. The Constitutions of Bolivia and Ecuador already declare that these countries are pluri-national states. What does this mean? Well, simply that in South America, the population of European descent is only one nation that coexists with a plurality of nations (Aymaras, Quechuas, Chiquitanos, nations of Afro descent). However, they identified themselves with the nation-state they themselves created in the process of repressing other nations. In Ecuador there are 33 indigenous nations, plus the nations of Afro descent. There is obviously no reason for one nation (that of European descent) to identify itself with the state. Obviously, the reference to Bolivia and Ecuador as pluri-national states was not an initiative from Creoles and Mestizos, nor from those of European descent. It came from indigenous initiatives. The United States is already a pluri-national state, although this is not recognized (yet) in the Constitution. Instead, the concepts of "minorities" and "multiculturalism" were created in official discourses as buffer zones to prevent the potential demands to rewrite the Constitution of the United States and declare it a pluri-national state.

Second, there is a considerable debate today in China on a civilization rather than a national state—a debate not promoted by the government, but deriving from an initiative of self-described "citizen intellectuals." What does it mean? It means that Chinese citizen intellectuals realize that the form of the nation-state was a mirage between the Chinese Revolution led by Sun Yat-sen and, today, passing through the Marxist-state Constitution of China. The idea of a civilizational state is connected with debates on Confucian constitutionalism. While adopting from Western experience the need for constitutional governance, the form of the nation-state may be potentially discarded. Confucian constitutionalism and civilizational states mean finding the structure of governance that fits the history of the Chinese and not the history of Western civilization. Similarly, Islamic states began to reconstitute themselves as civilizational states after their Sultanates were dismantled and replaced with nation-states. It is possible to think that in today's Turkey something of this sort is emerging: the memories of Ataturk's modern nation-state are beginning to be overruled by the memories of the Ottoman Sultanate, a civilizational state.

Third, there is the ongoing mobilization beyond the sphere of the state with the purpose of finding a form of governance that satisfies the needs of the people instead of the interests of the state. In this sphere decolonizing the state means liberating governance. However, the actors and institutions carrying out these projects are neither the existing states nor corporations and financial institutions. These are actors taking their destiny in their own hands, since neither the state nor capital cares about them—as became obvious in the critical conditions of increasing numbers of states within the European Union. Palestinians, at this point, are in the middle of the struggle at the heart of the crisis of the form nation-state and the possibility of its dismantling.

Whether the nation-state would remain the model for governance and interstate relations, it is difficult to say. The bottom line is that, while the State of Israel presupposed the secular European and modern form nation-state, a solution to the conflict Palestine/Israel could hardly be found within the same frame that created the conflict. Simultaneously, the planet is witnessing the politicization of civil society (growing manifestations demanding dignity) and the emergence of a global political society. The solution of the conflict of Palestine/Israel must be thought out in forms of governance that offer alternatives to the form-nation state, which created the conditions for the emergence of Zionism in the modern/colonial world order.

Notes

1   I am grateful to Santiago Slabodsky not only for reading this piece and making recommendations, but also for engaging in a discussion of his recommendations. I am also grateful to him for over ten years of conversion on Zionism, Judaism, anti-Semitism, and Decolonial Thinking, as well as for letting me read his chapter on Theodor Herzl from his forthcoming book *Decolonial Judaism* (Basingstoke: Palgrave, 2014).

2   For the sake of clarity: by "decolonizing the nation-state" I mean decolonizing the theory of the state since there is no state without a theory of it, just as there is no theory without a vision of the nation-state in modern European thought.
3   I qualify "modernity" as "Western" because "modernity" is not an entity or a historical period but the self-fashioned narrative by European actors of their own achievements and legitimization for dispossession, overruling, and invading.
4   Theodor Herzl had fully embraced the rhetoric of modernity in 1896, when he wrote his programmatic text, *The Jewish State* (http://www.jewishvirtuallibrary.org/jsource/Zionism/herzl2.html) [date accessed August 28, 2013]. At that point, he embraced the rhetoric of modernity from a subaltern position: there was no state yet to see the consequences of the implementation of his ideals. A case for reflection: projects of liberation from a subaltern position are just that—projects. We could remember many cases, like Vladimir Lenin's writings before the Russian Revolution and the advent of the Soviet Union. Lenin fully endorsed the rhetoric of modernity from a Marxist, rather than a Liberal, point of view.
5   Michael Prior, *The Bible and Colonialism. A Moral Critique* (London: Bloomsbury, 1997).
6   Marc Ellis, *Judaism Does Not Equal Israel* (New York: The News Press, 2009).
7   Ellis, *Judaism*, p. ix.
8   Giulio Meotti, "Tutu's War on Israel, Jews." Y-Net Magazine, August 11, 2011 (http://www.ynetnews.com/articles/0,7340,L-4107913,00.html) [date accessed August 28, 2013].
9   Alan M. Dershowitz, "Bishop Tutu Is No Saint When It Comes to Jews." Gatestone Institute. International Policy Council, December 20, 2010 (http://www.gatestoneinstitute.org/1742/bishop-tutu-is-no-saint-when-it-comes-to-jews) [date accessed August 28, 2013]; Robert Fine, "Blame Games Won't Lead Us to Peace." October 2010 (http://engageonline.wordpress.com/2010/10/08/robert-fine-responds-to-desmond-tutus-call-for-a-boycott-of-israel-in-the-south-african-mail-guardian/) [date accessed August 28, 2013].
10 See the report on *The Virtual Jewish Library* (http://www.jewishvirtuallibrary.org/jsource/History/67_War.html) [date accessed August 28, 2013].
11 An interesting effort in this direction is the book by Roxanne L. Euben, *Enemies in the Mirror. Islamic Fundamentalism and the Limits of Modern Rationalism* (Princeton, NJ: Princeton University Press, 1999).
12 I cannot go into the communities of beliefs in Asia (Confucianism, Buddhism), in Africa, and in the great civilizations of Tawantinsuyu and Anahuac (Incas, Mayas, and Aztecs).
13 The major European concentration of Jews by 1900, when political Zionism emerged, was in Russia (three millions plus) and, second, in the Austro-Hungarian Empire (one million two hundred plus). In the US by that time, the Jewish population was about 1.5 million. By 1942, the main concentration of Jews was in Central Europe, (http://www.jewishvirtuallibrary.org/jsource/History/totaljews.html) [date accessed August 28, 2013]. If, then, cultural Zionism had its point of origination in Russia and Poland, political Zionism emerged in Central Europe, where the winds of the West were blowing strong: the Austro-Hungarian Empire collapsed in 1918.
14 Franz Hinkelammert, "The Hidden Logic of Modernity: Locke and the Inversion of Human Rights." *WKO*, 2004 (http://globalstudies.trinity.duke.edu/wp-content/themes/cgsh/materials/WKO/v1d1_HinkelammertF.pdf) [date accessed August 28, 2013].

15 On the engineering aspect of Nazi genocide, see Zygmunt Bauman, *Modernity and the Holocaust* (Ithaca: Cornell University Press, 1991).
16 Gregory Blue, "Gobineau on China. Race Theory, the 'Yellow Peril' and the Critique of Modernity." *Journal of World History*, 10/1, 1999, pp. 93–111.
17 For a detailed account, see Michael Prior, *Zionism and the State of Israel. A Moral Inquiry* (London: Routledge, 1999).
18 A recent detailed and insightful account is available in David Nirenberg, *Anti-Judaism. The Western Tradition* (Chicago, IL: The University of Chicago Press, 2013), pp. 13–47, 217–68.
19 An account of the racial formation in the sixteenth century, as we know it today, is to be found in *Rereading the Black Legend. The Discourse of Religious and Racial Difference in the Renaissance Empire*, Margaret Greer, Walter Mignolo, and Maureen Quilligan (eds) (Chicago, IL: The University of Chicago Press, 2008).
20 The *Shah* was not an emperor in the same way that an *Emperor* was not a *Shah*. Consequently, Persia was not an *Empire* but a *Shahanate*, in the same way that Rome was not a *Shahanate* but an *Empire*. If we do not understand these differences across time and space, we run the risk of imagining fictional entities like *Empire*, for example.
21 Conrad Cherry, *God's New Israel: Religious Interpretations of American Destiny* (Chapel Hill: The University of North Carolina Press, 1998).
22 Michael Brenner, *Zionism: A Brief History*, trans. Shelley L. Frisch (Princeton, NJ: Marku and Wienner Publisher, 2003). However, from a decolonial perspective, "international nationalism" is not a paradox but a historical consequence of decolonial struggles in Asia and Africa (The Bandung Conference, 1955) and the Non-Aligned Countries (Yugoslavia, 1961). Still, the directionality of these projects is not concurrent: decolonial struggles were directed to end Western imperial control of their territories and to build their own state, while Zionism moved in the reverse direction, wishing to get a territory and build a state with the support of imperial forces.
23 Carl Schmitt, *The Nomos of the Earth in the International Law of the Jus Publicum Europaeum* [1950], trans. G. L. Ulmen (New York: Telos Press, 2006). For the "colonial matrix of power" as the grounding of Western civilization, see Walter D. Mignolo, *The Darker Side of Western Modernity: Global Futures, Decolonial Options* (Durham, NC: Duke University Press, 2011).
24 The (in)famous "*Requerimiento*" demanded the natives to submit themselves to Spanish rules and Christianity (http://www.milestonedocuments.com/documents/view/requerimiento) [date accessed August 28, 2013]. Factual dispossession followed suit. Two decades later, international law was put in place for the first time in the history of humanity to legitimize dispossession. Fernandez de Santa Maria, *The Discovery of America and the School of Salamanca* (Cambridge: Cambridge University Press, 1977).
25 Anthony Angie, *Imperialism, Sovereignty and the Making of International Law* (Cambridge: Cambridge University Press, 2007); Sba N' Zatioula Grovogui, *Sovereigns, Quasi-Sovereigns, and Africans* (Minneapolis: University of Minnesota Press, 2005).

5

Karl Marx and Hannah Arendt on the Jewish Question

Political Theology as a Critique[1]

Artemy Magun

Introduction

In this chapter, I will show the strange proximity between the arguments of Karl Marx and Hannah Arendt with regard to the "Jewish question." Both authors interpret the specific problems associated with the political role of Jews as a distinct ethno-religious group, in a larger context of the difference and debate between Judaism and Christianity as politico-theological doctrines. In Marx's essay "On the Jewish Question," the politico-theological context is more evident than in Arendt's *Eichmann in Jerusalem* where it remains latent. But I show that, essentially, it is the *same* context: the one that goes back to the Hegelian construction of the socio-political implications of Judaism and Christianity. Both Marx and Arendt read "Judaism" as a synonym of a political order where the particular is torn away from the universal. However, both authors are far from unilaterally "promoting" Christianity at the expense of Judaism: their argument consists rather in saying that modern post-Christian Europe, and more precisely the post-Christian representative state, are unable to overcome what seems to them problematic in "Judaism." Modern capitalism and the modern rule of law *fall back* on to the alienated "Judaic" order which had been a target of Christian and post-Christian criticism. A further, more radical, critique of religion and state, be it Christian or Judaic, is necessary, although Christianity and Judaism keep, paradoxically, providing *criteria* of this critique.

The problem of "political theology," famously restated and made popular by Carl Schmitt in 1922,[2] has an old history.[3] Most major religions before Christianity had had a direct socio-political content. Christianity originally abandoned any political theology, but it gradually became evident that the very *separation* of the spiritual from the earthly was itself a political doctrine. Indeed, throughout its existence, particularly in Western Europe, the Christian Church has played a crucial political role. Furthermore, the new modern epoch, which led to an impressive secularization of daily life and of ideology, originated, at least in part, in Reformation and Counter-reformation. The question remains open whether religion was here a motive for the change or its retrospective rationalization.

Reformation was, in many respects, an intra-religious critique of religion. Both of its political consequences—the revolutionary spirit that started as a theological creed[4] and the intensification of economic activity that started as a religious asceticism[5]—in different ways contributed to the fall of theocracy and to the emergence of a new secular state. As a paradoxical and unwilled consequence of the Reform, faith was gradually transferred to the "internal forum" of an individual and, in many cases, lost its earthly significance. Deism and atheism started spreading among the intellectuals and, later, among the masses—particularly after the French Revolution. It is at this moment that Hegel interpreted the modern state, itself a product of the Reform, as a "sublation" (*Aufhebung*) of religion that materially fulfills its program. While Hegel still thought that religion remained vital in the new state, his more radical followers, such as Bruno Bauer, were more consequent and saw a need to do away with the Christian religion (at least on the public level) *because* its program was fulfilled and materialized. This crucial argument of Hegel's school laid a foundation for a new tradition of political theology, which occupied itself with secular political analogies of the theological concepts, with a double task, either to criticize these seemingly secular political forms, and/or to make *sense* of them, to supply them with a meaning that would be transcendental and not simply empirical.

In the nineteenth and twentieth centuries, atheist liberals often presented politics and economics as a rational phenomenon based on the self-interest of individuals. Theology can only enter this picture as a secondary rationalization. However, several factors have kept a theological analysis of politics pertinent up until this moment:

1. The persistence and resurgence of actual religious belief.
2. The increasing role of this belief (or faith) in political life.
3. The ubiquity of *ideologies*, which often repeat the religious structures of meaning without grounding them in the actual structures of society.
4. The seemingly "irrational" phenomena of politics which can only be explained away or fetishized by the liberal rationalism (for example, as being "charismatic").

Thus, it appears that a serious consideration of the theological structures of meaning is required for the purpose of a critique, not just of religion, but of the politics which tacitly relies on it—including liberal politics. Moreover, a serious atheist reconceptualization of society is only possible through a serious internal polemics with religion and through a rethinking of its issues, such as the rupture between the universal and the particular—which have been perceived by theology but only resolved by theological means, such as the exaltation, ritualization, and alienation of a certain sphere of human life.

Carl Schmitt, in 1922, announced that "all significant concepts of the modern theory of the state [were] secularized theological concepts."[6] He immediately cited sovereignty as the utmost example of such "secularization." Sovereignty would, for him, be a right to decide on exception, and would therefore be inherently linked with what, in theology, is conceived of as a doctrine of the miracle. Theology for Schmitt (who follows Kirkegaard on this) comes in via the need for an *exception*.

Hans Blumenberg, a younger German thinker, argued against Schmitt in 1962 that the "secularization" of political concepts included a shift in their meaning.[7] Most importantly, Blumenberg insists on an epochal rupture linked with the apology of "curiosity," as a form of openness towards the future, toward the new, and toward the experiential knowledge.

From the opposite, Christian, side, Erik Peterson, an important twentieth century theologian, contested Schmitt's thesis on the ground that the true Christian religion (unlike the Roman and Judaic ones) had never been "political" or even, for that matter, monotheistic. The doctrine of *trinity* meant, according to Peterson, a determinate departure from the political use of religion, particularly from its use for the legitimization of a monarchy.[8] Therefore, a modern "political theology" was no Christian theology at all, but a simple atheism or paganism.

Schmitt, however, contended to Blumenberg that the very rupture with theology was itself an essential part of theology and responded to Peterson that the idea of Trinity already implied an internal rupture and an opposition (*stasis*) of God to himself.[9] *Nemo contra deum nisi deus ipse*—no one against God except God—thus lucidly finishes his response.[10] Theology, particularly Christian theology, has always already contained a critique of religion (critique of the overly material, fetishist, "idolatric" forms of cult; critique of the "monarchic," politically complicit cult: more broadly, critique of a blind servitude that is inappropriate for the true faith). But this also means that a critique of religion (or of a political application of religion) and struggle against it do not yet mean that one is finished with religion (or at least with political theology). A deeper contestation and a deeper analysis are necessary.

Perhaps the most important "internal" dispute of Christianity has for ages concerned its birthmark, its polemics with Judaism. This argument was not unilateral, since Judaism continues to exist and be practiced. The actual presence of the Jewish people in the European land provided this debate with a clear political sense. Moreover, the debate was originally political: does monotheism have to be expressed in a theocracy? Is monotheism (the religion of the *One*) also a politics of *one*—of the one, chosen people? Or is it a universalist religion of the One qua totality, which exists in excess to any given polity? In addition, if religion does play a role in society, then what does it produce in it: the alienation of law, or the mediation of love?

It is this set of questions that is constitutive for Christianity and which always remains fundamental for it, as long as Christianity preserves its Judaic monotheistic basis and as long as it remains a *religion* and a social force. The late modernity, which brought forward a large-scale re-politicization of society and which succeeded in creating a legal state (*Rechtstaat*) and a nation-state, problematized the status of Jews as subjects of law. As I will argue further in this chapter, this problem has to do not only with the fact that Jews, being a heterogeneous religious group, undermined the new legal national unity but also with the fact that the new European state, having secularized the monotheist religion, looked "Judaic" and "Christian" at the same time. Indeed, the German political philosophy considered the principle of purely legal, alienated authority to be a secularized version of Judaism, while secularized Christianity was associated with emancipation and the recognition of the individual. In what follows I will consider the two major political theories of the last two centuries, both of which focus on the political issue of the status of Jews, but both of which also present a critique of the modern liberal state and international community as such. These are the doctrines of Karl Marx and Hannah Arendt.

In the nineteenth century, the Jewish question was generalized to problematize the relationship between religion and the liberal democratic state, and the universality of nation-states. In the twentieth century, it obtained a new universal meaning: the catastrophe of European Jews exposed the dangers of nation-state and at the same time the powerless and non-democratic character of international law. The Shoah linked the Jewish question to the question of modern history at large—whether this history is oriented to progress or, on the opposite side, whether it leads to a "totalitarian" hell on Earth. Because, as a result of the Shoah, there emerged a Jewish nation-state, which remains in acute conflict with the Arabic population, the Jewish question became also tightly entangled in the problem of the European colonialism. Thus, in a secularized way, the Jewish question, and this means Christianity at its limit and origin, remains an important horizon of contemporary history, in both a theoretical and a practical way.

Karl Marx and the political theology of the nineteenth-century state

I will start with Karl Marx and his early essay "On the Jewish question" (1843).[11] Marx was a representative of the aforementioned Hegelian school of political theology—perhaps the first one to convert it into the critique of political theology. Unlike Hegel, who rejoiced in the Christian elements being realized in the liberal state, Marx thought that in this seemingly secular state there remained some rudimentary religious structures which needed to be uncovered and criticized.

The Jewish question appears then as the crucial one, because—as Hegel's disciple Bruno Bauer notes in his texts—Jews have to enter the new liberal democratic state on equal terms *but* they remain religious themselves. It is in response to this thesis of Bauer that Karl Marx, then a young beginning philosopher and journalist, wrote his short article "On the Jewish Question"—the work which was among the first to endow political theology with the meaning of political critique. Marx reviewed two works by Bauer: "The Jewish Question"[12] and "The Capacity of the Contemporary Jews and Christians to Become Free."[13] His criticism, to formulate it briefly for the moment, consisted in the fact that Bauer could only envision a "political emancipation" of Jews, but a political emancipation remained incomplete because it preserved a religious split between the state and civil society, between the "rights of citizens" and "rights of man." The problem therefore lay not in the Jews as a group or in their religion but in the very life of the modern state organized in a "Judaic" way. Marx writes this work, as most of his works, in a highly polemical, dialogical way, so that it is often difficult to say if he states something from his own point of view or from the point of view of the author he criticizes. This style fits well for the difficult and ambivalent character of the issue, in which what there is to save and to abandon in the Judeo-Christian religion is intricately intertwined.

Let us turn to the "Jewish" works of Bauer, which remain in many ways pertinent up to the present. Bauer criticized the German and French liberals who, from their non-Jewish point of view, struggled for the rights of Jews, for their full inclusion into the state. The problem of this approach to the rights of Jews, and to human rights at large, was that the subjects of these rights remained passive defendants, objects rather than true subjects. This is a familiar problem, and it is central for today's human rights ideology: more often than not, human rights are rights of victims defended by the stronger ones from abroad. For Bauer, the Jewish question was at his time an epitome of this problem. In his construction, Jews needed first of all to "emancipate" themselves, and this could only be done through their abandonment of the Jewish religion, which separated them from the rest of the nation and prevented them from acquiring a true public spirit. This religion had at least to be abandoned as a public institution, but Bauer allowed for it to remain in the private sphere. Christianity was a harmful institution, too, because, as Bauer stated, it was "the accomplished Judaism (*vollendete Judentum*),"[14] and because it despised "peoples," and dismissed public spirit and national unity.[15] "The question of emancipation is a universal [*allgemeine*] one. Not only Jews but also we ourselves want to be emancipated."[16] But Christianity had already accomplished the separation of state and religion and retreated into the public sphere. It was sublated and superseded by the popular state ("dissolved Christianity,"[17] Christianity qua dissolved)—the thing that had not yet happened to Judaism. This, however, was a problem not only for the Jews, but for secular Christians and for atheists as well: as long as the latter keep protecting the human rights of those who do not stand up for themselves, they are themselves unfree: the "general emancipation" is not accomplished. As for Bauer's proposed solutions to the question, they differed in the two of his "Jewish texts" reviewed by Marx. In the first one ("The Jewish Question"), the political goal was set as a republican state which would overcome the narrow legalism of Kant or Hobbes via democratic constitution and national unity. In the second, subsequent one ("The Capacity of Jews and Christians ..."), the program becomes more universalist: Bauer criticized Jewish national exceptionalism and noted:

> A human being [*Mensch*], born as a member of one people, is destined to become a citizen of a state to which he belongs by birth, but his destination [*Bestimmung*] as a human being goes beyond the limit of the state where he is born.[18]

Marx, in his review, concentrates on only one aspect of Bauer's argument—the need for Jews to become citizens of a state and to reduce their religion to the private sphere. But in some other aspects that he does not name, Marx seriously depends on Bauer: first (as we will see), in the politico-theological formulation of the question; second, in the appeal to the universal, or human, emancipation, which doesn't end with formally conferring rights on someone; third, in the critique of human rights as split into the rights of an active (sovereign) or a passive person (whose rights must be defended by someone else). Marx gives all of these ideas a new spin by applying them to the split between the state and civil society—something that Bauer had not done.

According to Marx, Bauer is right, of course, in that he sees any religion as a way of oppressing and artificially separating people from one another. But religion qua subjective faith is, to Marx, just an ideological expression of the more fundamental structural problems of the state as such. This is why the solution to the question on just the theological and political level, as the one suggested by Bauer, is insufficient. Indeed, we see that religion, far from dying out, is actually flourishing in most modern republican states, such as the USA. Therefore, says Marx, religion (qua ideology) is just a *symptom*—not just a symptom of a certain material "basis," as vulgar Marxism would present it, but a symptom of the deeply *religious* organization of the material life of society. "The members of the political state are religious owing to the dualism between individual life and species-life, between the life of civil society and political life."[19] Religion is a default in the organization of the totality. This default is the rupture between the particular and the universal, or, between the public and the private, or, between the state and "civil society" (Hegel's name for routine economic activity).

Let us take the rights of man, says Marx—the very heart of the liberal doctrine. The rights of man, as they are formulated in the great revolutions of the end of the eighteenth century, are, according to him, self-contradictory. On the one hand, they imply a collective universality at the level of civil rights—people's sovereignty, the voting rights, right to public statement, etc. But, on the other hand, they imply egoism and the right of particularity, at the level of rights that relate to the "private" sphere, namely economy and religion. Thus, liberty is defined in the declarations of the rights of man as "the right to do everything that harms no one else."[20] This means that this is just a question of the liberty of man as an isolated monad, withdrawn into himself. Analogously, the separation of the state from religion leads, not to freedom *from* religion, but to freedom *for* (one's particular) religion. Thus, the "human rights" sanctify the "civil society" of atomized individuals who live their own particular life and are united at the top by the state, in an external way only.

Notably, and importantly for the subsequent discussion of Arendt, Marx understands the atomized egotistic individual, not just as a *petit bourgeois*, but as a product of a catastrophic alienation.

> Political democracy is Christian since in it man, not merely one man but everyman, ranks as sovereign, as the highest being, but it is man in his uncivilized, unsocial form, man in his fortuitous existence, man just as he is, man as he has been corrupted by the whole organization of our society, who has lost himself, been alienated, and handed over to the rule of inhuman conditions and elements—in short, man who is not yet a real species-being. [21]

What is criticized is not just a bourgeois or a "huckster," but an abject and solitary man who is proclaimed a sovereign but is, indeed, an unhappy, anomic one.

Thus, to sum up, the *Aufhebung* of religion, says Marx, does not destroy this religion, but transfers it to a down-to-earth, non-public and unconscious, level.

Religion is nowadays *embodied,* and in this sense Hegel and Bauer are right. But it is embodied as a rupture between Heaven and Earth or, more precisely, as a rupture between the public and the private, the nature and the spirit, etc. Religion is realized not with its better, more progressive side (which would be the *mediation* between the universal and the particular), but with its worst side (which is that of alienation and servitude). But this alienation and the gap between the universal and the particular are, in Hegel's philosophical theology, precisely what characterizes Judaism in contrast with Christianity. Thus, Marx is saying that the embodiment of Christianity sends it back toward the Judaic religion from which it had emerged and which it attempted to sublate.

Since Hegel's early theological writings, Judaism had interested him greatly. Although his attitude toward Judaism changed from one to another period of his life—the account of it in the *Lectures on the Philosophy of Religion* is more respectful and ambivalent than the Frankfurt and Iena writings—generally, Judaism is for Hegel a religion of the split between the human being and nature, of positive external precepts and the respective slavery of an individual, etc. As such, it is also a necessary negative step on the road to the absolute religion and to the self-recognition of a free subject in the world. For the mature Hegel, the figure of Judaism becomes an important weapon in his polemics against Kant, whose insistence on the split between law and sensibility seems to him to be analogous to the mentality of the Old Testament.

Francesco Tomasoni, in his detailed history of "The Debate over Judaism from Kant to Young Hegelians,"[22] shows that Hegel's figure of Judaism, aimed against Kant as it was, was at the same time *borrowed* from Kant and, more broadly, from the late eighteenth century discussions of Judaism. It all started with Moses Mendelsohn, who claimed Judaism to be a perfect Enlightenment-like religion,[23] because, in the footsteps of Spinoza he conceived of it as a rational moral teaching without any supernatural illusions. Interestingly, Kant took up Mendelsohn's idea of such a rational religion, but, in *Religion in the Boundaries of Mere Reason,* he turned it into a defense of Christianity against Judaism, asserting that in Judaism, rational laws play a merely "statutory" role, since they "deal only with external actions."[24] Hegel makes another twist: for him, the very idea of a moral religion of Enlightenment is suspect: like Schiller, he searches for a way to unite morals with sensibility and with human material needs, and finds this mediation, first, in "love," later in "spirit." Both Mendelsohn and Kant are then "Judaic," and Kant himself is guilty of what he blames on Jews: statutory morals not penetrating the prosaic human life.

Christianity, in Hegel, is a religion which proposes to overcome the rupture between God and man via its *mediation.* Judaism, on the other hand, is understood by Hegel as a religion where an atomized individual, servant of God and of abstract law, is separated from the God and from Law which are distant and absolute.[25] Hegel develops this understanding of Christianity and Judaism already in his early text "The Spirit of Christianity and its Fate."[26] Here and elsewhere, he opposes Christianity, as a religion of fate, to the Judaic religion of abstract, "positive" legality. A large part of this work is dedicated to the treatment of *crime* and to the opposition between punishment and fate. "Fate" (or "destiny," as it may also be translated) is a dialectical logic that develops the meaning of one's deeds in time, in the concatenation of events it had provoked. "Punishment as fate is the equal reaction of the trespasser's own deed, of a power he himself has armed, of an enemy made an enemy by himself."[27] If one thus "pays," lightly or heavily, for his or her deed, this reckoning comes as one's own accomplishment, not as an external punishment. The punishment imposed by law opposes the universal to the particular, but the crime, as a particular act, is itself *universalized* as such. Thus, in the field of legality and punishment (i.e., of Judaism), we have two opposite principles in a desperate standoff. In contrast, when the "fate" comes into the picture, says Hegel, then:

> [T]he law is only a gap [or lack—*Lücke*] of life, defective life appearing as power. And life can heal its wounds again; the severed, hostile life can return into itself again and sublate [*aufheben*] the bungling achievement of a trespass, can annul law and punishment.[28]

This is early Hegel (the one that had not been read by the young Hegelians, since the relevant texts had not been published by then). Much later, in the Berlin *Lectures on the Philosophy of Religion* (taught since 1821), Hegel repeats and develops the opposition between Judaism and Christianity. He says of the Judaic God:

> God is absolute wisdom ... but he is this in the sense of being entirely abstract wisdom.... This indeterminate end thus devoid of content, changes in actual existence into immediate particularity, into the most perfect limitation.... God's real end is thus the family, and in fact this particular family.... We have here a noteworthy and absolutely rigid contrast—in fact, the most rigid possible contrast. God is, on the one hand, the God of heaven and of earth, absolute wisdom, universal power, and the end aimed at by this God is at the same time so limited that it concerns only one family, only this one people.... In politics, if it is only universal laws which are to hold sway, then the governing element is force, the arbitrary will of the individual.[29]

In Judaic law:

> Penalty attached to disobedience is not an absolute penalty, but is merely external misfortune.... The penalties which are threatened are of an external earthly sort.... Just as the obedience demanded is not of a spiritual and moral sort, but is merely the definite blind obedience of men who are not morally free, so also the penalties have an external character.[30]

In Judaism, evil constitutes only an external accident, Hegel says.

> Evil accordingly appears as an external accident ... God punishes evil as that which ought not to be. It is good only that ought to be, since it is what the Lord has enjoined. There is here as yet no freedom.... The characteristics of the Good ... derive their worth from the fact that they are rules laid down by the Lord, and the Lord punishes any transgression of these.[31]

Hegel and his disciples view Judaism as a religion of rupture, which combines everyday egoism with spiritual servitude, *and* as a religion of *exceptionality*, of a subject who treats its own collective egoism as a sign of selection and singularity. This exceptionality grounds egoism and egocentrism. But—as we see in Marx and particularly in Arendt—it can also lead to an abject, outlawed status of an individual or a collective, in the same sense that, in Giorgio Agamben's well-known construction,[32] the logic of sovereignty coincides with the logic of exclusion and "ban."

It is clear that this, mildly speaking, is an incorrect presentation of the actual *historical* Judaism. But Hegel was interested in Judaism as in something from which Christianity had once started off, in the obverse side of Christianity and of religion as such. Moreover, he projects on to this religion his critique of the abstract rationalism of the Enlightenment as represented by Kant (whom Hölderlin once called "the Moses of our nation").

Bruno Bauer, in his ironical pamphlet "The Trumpet of the Last Judgment over Hegel, an Atheist and Antichrist" (in which Marx probably collaborated with him), strengthens Hegel's respectful criticism of Judaism. A whole section of Bauer's pamphlet (#7) is entitled "Hatred of Judaism." It says, among other things:

> The fundamental attitude of the religious attitude to Judaism, Hegel says, is "fear of the master". The self-consciousness is here fully alienated from itself, "ego" is only the empty consciousness of ego, in its raw, barbarian, and stupid singularity—and self-consciousness qua infinite power. Ego is only here "in the abstract relation to itself", that is, it is a pure and frightening *egoism*, because it's "deprived of breadth or extension, has not taken up spiritual intentions, inclinations."[33]

Bauer interprets Hegel's notion of a singular abstract consciousness as "egoism," and Marx picks up this interpretation. Like Bauer, Marx discovers a "Jewish question" both in the empirical and in the theological sense.

In Bauer's "Jewish Question"—the first of the two works reviewed by Marx—Bauer develops the same approach, applying the critique of Judaism to the question about the status of present-day Jews. He notes their ahistorical character (i.e. the incapacity of actively changing themselves),[34] their tendency to "isolation" and, most importantly, points out that the spirit of Judaism is the spirit of "positive laws" "without a universal reason."[35]

> The Jewish people could never produce a true state law or people's law and was therefore only a collection of atoms. This isolation is rooted in the essence of Judaism [*Judentum*], but it had to be accomplished in Christianity where it became the highest obligation of a believer.[36]

An argument in this sense close to Bauer is advanced by another young Hegelian, and another mentor of Marx, Ludwig Feuerbach. Bauer tended toward liberal republicanism, and Feuerbach to socialism, but at the time these divisions were not that strong. In his "Essence of Christianity" (1841), Feuerbach writes:

> Jews have maintained their peculiarity to this day. Their principle, their God, is the most practical principle in the world—namely, egoism, and moreover egoism

in the form of religion. Egoism is the God who will not let his servants come to shame. Egoism is essentially monotheistic, for it has only one, only self, as its end.[37]

Feuerbach believes that Judaism is grounded, univocally, on the affirmative nature of man, on its *will*, but that Christianity has overcome the "solitude" of God and introduced the Godmother—a *sensitive*, receptive image.

However, he says that in the ultimate analysis, "Judaism is worldly Christianity; Christianity, spiritual Judaism."[38] "Christianity has spiritualized the egoism of Judaism into subjectivity (though even within Christianity this subjectivity is again expressed as pure egoism)."[39] This means that religion per se is ego-bound, "egotistic," although Christianity does take a step toward its overcoming, to the "opening up" of an individual, and to the productive communication of people among themselves, not just with God.

Now it must be clear to us *why* Marx, after having rejected the false, political solution of the Jewish question by Bauer, declares this very solution … a Judaic one! He tries to show that, under the Christian façade of the Modern state, there hides a generalized "Judaism," so that the "Jewish question" is in fact not just the problem of Jews, but the problem of the modern state as such.

In the second part of "On the Jewish Question" (review of the "Aptitude of the Jews the Christians …"), Marx moves to the openly theological discussion:

> The Jew has emancipated himself in a Jewish manner, not only because he has acquired financial power, but also because, through him and also apart from him, *money* has become a world power and the practical Jewish spirit has become the practical spirit of the Christian nations. The Jews have emancipated themselves insofar as the Christians have become Jews.[40]

There is a certain anti-Semitism distinguishable here. But Marx forms a conclusion that is not at all anti-Semitic: he says that the problem lies not in the Jews but in the very structure of the Christian (i.e. liberal) state and society. That is, everyone gradually becomes a "Jew" or an "egoist." Because the public, "generic" (another Feuerbachean term in Marx) life retreats in the face of the individualist, economically oriented "civil society," the Christian embodiment of a generic human being in the state increasingly turns into a sublime fiction used to legitimize the everyday egoism and the mutual alienation of people. Hence, the difference between Judaism and Christianity vanishes day by day! "Christianity sprang from Judaism. It has merged again in Judaism."[41]

This is similar to Feuerbach, who claims Christianity to be the spiritualized Judaism. However, Marx adds the moment of a non-linear movement, of a *regression* with regard to the achievements of Christianity. Thus, the apparent overcoming of the Christian religion in a liberal secular state reproduces the very structure of the religious rupture between the universal and the particular. The post-Christian condition is the prevalence of the dead letter of law (both moral and political), the pluralism of ideologies and religions. As such it does not overcome but *fixes down* the archaic structure of religion which Christianity has promised to sublate. This is why, in his "positive" program, Marx restores, in a secularized way, the messianism of the Christian kind: he makes his bet on an uprising of outcasts who would destroy the structures of alienation and redeem the whole world. Marx calls for a new, earthly Christianity supposed to win, once again, over the old Christianity that became Judaism, that is, over a new phariseanism.

There is, however, an ambivalence here: the idea of an earthly, "economical" Messiah sounds Christian, the address to this messiah as to someone who comes in the *future* is closer to the Judaic theology. Marx is a prophet rather than a saint. To the Judaism in the Christian form which produces alienation, he opposes a Christianity (the embodied universal) in the Judaic form of the futurist messianism.[42]

Hannah Arendt on the Jewish question in the twentieth century

Now, let us jump a hundred years ahead and turn to the work of another great political thinker, Hannah Arendt. Like Marx, Arendt was an assimilated, secular Jew and received a Christian school education, although, unlike him, she always recognized her Jewish "identity" as a fact of life (without accepting the Jewish religion). In her philosophy, she explicitly relied on such emphatically Christian thinkers as St. Augustine, even though she interpreted them in a secular, "ontological" way.

Arendt had very little sympathy for Marx, although in the late 1950s/early 1960s she wanted to write a book on him—the book that eventually turned into "On Revolution." However, there are two themes that unite Arendt with early Marx. The first one is *alienation*. In *The Human Condition*, Arendt introduces the concept of "world alienation"[43] in sympathetically quoting *early* Marx.[44] Significantly, she points out that this modern world alienation is, in a way, a continuation of the religious withdrawal from the world which the "secularization" has never annulled:

> We tend to overlook the central importance of this alienation for the modern age because we usually stress its secular character and identify the term secularity with worldliness. Yet secularization as a tangible historical event means no more than separation of Church and State, of religion and politics, and this, from a religious viewpoint, implies a return to the early Christian attitude ... rather than a loss of faith and transcendence of a new and emphatic interest in the things of this world.[45]

Thus, Arendt sees alienation as a transformed version of political theology, a result of the failure to get rid of religion, in the abandonment of the Christian cult. This argument, needless to say, is close to the one of Marx: the modern state claims to overcome religion but, in fact, perpetuates it by isolating and degrading man's "worldly" activity. It is not hard to see the decisive influence of Heidegger on this argument (Heidegger famously praises Marx's concept of alienation in "Letter on Humanism"[46]), but the evocation of theology is Arendt's own.

The second theme is the philosophical critique of the theory and practice of human rights. In her *Origins of Totalitarianism*,[47] Arendt, like Marx, shows that the doctrine of human rights is internally contradictory. In her view, they are, on the one hand, rights of a citizen, which are guaranteed by a state; on the other hand, they are rights of a victim to a biological survival which can be protected only by an outside benefactor (this analysis is even closer to Bauer than to Marx). The "naked being" (she uses Benjamin's formula) becomes the destiny of a stateless person. The central example of such stateless persons are Jews—who have not had their own state (at least for the past 2000 years) and who, when expelled from Germany, were not given citizenship by any European state.

Arendt notes that "human rights" emerge in the process of dissolution of the medieval "civil society": "[I]n a new secularized and emancipated society, men were no longer sure of these social and human rights which until then had been outside the political order and guaranteed not by government and constitution, but by social, spiritual, and religious forces."[48] Further, she contrasts "general human rights" and the "rights of the citizen", saying that the former are not guaranteed by any instance and are thus not rights at all. Stateless people can be helped by a "charity"[49] but they do not have rights. They live in a hierarchical condition (in contrast to political equality) and are doomed to a sheer "individuality as such."[50] *Mutatis mutandis*, this argument is analogous to the one of Marx, only instead of the state/civil society division we here have the dichotomy of the nation-state and the stateless persons and, in both cases, this argument has Jews as its paradigm (respectively, Jews of the nineteenth and of the twentieth century). Arendt agrees with Marx's analysis in that the subject of abstract right is not just "*egotistic*," but that s/he exists in an *exceptional*, outcast situation, which is implied and presumed by the nation-state (we need to remember that *privilege* was central, for Bauer, for the definition of Jews). An exceptional singularity precedes a standardized individual unit, but it is equally a result of alienation.

Arendt was a secular, assimilated Jew, but she insisted on her Jewish identity. In her letter to G. Scholem, she writes that she "always regarded [her] Jewishness as one of the indisputable factual data of [her] life, and ha[s] never had the wish to change or disclaim facts of this kind."[51] Moreover, throughout her life, Arendt had had an interest in the "Jewish Question," but never in the Judaic theology.[52] The acute interest emerged in the 1930s when she was writing a book about Rahel Varnhagen—a book criticizing enlightened Jews of the nineteenth century for an attempt to escape from the world into a self-enclosed circle. After the Nazis had come to power and Arendt had fled Germany, she started working for Zionist organizations and publishing articles sympathetic to Zionism. At the end of the 1940s she emerged, however, as a fierce critic of the newly founded State of Israel and broke her ties to Zionism, choosing to make an academic career. The first part of *The Origins of Totalitarianism* (1951) is dedicated to "Antisemitism" and contains a brilliant analysis of the social condition of Jews in Europe. In this work, Arendt cites Marx's "On the Jewish Question" as evidence of the fact that the "anti-Jewish" writing of this sort, often written by Jews themselves, had little to do with a "full-fledged anti-Semitism." She also explains Marx's "anti-Jewish" text as an expression of a social clash within Jewry, between the Jewish intellectuals and the Jewish financiers.[53] The details of Marx's text are not further discussed, but the reference is important because it shows Arendt's familiarity with Marx's important work, some of the ideas of which she echoes in her critique of the human rights, in the second part of *The Origins of Totalitarianism*.

After this book, Arendt abandoned the Jewish theme for a long time but returned to it magisterially during the Eichmann process in 1961. The resulting *Eichmann in Jerusalem*[54] became a culmination of her "Jewish" reflections, her main "Jewish question" book. I will briefly remind readers about the core argument of the *Eichmann* book. Arendt reflects on the nature of the Nazi "evil" and applies to it the Augustinian "privative" concept of evil, of evil as a *lack* of the good. She explains, then, the crime of Eichmann (and of the majority of Germans) as the incapacity to produce a free, responsible judgment. Eichmann, in Arendt's view, is not a demonic monster (which the prosecution construed him to be), but a "banal" individual who committed his horrible crime out of conformism. The point she makes is ethical: the one who presents a criminal as a satanic anti-Semite excludes him/herself out of the consideration and regards evil as something external. If, in contrast, evil has a privative, not substantial, nature, then each of us could be in the place of a criminal. To be good a risky effort is needed, and if a human being is left to the inertia of its own "nature" it inevitably slides into evil.

Arendt's book is difficult to read, because in part it is dedicated to the retelling of the standpoints of Eichmann and of his Israeli prosecutors. It is not always clear from this retelling whether Arendt is ironic or not, and what her own position is. This contributed, in part, to the acclaim that started after the publication of the book: many thought that Arendt defended Eichmann or that she opposed his punishment (neither is true). There is a parallel here with the dialogical style in which Marx's "On the Jewish Question" is written.

Arendt builds her book around three main topics: critique of the trial, the story of Eichmann's life and deed, and the "Jewish councils" in Nazi Germany which collaborated with the regime and which, according to Arendt, bore some responsibility for the genocide. Here, I will focus mainly on the two former topics: prosecutors and the defendant.

The prosecutors of Eichmann, says Arendt, were insensitive to the uniqueness and "unprecedentedness" of his deed and, even more so, to the unprecedentedness of the mass murder of Jews committed by Nazis. Instead of the actual person and his actions, instead of the concrete event, the judgment applies to the age-old "antisemitism":

> This was the tone set by Ben Gurion and faithfully followed by Mr Hausner who began his opening address ... with Pharaoh in Egypt and with Haman's decree "to destroy, to slay, and to cause them to perish". He then proceeded to quote Ezekiel: "and when I [The Lord] passed by thee, and saw thee polluted in thine own blood, I said unto thee, in thy blood, live," explaining that these words must be understood as "the imperative that has confronted this nation ever since its first appearance on the stage of history". It was bad history and cheap rhetoric; worse, it was really at cross-purposes with putting Eichmann on trial, suggesting that perhaps he was

only an innocent executor of some mysteriously preordained destiny or, for that matter, even of antisemitism, which perhaps was necessary to blaze the trail of "the bloodstained road traveled by this people" to fulfill its destiny.[55]

For Arendt, such an approach is the epitome of all that she had criticized in Zionism and Israel's ideology: namely the nationalist egocentrism and the confidence of one's righteousness. But, at the same time, the behavior of the Israeli politicians elucidates a larger philosophical problem: how to judge a *deed* which has, by the definition of judgment, to be seen as *unique*. Any court must necessarily use some generalized criteria of judgment, be it laws or precedents. But laws and precedents normalize, domesticate the evil and cannot account for a unique individual decision to commit it. This paradox is constitutive for any court, but the Jerusalem judges did not even attempt to resolve it. "The court … never rose to the challenge of the unprecedented … instead, it buried the proceedings under the flood of precedents."[56]

Judging history and accusing the past is an activity that runs the risk of legitimizing and normalizing this past. This problem has a considerable history. During the French Revolution, Robespierre and Saint-Just noted that the execution of Louis XVI is neither legitimate if he is judged as a king (a king is above all law, he is sovereign) nor if he is judged as simple citizen Louis Capet (as such, he had not committed any crime). Moreover, an execution of Louis qua king would be a recognition of kingly status and would lead to his posthumous "crowning." This is why Robespierre suggested that the execution of Louis would best be defended as the killing of an external enemy.[57]

Moreover, even the murder of Jews by the Nazis followed a somewhat analogous logic. As we have already seen in the beginning, the "Jewish question," as described, for instance, by Bauer, consisted in the dilemma: Jews cannot be included into the German state as a group apart (Germans are supposed to be building an egalitarian, integrated nation), but they cannot—from a certain perspective—be included there as simple citizens. Being almost indistinguishable from other Germans physically and culturally, they practice a political religion that would damage their allegiance to the state. Hence the hysterical "final solution," just to take these irritating internal aliens "off the radar screen"—to kill them as animals.[58]

It is because of this deadlock that Arendt, in her book, suggests that murdering Eichmann on the streets of Buenos Aires would perhaps be a better idea than staging a public trial.[59] Evil is, in such trial, sublimated; it looks attractively demonic. By killing Eichmann, one would emphasize his status as an outlaw of humanity: *hostis generis humanis*. She evokes two examples of such killings. One is Shalom Schwartzbard who murdered Petliura, and the other is Sohomon Tehlirian who killed Talaat Bey. Both avengers gave themselves up to the authorities, and both were acquitted in court. There was also a trial, but in the case of Schwartzbard and Tehlirian, the court discussed the "judgment" that was itself an illegal, extraordinary act: the singularity of the act of judgment is a match for the singularity of the crime itself. In contrast, the trial of Eichmann was incapable either of recognizing the Nazis' crime as an *act* or of establishing a new law out of his prosecution. Everything was dissolved in precedents and in the bureaucratic machine of a nation-state.

In this situation, Arendt decides to take the judgment *upon herself*. From the critique of the court, she moves to the critique of Eichmann as a person and, thus, of the Nazi subjectivity he exemplifies. Arendt fills the gap left by the judges and narratively reconstructs the biography and the career of Eichmann. To use a Hegelian term, Arendt tries to figure out Eichmann's "fate" (or "destiny"), not just the formal legal qualification of his deed. But, as a result of her long effort of narrating Eichmann's life in search of a decisive act, she comes to the conclusion that Eichmann was himself not a Jew hater but committed his deeds out of bureaucratic accuracy, for the sake of his career ambitions. Thus, during the trial, Eichmann does not even understand that he commits a certain crime.

There follow a number of ironic comparisons of Eichmann with his judges. First, Eichmann, says Arendt, became a "Zionist" for a while, because, like Zionists, he believed that Jews should create their own state. Second, Eichmann is unable to take the Other's point of view and is thus guilty of egocentrism. "His [Eichmann's] inability to speak was associated with his inability to think, that is, to think from the standpoint of someone else."[60] But so are his judges, who cannot view the situation from Eichmann's perspective. Third, Eichmann always follows the law meticulously. Arendt shows that Eichmann uses for his defense the Kantian conception of moral duty. In his words, he followed the categorical imperative (at least in Hans Frank's version: "Act in such a way that Führer, if he knew your action, would approve it"[61]). Of course, Arendt notes, this is a wrong understanding of Kant (for Kant, each person, when acting, turns into a legislator), but it agrees with what he himself called "the version of Kant for the household usage of little man." "There is not the slightest doubt—says Arendt—that in one respect Eichmann did indeed follow Kant's precepts: a law was a law, there could be no exceptions."[62] This reproach to Kant reminds one of Hegel's critique of Kant's abstract legalism and of the Judaic religion construed in the terms of Kant's metaphysics.

However, in saying that law knows no exception, Eichmann himself, as an individual, can only be an exception from law! Eichmann is an egoist, an atomized individual. Moreover, in another ironic turn, Arendt calls him a "stateless" person, and compares him to a pirate—not only because he was stolen in Argentina and judged in Israel, but also because of the very nature of his act, which, on the one hand, falls out of the general categories or precedents, and on the other, is deprived of a positive, substantial meaning.[63]

A stateless person is by definition a *passive* object of human rights. Arendt sends the reader back to her criticism of human rights in *The Origins of Totalitarianism*.[64] In her analysis, human rights are either protected by a certain concrete political order, or they turn into the rights of entirely alienated stateless persons, deprived of any agency in defending their own rights.

This analysis is in some aspects close to the criticism that Bruno Bauer turns against the defenders of the Jews' rights in "The Jewish Question." Eichmann, like these stateless persons, is a despaired social atom who therefore has neither legitimate authority to judge his ominous deeds and nor can he assume any active responsibility for those deeds. But, as we have seen, Arendt's critique of human rights is even closer to Marx's "On the Jewish Question." Like Marx, Arendt claims that "human rights" are torn between the rights of a citizen and the rights of "man" who, for Marx, is a human being in civil society, and for Arendt, a "stateless" human being directly deprived of citizenship. For both, "rights of man" are a dark obverse of the "rights of citizen," and the former annul the latter.

One more element in Arendt's portrayal of Eichmann is the fact that in his final speech he is unable to speak from his own position but proceeds as though he were an external observer of his own action, as though he were mourning himself from the position of a survivor.[65] It would seem that this example is contrary to Arendt's insistence that Eichmann is an egocentric; but in fact, there is no contradiction. In the speech, Eichmann assumes not a standpoint of another person, but the abstract standpoint of the blind impersonal public. He thinks "abstractly," as Hegel would say.[66] This demonstrates that the rupture between abstract egoism and abstract law goes inside Eichmann and prevents him from coming into contact with himself. However, since Eichmann shows this in his *speech,* this serves as final proof that the impersonal judgment of the Jerusalem court is reflected by Eichmann as a subject who refuses to be a subject. Or, rather, it is Arendt who produces this operation of *reflection,* to give both Eichmann and the legal order of a nation-state their *justice.*

As a result of Arendt's analysis it turns out that to the abstract, formalist, and egocentric thinking of judges, there corresponds an abstract, formalist and egocentric thinking of Eichmann. Arendt *attempted* to present Eichmann narratively, as a "hero" of his crime, but she could not find any hero. Instead, she found the "banality of evil"—the incapacity to commit a risky act, a negative (privative), not a positive phenomenon. St. Augustine's doctrine of the privative nature of evil was proven "experimentally." *The probe thus failed—but the judgment did not, because the failure itself constituted a result.*

As a result, Arendt comes to the conclusion that Eichmann was executed *justly.* Judges applied their abstract judgment to someone who happened to be thinking as abstractly as they did. In the Conclusion, Arendt herself sentences Eichmann and tells "him" that he is guilty simply by virtue of the factual things he did. This is all that is *left,* since we have not found either a personality or a preconception of the deed in the accused.

In the absence of an act we return to a naked being which can only be murdered, not hanged. In her improvised "sentence," Arendt concludes brutally: "This is the reason, and the only reason, you must hang."[67] Thus, justice is realized here as *non-recognition* of the criminal. Having criticized the Jerusalem court for its failure to recognize Eichmann's personality, Arendt probes such recognition but fails and concludes that it is unrecognizable, impossible to judge.

Note the logic of *exception* that is involved here. In fact, Arendt's "judgment" of Eichmann reproduces the paradox that the trial itself demonstrates. The court judges the unjudgable, and the law of recognition realizes itself in the form of its self-annulment. The "naked life" incapable of action is not possible to narrate or judge. This is what Schmitt, and later, Agamben, analyzed as a sovereign self-annulment of law.[68] Like Schmitt and unlike Agamben, Arendt is not necessarily horrified by this logic: when applied abstractly and unilaterally by the state to humans it is disastrous, but when reflection of the excluded subject him/herself (remember Bauer and "his" Jews!) enters the equation, and when the recognition is actively probed, then the outlawing can be affirmed, by a sovereign, to a "sovereign" outcast.

There are obvious analogies between this argument and the argument of Marx's "On the Jewish Question." Both texts deal with the political, secular problems of Jewish people, and both encounter the philosophical problems that, at least in the German tradition, were framed around the opposition between Christianity and Judaism, and, moreover, around the problem of religion as such.

Arendt does not cover up the theological context of her argument. *Eichmann in Jerusalem* abounds with references to God and to the Torah. Thus, for example, she says:

> [W]e can read in the postwar statement of the Evangelische Kirche in Deutschland, a Protestant Church, as follows: "we aver that before the God of Mercy we share in the guilt for the outrage committed against the Jews by our own people through omission and silence". It seems to me that a Christian is guilty before the God of Mercy when he repays evil with evil, hence that the churches would sin before the God of mercy if millions of jews would be killed for some evil they committed. But if the churches shared in the guilt for an outrage pure and simple, as they themselves attest, then the matter must still be considered to fall within the purview of the God of *Justice*.[69]

Even though, in truth, both mercy and justice are attributes of both the Judaic and the Christian God, for Arendt, justice is a "traditionally Jewish passion,"[70] and within the context of the book it falls clearly on the side of the blind, physical law rather than the considerate, recognizing judgment. In the letter to Scholem, she continues the same argument:

> Mercy was out of the question, not on juridical grounds – pardon is anyhow not a prerogative of the juridical system – but because mercy is applicable to the person rather than to the deed; the act of mercy does not forgive murder but pardons he murderer insofar as he, as a person, may be more than anything he ever did. This was not true of Eichmann. And to spare his life without pardoning him was impossible on juridical grounds.[71]

Thus, mercy and justice are not just characteristics of a court, but also of the subject who is under prosecution. To the deed of Eichmann, there corresponds the blind, abstract logic of law and of exteriority—because he is not a "personality." Although Arendt does not view justice unilaterally negatively, it appears as the best way out of the collision between an egocentric individual and the blind law. Because it is opposed to mercy, justice is clearly not the way to truly recognize or judge an *act*. But it fits for *inaction*.

Arendt's opposition between the legalistic, abstract judgment and the narrative recognition of the human personality is the traditional argument of Christian theology emphasizing its difference from the "pharisaeic" Judaism. As we saw above, Hegel, in the "Spirit of Christianity and its Fate," identifies Christianity with the capacity of the narrative constitution of personality, as opposed to the purely legal, abstract qualifications which characterize Judaism. Moreover, Hegel proposes "fate" as a means to reduce law to a mere *lack*.

The very issue of the mass murder of Jews as a unique event has clear theological repercussions. Jerusalem judges refuse to see the so-called "Holocaust" as a new precedent and as a historical rupture of the tradition (Arendt frequently insists on this latter perspective). This is precisely what traditionally separates Jews and Christians: the latter always accuse the former of their blindness to the event. However, in our case, Arendt comes to the conclusion that the event has indeed never taken place or was in truth a pseudo-event. The Israeli judges would be right in their judgment were they to distinguish events from non-events. Thus, curiously, Arendt, like Marx, emphasizes the *failure* of the Christian logic to triumph. Its superficial show character leads to the triumph of the older, legalist logic of Judaism. The argument of historical regression is evident in both constructions.

Arendt's critique of the court for its incapacity to go beyond the horizon of one, Jewish people, for the statement of its own exceptionality, also traditionally belongs to the arsenal of the Christian critique of Judaism. In her 1965 to 1966 lectures on "Some questions of moral philosophy,"[72] Arendt states that the only difference between the Christian commandments and the Judaic ones consists in the fact that in Christianity the other, not myself, becomes a criterion of action. 'This curious selflessness, the deliberate attempt at self-extinction for the sake of God or for the sake of my neighbour, is the very quintessence of all Christian ethics that deserves this name."[73]

Today, this apology of Christianity sounds odd, because the apology of the Other recently became the main point of the neo-Judaic doctrine of such thinkers as Cohen, Rosenzweig, Buber, Levinas, Derrida, and Lyotard. Richard Bernstein even uses Arendt's insistence on the Other's point of view as proof of her unconscious sympathy for Judaism.[74] But, as we have just seen, Arendt explicitly attributes this approach to Christianity, thus continuing in the footsteps of Feuerbach rather than Rosenzweig and Buber.[75]

If we look at Arendt's "positive" program, as developed, for instance, in *The Human Condition*, we see that it consists in the openness to novelty, the capacity of beginning anew. As in the case of Marx's messianism of proletariat, this argument seems to be ambivalent: on the one hand, it is this "Judaic" attitude of expectation, on the other it is the consciously Christian, Augustinian motif on "natality" and epochal beginnings. Arendt, like Marx, puts herself on the "prophetic" side, somewhere between Christianity and Judaism.

Conclusion

We see that Arendt, like Marx, uses the whole apparatus of the Christian critique of Judaism, or of the self-criticism of religion *tout court*, and comes to the conclusion that, behind the apparent overcoming of religion and behind its supposed embodiment in the liberal state, there lies a regression of religion from the logic of universality and mediation to the logic of rupture and alienation. Under the mask of the fulfilled Christianity (of representation, recognition, and humanism), there hides "Judaism" qua religion of alienation. But in fact the problem is *religion itself*, or, rather, what is religious in the bad sense of the word, as the spirit of servitude and alienation.

Arendt's critical political theology is similar to Marx's and, like Marx's, it continues in the footsteps of the German post-Kantian tradition. The difference between the two lies, first, in their *politics* (radical messianism in Marx, liberal openness in Arendt) and in their definition of *particularity*. For Marx, the particular is an egoistic individual. For Arendt, it is an outcast, the result of the inevitable *exception* and *exemption* from law that is produced by law itself. Exceptionality precedes individuality and particularity; the evil is not just exploitation of the poor, but the pastoral treatment of the stateless who are reduced to the status of animals. Arendt follows in the footsteps of the twentieth century political theology, namely that of Schmitt and Benjamin who saw the theological element of modernity, for its worst and for its best, in the "state of exception."

This critical political theology remains highly relevant today. In past decades, the abstract legalistic spirit has once more reaffirmed itself on the global level (in the "globalization" understood as an international expansion and unification of the rule of law and formally rational "governance"). It is a spirit which interprets human rights as rights of a passive victim, which denounces and punishes any overly disruptive violence as demonic "evil" and which, under the pretext of the care of a unitary legal space, proliferates the zones of exception where humans are left alone with their "naked being." The religious nature of this spirit increasingly shows itself and in the footsteps of the religious *structure* there follows the religious *belief*. The regime of the Enlightenment subjectivity, which had finally delegitimized itself by obliterating its revolutionary foundations, calls for religion as an external ontology of meaning. The Christian universalism returns but, as Marx may have put it, it returns in the Judaic form. Arendt opposes to this new phariseanism, not a new messiah, but readiness to a new radical act and readiness to recognize it. Both Arendt and Marx see the alternative to religion in a synthesis of decisiveness and opennesss. Their Christian critique of Judaism and of Christianity regressing to Judaism sounds attractive. But it is also dangerous as long as it is still determined by the theological structure of thinking, and implies a sublimated, exalted irrational moment (an ultimate proletarian uprising or a heroic action). In fact, heroism is, I believe, to be criticized as much as the cowardly banality. There is a chance that they are chains of the same jigsaw puzzle. What can effectively oppose and supersede religion would be the concrete socio-economic, practical structures that would enable free action. In a sense, only certain routines or machines of inventive freedom can be alternatives to divine intervention.

Notes

1 This chapter has been previously published in *Continental Philosophy Review*, Vol. 45(4), 2012, 545–68. It is reproduced with the permission of the copyright holders.
2 Carl Schmitt, *Political Theology. Four Chapters on the Theory of Sovereignty* (Chicago, IL: The University of Chicago Press, 1985).
3 The word usage goes to late stoic Panaetius; in Rome, Varro spoke of "theologia civilis."
4 Cf. Michael Walzer, *The Revolution of the Saints* (Cambridge, MA: Harvard University Press, 1982).

5. Cf. Max Weber, *The Protestant Ethic and the Spirit of Capitalism* (New York: Penguin Classics, 2002).
6. Carl Schmitt, *Political Theology. Four Chapters on the Theory of Sovereignty*, p. 36.
7. Hans Blumenberg, *The Legitimacy of the Modern Age*, trans. R. Wallace, (New York: MIT Press, 1983 [1966]), see esp. 92–105.
8. Erik Peterson, "Der Monotheismus als politisches Problem," in *Theologische Traktate* (München: Kösel, 1951), 45–147.
9. Carl Schmitt, *Politische Theologie II* (Berlin: Duncker und Humblot, 1970). On the "stasis"—a stagnant internal contradiction—as the very essence of the relationship between politics and theology, see a brilliant article by Dimitris Vardoulakis, "Stasis. Beyond Political Theology," *Cultural Critique*, vol. 73, fall 2009, 125–47. The argument of this article, which written from the Derridean perspective, is in many ways similar to mine, and the relationship of Christianity to Judaism reminds one of what Vardoulakis calls "stasis."
10. Ibid., 122.
11. Karl Marx, "On the Jewish Question," in Marx and Engels, *Collected Works* (New York: Lawrence & Wishart, 1975–2005), vol. 3, 146–74.
    My reading of "On the Jewish Question" is indebted to the seminar that Philippe Lacoue-Labarthe taught in Strasbourg on early Marx in 2001/2002. Unfortunately, Lacoue-Labarthe did not have time to publish or even finish this project during his life, but hopefully there will eventually appear a publication of the notes of his seminar.
12. Bruno Bauer, *Die Judenfrage* (Brauschweig: Friedrich Otto, 1843).
13. *Die Fähigkeit der heutigen Juden und Christen, frei zu sein: einundzwanzig Bogen aus der Schweiz*, hg. v. Georg Herwegh (Zürich: u. Winterthur, 1843), 56–71.
14. *Die Judenfrage*, 49.
15. Ibid., 47.
16. Ibid., 61.
17. *Die Fähigkeit der heutigen Juden und Christen, frei zu sein*, 70.
18. Ibid., 67.
19. "On the Jewish Question," 159.
20. Ibid., 162.
21. Ibid., 159.
22. Francesco Tomasoni, *Modernity and the Final Aim of History. The Debate over Judaism from Kant to the Young Hegelians* (Amsterdam: Kluwer Academic, 2010).
23. Moses Mendelsohn, *Jerusalem, or, on Religious Power and Judaism*, trans. A. Arkush (Hannover and London: University Press of New England, 1983).
24. Immanuel Kant, *Religion in the Boundaries of Mere Reason* (Cambridge: Cambridge University Press, 1998), 130 (6:125).
25. Cf. Takayuki Shibata, "Kritik der Juden- und Christentums bei Feuerbach und dem jungen Hegel," in *Feuerbach und der Judaismus*, 113–121. Shibata emphasizes that for Hegel, Judaism was a religion which opposed itself to the hostile nature and strived for domination over it, but, unable to do so, conferred this task on the all-mighty God. Ibid., 115.
26. G. W. F. Hegel, "The Spirit of Christianity and its Fate," in *Early Theological Writings*, trans. T. Knox (Philadelphia: University of Pennsylvania Press, 1971), 182–301.
27. "The Spirit of Christianity and its Fate," 230, translation modified.
28. Ibid., 230, translation modified.

29 G. W. F. Hegel, *Lectures on the Philosophy of Religion,* trans. E. B. Speirs and J. B. Sanderson, in 3 volumes (London: Kegan Paul, Trench, Trübner, 1895), Vol. 2, 196.
30 Ibid., Vol. 2, 216.
31 Ibid., Vol. 2, 218.
32 Giorgio Agamben, *Homo Sacer* (Stanford, CA: Stanford University Press, 1998).
33 Bruno Bauer, *Die Posaune des jungsten Gerichts über Hegel: den Atheisten und Antichristen: ein Ultimatum* (Wigand, 1841), 107. My translation.
34 *Die Judenfrage,* 30–5.
35 Ibid., 12. Bauer quotes Moses Mendelsohn who made the same observation in the apologetic sense.
36 Ibid., 48.
37 Ludwig Feuerbach, *Essence of Christianity,* trans. G. Eliot (New York and London: Harper & Row, 1957), 114. Cf. M. Vogel, "Feuerbachs Religionskritik, die Frage des Judaismus," in *Ludwig Feuerbach und die Philosophie der Zukunft,* ed. H.-J. Braun, H.-M. Sass, W. Schuffenhauer and F. Tomasoni (Berlin, 1990). It should be noted, however, that Feuerbach's relationship to Judaism was complicated. Since the *Essence of Christianity,* his attitude toward Judaism had significantly evolved, becoming more positive. Feuerbach felt interest and sympathy for the mystical element of the Jewish tradition: he took private lessons from Rabbis, tried to study Hebrew, and befriended David Friedländer, a well-known German Jewish banker, activist, and intellectual. See on this point Doninique Bourel, in *Feuerbach und der Judaismus,* 127; also Francesco Tomasoni, "Feuerbachs Studium der Kabbala," in *Sinnlichkeit und Rationalität. Der Umbruch in der Philosophie des 19. Jahrhunderts,* ed. W. Jaeschke (Berlin: Akademie Verlag, 1992), 57–67.
38 *Essence of Christianity,* 120.
39 Ibid., 121.
40 "On the Jewish Question," 170.
41 Ibid., 173.
42 Interestingly, Francesco Tomasoni, in his above-quoted book *Modernity and the Final Aim of History. The Debate over Judaism from Kant to the Young Hegelians,* does not give a convincing interpretation of Marx's text on the Jewish question. He erroneously attributes to Marx a more moderate denunciation of Judaism than Bauer's because Marx, to him, would be interested in economics more than in theology and would therefore see the Jew as an earthly, concrete figure, which "rather than condemning him to immobility and relegating him to the margins of history, put him at the very heart of the transformations" (184). Moreover, Tomasoni says that "religious doctrine interested [Marx] little … the economic practice was more his line … [and] the incentive to grasp its importance came more from the concreteness of Judaism than from the abstractness of Christianity" (186). Nothing could be further from the actual intentions of Marx. First, the interest in theology and economy is for him (as for Hegel) one and the same. "On the Jewish Question" is a work on theology, on the religious rupture within the modern state. Second, the materialist, prosaic character of Judaism is for Marx precisely *abstract,* not "concrete," because it depends on the rupture between the universal and the particular. Third, the sheer materiality of the "Jew" shows the victory of Judaism over Christianity in our time, but it is far from being the final word of history, since this is the materiality artificially separated from its ideal meaning. Tomasoni, in the title and in the introduction to his book, denounces the Hegelian vision of "the final aim of history,"

and perhaps he is right, but nevertheless for Hegel and for Marx, "Judaism" is a concept strictly correlate with the Christian and Enlightenment eschatology. In Hegel and Bauer it represents the resistance to *Aufhebung*; in Marx it appears as its hidden truth, regression under the guise of redemption. However, Marx is indeed ambivalent toward Judaism, not because Judaism is "materialist" but because it is messianic. Reduced to sheer material existence, a human being turns to the *future* redemption, concrete but as yet unaccomplished (Tomasoni rightly points at this other aspect of Judaism, obliterated but sometimes surfacing in the Hegelian tradition, on p. 15).

43 Hannah Arendt, *The Human Condition*, 248–57.
44 Ibid., 254.
45 Ibid., 253.
46 Martin Heidegger, *Basic Writings* (London: Harperperennial, 2008), 213–67, cit. 243: "What Marx recognized in an essential and significant sense, though derived from Hegel, as the estrangement [*Entfremdung*] of man has its roots in the homelessness of the Modern man."
47 *The Origins of Totalitarianism*, 290–302.
48 Ibid., 291.
49 Ibid., 296.
50 Ibid., 301.
51 Arendt, Hannah *Jew as Pariah*. (New York: Grove Books, 1978), 246.
52 This is rightly noted by Richard Bernstein in his book *Hannah Arendt and the Jewish Question* (Cambridge, MA: MIT Press, 1996), 15, 185. But Bernstein looks for the traces of the Judaic tradition in Arendt's work, such as her notion of "love of the world" or the criticism of the fixation on the ego in the modern culture (Ibid., 188–9). This attempt is not overly persuasive, because the arguments in question may be equally attributed to the Christian tradition and because Bernstein does not take into account Arendt's latent polemic against Judaism. Thus, as we saw, for Bauer and Feuerbach it is precisely Judaism, as opposed to Christianity, that is egoistic and egocentric. See also an interesting book by Martine Leibovici, *Hannah Arendt, une Juive* (Paris: Desclée de Brouwer, 1998). Leibovici pays little attention to the theological side of Arendt's argument in the Jewish question, but she notes that Arendt had consistently criticized the "acosmism" of the Jewish people (ibid., 279–340). Acosmism is also a theological motif, used by Hegel, for instance, in his critique of the Jewish thinker Spinoza. But acosmism often figures as an argument against the religion as such.
53 Hannah Arendt, *The Origins of Totalitarianism* (New York: Harcourt Brace, 1979 [1951]), 34; 47–8.
54 Hannah Arendt, *Eichmann in Jerusalem. A Report on the Banality of Evil* (New York and London: Penguin Books, 1994 [Viking Press, 1963]).
55 *Eichmann in Jerusalem*, 19.
56 Ibid., 263.
57 M. Robespierre, "Sur le procès du roi," in *Pour le bonheur et la liberté. Discours* (Paris: La fabrique, 2000), 195.
58 See on this Georgio Agamben, *Homo Sacer* (Stanford, CA: Stanford University Press, 1998).
59 *Eichmann in Jerusalem*, 396.
60 Ibid., 49.
61 Ibid., 137.

62 Loc. cit.
63 *Eichmann in Jerusalem*, 263.
64 *The Origins of Totalitarianism*, 290–302.
65 *Eichmann in Jerusalem*, 252.
66 To Hegel, not only a general law, but a brutal senseless fact, or an isolated individual, are "abstract." In the text "Who thinks abstractly" (in Walter Kaufmann, *Hegel: Texts and Commentary* (Garden City, NY: Anchor Books, 1966), 113–18, Hegel discusses the generalized judgment of a criminal as an example of an abstraction. "This is abstract thinking: to see nothing in the murderer except the abstract fact that he is a murderer, and to annul all other human essence in him with this simple quality" (ibid., 117).
67 *Eichmann in Jerusalem*, 279.
68 See Carl Schmitt, *Political Theology. Four Chapters on the Concept of Sovereignty* (Chicago, IL: The University of Chicago Press, 2005); Agamben, *Homo Sacer*.
69 *Eichmann in Jerusalem*, 296.
70 Hannah Arendt, "The Jew as Pariah: A Hidden Tradition," in *The Jew as a Pariah*, 72.
71 Hannah Arendt, *The Jew as a Pariah*, 250.
72 "Some questions of moral philosophy," in Hannah Arendt, *Responsibility and Judgment* (NY: Schocken Books, 2003), 49–146.
73 Ibid., 116.
74 Richard Bernstein, *Hannah Arendt and the Jewish Question*, 188–9.
75 Both Rosenzweig and Buber knew Feuerbach's philosophy. Rosenzweig acknowledges his role in "The New Thinking" (Syracuse, NY: Syracuse University Press, 1999), 87. Buber refers to the "extraordinary importance of Feuerbach," for instance, in "Das Problem des Menschen," in Martin Buber, *Werke*. Bd. III, München/Heidelberg, 1926, 339–42. On Feuerbach's Jewish reception (which started as early as the mid-nineteenth century), see Dominique Bourel, "Lüdwig Feuerbach die jüdische Lektüre," in *Feuerbach und der Judaismus*, Ursula Reitemeyer and Takayuki Shibata, Francesco Tomasoni (eds), Vol. 4 (Waxmann Verlag, 2009), 125–34. It is highly ironic, however, that Feuerbach, with his critique of Judaism, was a predecessor of the neo-Judaic twentieth century tradition.

6

Notes on the Prophetic Instability of Zionism

Marc H. Ellis

Prelude

When it comes to issues pertaining to Jews and Jewish identity, we enter a historical and iconic minefield. In the long arc of Jewish history, identity constructions—and deconstructions—of "Jewish" have been diverse and ongoing. Yet, after each construction/deconstruction we are left with something that lives beyond any particular historical moment.[1]

There is a fixed reality to "Jewish" that belies its many permutations. So it is with Zionism. Diverse understandings of "Zion" are ancient and contemporary. When we deconstruct Zionism and expose its many varieties, we are left with something else that lives beyond any particular historical moment.[2]

When articulated by Jews, that "something else" is contested. If we add to this historical sweep the iconic nature of how Jews, Jewish, and Zionism are seen in the non-Jewish world, the subject becomes even more complicated. As we know from history, separating reality and myth relating to Jews is difficult if not impossible. Although the deconstruction of communal identities across the board is always contested, Jewish identity has a particular and peculiar valence. Throughout history, Jewish identity has been up for grabs. The results have rarely been benign.

With the addition of the concern for and about Jews in the non-Jewish world, an additional issue is thrust upon us: Who has the right to deconstruct "Jewish"? After all, depending on one's viewpoint, both philo-Semitism and anti-Semitism may be seen as deconstructing certain definitions of "Jewish." Jews only partly control their own image and, of course, different parts of the Jewish community define "Jewish" differently. At certain times, it seems that Jews are only bit players in their own history. At other times, Jews are involved in an internal civil war over what it means to be Jewish.

Jean-François Lyotard, a French philosopher, offers a distinction that further complicates matters by differentiating between "Jew" and "jew." For Lyotard, Jew stands for real flesh-and-blood Jews; jew stands for the concept attached to Jews in history. Lyotard understands jews in a positive light, though obviously jews have been seen in a negative light as well. For Lyotard, jews are disturbers of the peace. They break through what is acceptable in the broader society. Moreover, jews are important because they refuse assimilation to whatever is the fashion of the moment. Often Jews act as they are viewed. For Lyotard, there is a connection between the real and the conceptual J/jew.[3]

Since society identifies jew as something beyond Jews, the connection is also tentative. There can be a separation between the two, and we know from history that jews can exist in the individual and societal imaginations without Jews being present. As well, the conceptual jew may be only marginally related to the Jews that actually live in a particular society. Hence, as often as not, Jews are defined by the conceptual jews of the mythic imagination.

If we apply Lyotard's analysis to the contemporary scene, we now have "Israel"—that is, the real Israel in its complex, difficult and interesting configurations—and "israel"—the conceptual Israel that is endlessly held up as the archetype of goodness by some and the epitome of evil by others. This is true of the Holocaust as well. In many ways, the real "Holocaust" of unimaginable suffering has been eclipsed by the conceptual "holocaust." Here, the Holocaust is either beyond analysis or is a made-up conspiracy of the J/jews.[4]

When attempting to discuss Zionism, we encounter a similar complexity. Because of the political, religious and geo-political intensity of Israel, it is almost impossible to separate "Zionism" and "zionism." We immediately encounter further difficulties. As with Jew/jew, Israel/israel, Holocaust/holocaust, Zionism and zionism have a variety of historical and contemporary angles. Both have real histories with consequences. Both have mythic histories of interpretation.

So, for example, historic Zionism has different religious and secular strands. Zionism is further differentiated by mainstream state and homeland Zionism. In turn, each has various and diverse strands. If we separate Zionism into historical eras (for example, pre- and post-state Zionism), and then further specify a timeline, say, Zionism before and after the 1967 Arab–Israeli war, further issues arise. Complicating Zionism's landscape even further is anti-Zionism, itself a reaction to various Zionism(s). All appear in different guises depending on the historical period we are dealing with.[5]

If history is a reconstruction from the present, then our present heavily influences our deconstruction as well. Before Zionism also became zionism in its mythic form, what was it really about? Since Zionism and zionism are now so deeply entwined in the public perception, is it possible to disentangle the two, if only for historical accuracy? Or, by disentangling the two, do we inadvertently serve political interests that seek to defend against or extend the reach of Israel's power over and against the Palestinian people?[6]

Deconstructing Zionism is a philosophical act but it is also always a political act—with important consequences. The consequences of state Zionism are visible on the ground in Israel/Palestine in the real lives of Jews and Palestinians. The conflict surrounding Zionism in academic and political discourse among Jews and Palestinians outside of the Middle East is also impactful in real terms. Therefore, deconstructing such a history, especially when it influences a narrative of historically displaced peoples with their further displacement up in the air, should give us pause.

Now add to the mix the highly charged city of Jerusalem, the broken-middle of Israel/Palestine. Jerusalem itself has multiple lives in the world's monotheistic religions and beyond. As we know from history and the present, "Jerusalem" is also "jerusalem." The historical baggage and surplus meaning of jerusalem often obscures the ordinary life of those who actually live in the city. In our postmodern world, it is surprising that Jerusalem/jerusalem has once again surfaced as a global flashpoint for violence and hope. It is also testimony that the real and mythic J/jews continue to resonate on the world scene.

Despite such variety and ambiguity, a deconstruction of Zionism must take place. Justice demands it. A future for Jews and Palestinians in the land is at stake. Yet, with all our caveats, a further question demands our attention. Are we primarily interested in the historical or present-day consequences of Zionism?

If only for a philosophical discussion, can history and the present be separated? Or are both necessarily entwined? Although this may be seen as splitting hairs, the view of the Israeli–Palestinian conflict and a just resolution of it depends heavily on where one starts in relation to Zionism. Since deconstructing Zionism is not simply an academic or philosophical enterprise, we should assume the way Zionism is deconstructed will be influenced, if not determined, by the end result of the Israeli–Palestinian conflict the deconstructor envisions.

From the political angle, it is important to know if one's deconstruction seeks a two-state or one-state solution to the Israeli–Palestinian conflict. From the Jewish perspective, it is important to understand whether one's deconstruction seeks solidarity with Jews or a demeaning of Jews. In the framework of deconstructing Zionism, solidarity here means a critical embrace of Jewish history and contemporary Jews with the hope that the end of the violence of the Jewish state will bring Jews back to an ethical path.

The point of view of the observer is crucial. For Jews, the deconstruction of Zionism is viewed in light of Jewish history, Jewish affiliation and a Jewish future. For Palestinians, the deconstruction of Zionism is viewed in light of Palestinian history, Palestinian affiliation and a Palestinian future. When such a deconstruction is being carried out by a third-party observer, the issue revolves around where the observer is from, what affiliation they have and what future for Jews and Palestinians they seek.

If we reverse the proposition and try to construct Zionism, if only to have a definition to deconstruct, we encounter obstacles as well. If we limit a definition of Zionism to the present, what does it include? To be more than theoretical, a definition of Zionism today has to include Israel as a Jewish state, Jewish support in the Diaspora for a Jewish state, and the priority of a Jewish state over Palestinian history inherent in the State of Israel today. A robust contemporary Zionism includes a united Jerusalem with control over the Jewish and Palestinian sectors of the city, as well as the major Jewish settlements in the West Bank. While a contemporary definition of Zionism does not preclude the possibility of a Palestinian state, it necessarily limits its borders and its potential independence.

What is the rationale for the State of Israel in a contemporary definition of Zionism? This includes secular and religious themes as well as historical and geo-political understandings. Although originally, at least in its contemporary form, Zionism was mostly secular, religious Jews have a much more substantial stake in defining contemporary Zionism. An unannounced religious framework has become part of the Israeli secular consciousness over past years. This is true of Holocaust consciousness as well. Originally rejected by Zionism as a demonstration of the weakness of the Diaspora, the Holocaust has become more intrinsic to Israeli culture.

Here is an attempt at a positive—Jewish—construction of Zionism today:

> Zionism is the return of the Jewish people to the land of Israel, now embodied in a state, which seeks to maintain and extend its territory so that Jews living in Israel and Jews around the world can live in their natural home that was promised by God and needed in history after the Holocaust.

Here is an attempt at a negative—Palestinian—construction of Zionism today:

> Zionism is the colonial appropriation of the land of Palestine, now embodied in a Jewish state, which seeks to displace Palestinian life and culture in our homeland.

Although there are ways to extend and refine these definitions of Zionism, these should suffice for the realization of what is at stake in deconstructing Zionism.[7]

Zionism, Holocaust theology, and Jewish particularity

Is deconstructing Zionism deconstructing Jewish particularity? The reverse—as a way reconstructing Jewish particularity—is also in play. We have noted that Jewish cannot be viewed through a single frame. The deconstruction/reconstruction of Zionism and Jewish are closely intertwined in the modern era.

The connection of Jewish and Zionism is a major theme in Zionist literature in the nineteenth, twentieth, and now twenty-first centuries. Throughout Zionist literature, Zionism and the survival of Jewishness, Judaism and Jews are conjoined. Even homeland Zionists who dissented against state Zionism were deeply involved in the Jewish question of survival and flourishing in a changing European landscape.[8]

If Zionist concern for the future of Jewish life was noticeable before the Holocaust, it increased after the Holocaust. We can look at Zionism before and after the Holocaust *as* a desire to continue Jewish history *even as* political, military, and modern concerns impinged on the possibility and credibility of Jewish affiliation in modern Europe and beyond. Early Zionists and the post-Holocaust Jewish world share the worry of what is to become of Jews and Jewish.

In the twentieth century, external political/cultural pressures came together with internal Jewish searching. Is there a future for Jewish life? If there is a Jewish future, where will that take place geographically? After the Holocaust and with the founding of the State of Israel, the demographic map of world Jewry changed dramatically. Thus, the geography to nurture and sustain a Jewish future narrowed considerably.

That the subject of geography plays such a role in the Jewish imagination seems overdetermined. Communal life evolves in the place where the community lives. The future of a community is where it lives. For Jews, of course, geography has rarely been secure as the place of the future's evolution. In the twentieth century, that insecurity was magnified. The early Zionists' questions about the physical future of Jews in Europe were complemented by their fear that diminishing cultural and linguistic resources for Jewish identity would be the order of the day. Both fears materialized in the Holocaust. In fact, the reality of Jewish displacement and death went far beyond the early Zionist imagination.

The fear that Jews and Jewishness might disappear is an ongoing theme in Jewish history. Therefore, it has been a major premise in constructing and deconstructing Jewish identity over time. The Hebrew Bible is already deeply involved in this construction/deconstruction. At stake in the biblical narrative is whether the people of Israel will coalesce and survive or whether internal and external forces will bring about Israel's demise before she has been launched into the world.

The biblical framework revolves around the construction of "Israel" and what Israel means to itself and to the world. Bound up with that meaning is a God who, though God of the universe, is first and foremost Israel's God. In the biblical narrative, God becomes known to the world through the people of Israel. God demonstrates to the world that He exists and is a force to be reckoned with through the liberation and flourishing of Israel itself. From the beginning, God and the people of Israel are bound together.[9]

The covenantal relationship between God and Israel is highly charged. Having a joint destiny, their future requires companionship and solidarity. The intensity of the covenant challenges both parties. While their potential is great, a shadowy side exists as well. The biblical narrative is promising and ominous. At any moment, Israel may be destroyed. Then where will God be?

The promising side of their relationship is God's pledge of the land to Israel. The ominous side is God sending the prophets to judge Israel's behavior in the land. The key here is the essential instability that characterizes God's and Israel's relationship. The instability of Israel's self-narrated origins forms the center of the Jewish canon carried through the generations. It remains the optic through which Jews form their post-Holocaust/Israel identity today.

The instability of the covenantal relationship between God and Israel has to do with the essential demands of both. God wants a people to call His own and who will obey His commandments. God also wants Israel to internalize these commandments. Through these commandments, Israel's—and God's—destiny unfolds.

As might be expected, God's commandments and Israel's internalization of them are subject to interpretation and contestation. While God thinks His commands are self-evident, Israel is far from sure. Israel is reluctant and at times unwilling to tow a line that seems unnatural and life-threatening. At various points in the biblical narrative, the bond between God and Israel unravels. On more than one occasion, God and Israel announce they are breaking the covenant altogether. God and Israel will go it alone.

In the biblical narrative, the final break does not occur. Against their better judgment, it seems that God and Israel cannot navigate life each without the other.

An unstated dependency, even a co-dependency, forces both parties to stay together. Although the relationship of God and Israel is unstable, there is something even more important to note. To be sure, God and Israel are unstable together. They are also unstable alone.

Perhaps it is this individual instability that cements their bond. If their individual instability complements their unstable relationship, their instability also provides an asymmetric stability. In the Hebrew Bible, instability is the foundation of a peculiar stability. This stability within instability is another key to Jewish identity down through the ages.

What is the foundation of this instability? Since this instability persists through the ages this is an important question. It is also the factor that makes Zionism in its various forms unstable as well. The foundation of the instability is the prophetic, originating and being honed in the narrative formation of Israel. It is the prophetic impulse that sends Israel on its way out of oppressive Egypt and ultimately out of the Promised Land. Paradoxically, it is the same impulse that also forms the other side of the Jewish dynamic through the ages, the desire to escape prophetic criticism through empire.

Israel's instability because of the prophetic element is legendary. So is Israel's desire to become stable through empire. It is for this reason that throughout history Jews have existed on both sides of the 'empire divide.' This is likewise the reason that Jewish identity rarely remains satisfied with its current incarnation. We see this historically in a variety of eras, and today in the promulgation of and dissent against Zionism. After the Holocaust, Zionism reintroduced this central empire divide dynamic in Jewish life with a fervor that only a history that narrates a unique destiny can produce.[10]

Looked at from this angle, the history of Holocaust consciousness, so triumphant in contemporary Jewish life, is important to the discussion of Zionism. Holocaust consciousness, evolving into a theology, is constructed like other interpretative identity frameworks. At first, the elements of Holocaust theology seem obvious. The first order of Holocaust theology is to speak about the unspeakable horror which Europe's Jews underwent during the Nazi era. The second order of Holocaust theology is to respond to the destruction of Europe's Jews. Both are explicit in the Holocaust narrative.[11]

The first response is to address the Holocaust in speech, literature, and memorialization. The second response is for Jews to seek empowerment, most explicitly in the State of Israel. Other parts of Holocaust theology involve the absence of God and the breaking of Israel's and God's covenantal bond.

Since God was absent in the Holocaust, the Jewish people take up the task of empowerment. The question of where God was in Auschwitz is complemented by the command that issues from Auschwitz: Never again will Jews be weak or depend on others for their safety. The State of Israel is the response to both questions. With God absent, Jews are responsible for their own fate. That fate is concretely embodied in the State of Israel.

Among the most popular and established of Holocaust theologians, the unstated element is the Jewish need for empire following the Holocaust. Assumed as a corollary is the need for the Jewish community to discipline the Jewish prophetic impulse. The Holocaust saw over one-third of the Jewish people systematically murdered. In the post-Holocaust era, Holocaust theologians cite the need for Jewish empowerment. It is only through empowerment that Jews can replenish and protect what is left of the community and the tradition.

Paradoxically, what threatens Jewish empowerment is the prophetic impulse which Jews have so often applied to others who commit injustice. Holocaust theologians know intuitively that, notwithstanding the post-Holocaust context, the Jewish prophetic impulse lurks in the corner. If applied within an empowered Jewish community as it was in its biblical origins, the prophetic impulse endangers the State of Israel.

A subtext of Holocaust theology is the fear that if the State of Israel's power wanes, Jews will be thrown back into another Holocaust situation. Much of Holocaust theology carries the implicit and, at times, explicit warning that Jewish dissent—the occasion for Jewish instability in an era of empowerment—will bring about Israel's destruction. That destruction would occasion a second and final Holocaust.[12]

Holocaust theology rarely mentions Zionism by name. Holocaust theologians do invoke the State of Israel by name. However, invoking Israel is more in the defense of its need to exist than any practical discussion of the state and its history. In Holocaust theology, the need for Israel is understood. Why get into the messy details of what fulfilling that need entails?

Differently stated, in Holocaust theology, Israel is a self-understood need that transcends the normal give-and-take of practical and contested politics. Holocaust theologians envision the State of Israel as transcending politics. They structure their Holocaust narrative in such a fashion that a practical and ethical critique of the State of Israel's right to exist or a critique of Israel's policies toward Palestinians is off-limits. According to Holocaust theologians, only anti-Semites—or self-hating Jews—go down that route.

Are Zionism and Israel declared off-limits because Holocaust theologians fear that a deconstruction of Israel would lead to a deconstruction of the Holocaust, at least as it is narrated in relation to Jewish empowerment? As it is instrumentalized by Holocaust theology, the Holocaust is the critical engine of Israel's legitimacy. Where a critical understanding of Israel, and by extension Zionism, is off-limits, the Holocaust as it is narratively constructed is off-limits as well.

Like the bonding of the people of Israel and God, Holocaust and Israel constitute an unstable coupling. Since they need each other, a threatened divorce is to be avoided at all costs.

A prophetic deconstruction of Zionism?

The phrase "after Auschwitz" has almost become a cliché. Indeed, Jews do come after the Holocaust. They also come after Israel.

Since the State of Israel continues on into the present, what does 'after Israel' mean? 'After Israel' means after what Jews have done and are doing to the Palestinian people.

It means that though Jews were innocent in the suffering of the Holocaust, Jews are not innocent in their empowerment. It means that the details of Jewish empowerment in Israel include the ethnic cleansing of Palestinians in 1948 and beyond. It means that the continuing expansion of the State of Israel, occupation of East Jerusalem and the West Bank, and Jewish settlements in Palestinian territories position the ideology of Zionism for a historical test. This means as well that the Jewish identity formation which binds the Holocaust and Israel is in play. It is the Jewish prophetic impulse that forces this analysis.[13]

As it has many times in Jewish history, the prophetic impulse challenges contemporary Jewish identity at its most basic level. In turn, that root exposure further emboldens the prophetic drive and exposes the contemporary empire dynamic. The prophetic and empire are once again at odds—such is the battle Holocaust theology seeks to bury in its mourning for the victims of the Holocaust. Such exposure does not necessarily invalidate Zionism itself; nor can it reverse Zionism's role in the establishment of the State of Israel. But the prophetic impulse does raise questions about Jewish empire and its extension as normative.

The prophetic impulse demands an accounting of Zionism and the State of Israel. In its narrative and implementation, the prophetic view of Jewish destiny forces a detailed historical accounting of what Jews have done to Palestine and Palestinians, and thus to Jewish ethics and Jewish destiny. In the name of Jewish stability after the Holocaust, have Holocaust theology, Zionism, and the State of Israel confined Jewish destiny to empire and the oppression of another people?

Here, some separate the Holocaust, Zionism, and the State of Israel. The Holocaust is over; Zionism established the State of Israel. When the State of Israel was established, Zionism, as an ideological force, became a platitude used—and at times disciplined—by the state apparatus. If this is the case, then the subject of Israel's continual expansion as a state must be raised, as well as the reality and motivations of the settlers in Jerusalem and the West Bank.

A series of important questions ensue. Is the continuing expansion of the State of Israel directly related to the religious and secular Zionism flourishing within Israel, or does it have more to do with normal prerogatives of a state that has the power to expand at the expense of weaker non-state actors? If indeed the problematic comes from a combination of Zionism, a particular Jewish phenomenon, and Israel as a state like any other state, what approach is to be taken with regard to Israel as it is presently constituted? Should Zionism be handled within the framework of Jewish particularity or in the framework of international law? Is it best to deconstruct Zionism Jewishly or internationally?[14]

The conflation of Zionism and Israel make the philosophical and theoretical distinctions between the two less and less meaningful. The matter at hand is preventing the State of Israel from a further dispossession of Palestinian land and hope for their future. Initially this falls into the framework of the two-state solution, namely Israel and Palestine as two distinct states existing side by side. But since most analysts see such a solution as foreclosed by the expansion of Israel, Jewish dissidents are more and more drawn to the one-state vision of Israel/Palestine as a democratic secular state with equal citizenship without regard to ethnic or religious distinction. Since the one-state option signals the end of Israel as a Jewish state, this returns us to the issue of whether the one-state solution should be argued for Jewishly or internationally.[15]

Does arguing for the one-state solution demand a further deconstruction of Zionism as the ideological origin of the Jewish State of Israel? In this case, Zionism and the State of Israel, though bound in birth, are now separated, thus undermining not only Zionism but the Jewish State of Israel as well. If this were to happen, the foundations of contemporary Jewish identity might quickly collapse.[16]

Although Holocaust theology does not explicitly address the issue, the Holocaust in its narrative form assumes Zionism and Israel as central. Without Zionism and Israel, the Holocaust as an ideological and identity-building force would recede. Jews would thus come 'after' the Holocaust and Israel in a way not yet thought of.

Would Jewish identity then return to 'before' the Holocaust and Israel? Once the Holocaust, Zionism, and Israel recede, there is no possibility of going back. Although some have speculated about identity in a post-Zionist age, almost all of the speculation has involved a Jewish State of Israel with Zionism and the Holocaust remaining in a place of historical honor. What has not been thought through in relation to Jewish identity is what comes after the discredited misuse of the Holocaust, Zionism and Israel.[17]

There is an important difference between deconstructing Zionism within the framework of a Jewish state and deconstructing Zionism without a Jewish state. The contrast is the type of Jewish particularity that flows from either choice. But since the great majority of Jews alive today were born after the Holocaust and after Israel was formed, contemporary Jews have no experiential memory of living without a Jewish state. Appealing to the Jewish tradition before the Holocaust and before Israel may be instructive in some areas. However, such appeals have depended implicitly on Jewish empowerment, even as they criticize it.[18]

What does the Jewish prophetic impulse say to these conundrums? The answer is mixed. On the one hand, the biblical prophets appear within eras of Jewish empowerment. Their critique of Israel is harsh, much harsher than that of today's Jewish dissidents. Further, the biblical prophetic critique was always articulated within the framework of an assumed responsibility for the people of Israel to create a new kind of internally generated Jewish society, one based on justice and peace.

Thus the prophetic call for Israel's disbursement among the peoples, that is the end of Jewish priority and specific Jewish empowerment, was punishment for waywardness. Aside from some universal sentiments, the prophets were Israel-centric. The people of Israel had a destiny that only Israel could accomplish. In today's parlance, the prophets were not advocates of one-state solutions.

For most of Jewish history, Jews have existed without a state of their own. Zionism was confined to visions of the land Jews did not live in and, even when they had the chance, few chose to live there. This occasioned the expansion of the Jewish prophetic impulse outward toward societies and cultures Jews lived within as minorities. In the present situation, we have the Jewish prophetic drive once again reaching out, especially to others, Palestinians. But this outreach occurs in an unprecedented way—within Jewish empowerment and a Jewish state. The contemporary prophetic critique of Zionism and Israel is a *novum* in Jewish history.

When the biblical prophets reached the end of their patience, which was also the end of God's patience, the people of Israel were condemned to exile from the land. As narrated in the Bible, the exile was neither orderly nor benign. Exile was horrific. The people of Israel suffered imprisonment, rape, and massacre. Most Jewish critiques of Zionism and the State of Israel, including the end of Israel as a Jewish state, are quite obvious. They presuppose an orderly transition, with Jewish empowerment remaining in place during the transition. They likewise assume the continuing acceptance of millions of Jews in the Middle East following the demise of the Jewish character of the State of Israel.

Few anti-Zionist Jewish thinkers have dealt practically with this transition, and the truth of the matter is that no one from any perspective or community really knows how or whether such a transition would work. At least in the present, the very announcement of a process of ending a Jewish State of Israel would probably precipitate a mass exodus of Jewish Israelis to Europe and the United States—if, that is, the borders of the various states would accept millions of Jewish Israelis.

Without ascribing any intent to the warring parties, the resolution of the Israeli/Palestinian situation through the voluntary dissolution of the Jewish state is barely thinkable in contemporary Jewish politics and thought. It is fraught in the actual give-and-take of the geo-political world. The heightened symbolic significance of Jews, Israel, Jerusalem, and the religions of Christianity and Islam make practical steps toward the deconstruction of Zionism and the Jewish character of the State of Israel problematic, if not foreboding.

But, then, since the injustice done to Palestinians continues into an indefinite future, the question remains: What is there to do except to deconstruct an ideology, now embodied in a state, that will not stop and, at least in the foreseeable future, cannot be stopped?

In this indefinite future, a further fracturing of the Jewish community is in progress. Confronting the combined power of the Holocaust, Zionism, and Israel, the numbers of Jews of Conscience continue to increase.

Like Progressive Jews, Jews of Conscience oppose Israeli policies toward Palestinians. Their opposition, however, moves into another realm. While Progressive Jews oppose the Jewish establishment's view of an innocent Israel, they support the establishment and continuance of Israel as a Jewish state. On Zionism and Israel's birth as a state in the ethnic cleansing of over 700,000 Palestinians, Progressive Jews are silent. For Progressive Jews the fault line is the Israeli occupation and settlements following the 1967 Arab–Israeli war. If Israel withdraws from the West Bank and a Palestinian state is created, Zionism and Israel can reclaim their historic mission of creating a place for Jews to live in their own homeland.[19]

Jews of Conscience have come to the end of Israel's innocence; that is, Jews of Conscience believe that Israel's state project is fundamentally flawed. Zionism in its practical application in Palestine was and is a colonial and racist project. Taking this position, Jews of Conscience break with Progressive Jews and the Jewish establishment. They see the conflict between Progressive Jews and the Jewish establishment as false and misleading. In general, Jews of Conscience interpret Progressive Jews as the left wing of the Jewish establishment.

To the untrained eye there is a civil war between Progressive Jews and the Jewish establishment over Israel's policies toward the Palestinians. Since Jews of Conscience understand the connection between Progressive Jews and the Jewish establishment, the civil war is much less than it seems. In fact, Jews of Conscience see this as a false civil war. The effect: Israel continues on its way.

For Jews of Conscience, the break with Progressive Jews and the Jewish establishment has to be clarified politically. The theoretical underpinnings of this break are less explored. It may be that the historical situation of Israel's existence is too complex and immediate for Jews of Conscience to probe. It may be that the sheer existence of Israel makes the theoretical work less compelling. At the end of the day, the political opposition to Israel's policies and even to Israel's existence as a Jewish state may be too involved to dabble in the philosophical identity underpinnings of contemporary Jewish life. Then, there is the Holocaust and the perception at least in Europe and the United States that opposition to Israel and Zionism is anti-Semitic. Why raise philosophical points when politically so much is on the line?

The constraints on the critique of Zionism and Israel are real. Such constraints may be used as a cover for injustice but they also represent an historical impasse. After the Holocaust and after Israel, how free are Jews and non-Jews to think about the end of the Jewish state and the very Zionism that animated its birth and expansion?

Obviously the question of the day is about the political efficacy of such thought. What if Zionism is thoroughly deconstructed and Israel continues to oppress Palestinians? It could be that the deconstruction of Zionism will have long-range political effects. By hollowing out the Jewish claim to Palestinian land, eventually Jews in Israel and around the world will acknowledge the wrong done to Palestinian people. Then, Jews will embark with Palestinians in creating an Israel/Palestine where both live together in equality, justice, and peace.

Notes

1 For one take on the different identity constructions in Jewish history see Ephraim Shmueli, *Seven Jewish Cultures: A Reinterpretation of Jewish History and Thought* (Cambridge: Cambridge University Press, 1990). See also David Biale, ed., *Cultures of the Jews: A New History* (New York: Schocken Books, 1990).
2 For the most recent attempt to discuss Jewish and Zionism see Judith Butler, *Parting Ways: Jewishness and the Critique of Zionism* (New York: Columbia University Press, 2012).
3 Jean-François Lyotard, *Heidegger and the "the jews"* (Minneapolis: University of Minnesota Press, 1990), pp. 1–48. Lyotard's use of terms is multi-layered. Thus I am adopting a certain direction for his use of terminology in this chapter.

4   For a fascinating attempt at reclaiming what actually occurred during the Holocaust see Timothy Snyder, *Bloodlands: Europe Between Hitler and Stalin* (New York: Basic Books, 2010).
5   For a diverse collection of Zionist writings see Arthur Hertzberg, *The Zionist Idea: A Historical Analysis and Reader* (Philadelphia, PA: Jewish Publication Society of America, 1997).
6   For a recent example of deconstructing Zionism with a political purpose in mind, see Sholmo Sand, *The Invention of the Land of Israel: From Holy Land to Homeland* (New York: Verso, 2012).
7   Palestinian perspectives on Zionism are crucial for Jews to face the question of Zionism within Jewish history. For some Palestinian perspectives see Nur Masalha, *The Palestine Nakba: Decolonising History, Narrating the Subaltern, Reclaiming Memory* (London: Zed Books, 2012).
8   On homeland Zionism see the writings of Paul Mendes-Flohr, ed., *A Land of Two Peoples: Martin Buber on Jews and Arabs* (Chicago, IL: University of Chicago Press, 2005). See also Jerome Kohn and Ron H. Feldman (eds), *The Jewish Writings: Hannah Arendt* (New York: Schocken Books, 2007).
9   I explore some of these issues in my latest book, *Future Prophetic: Re-presenting Israel's Ancient Wisdom*, forthcoming from Fortress Press, 2014.
10 For my understanding of Jews being on both sides of the empire divide see *Future Prophetic*.
11 On Holocaust theology in Jewish life see my *Toward a Jewish Theology of Liberation: The Challenge of the 21st Century* (Waco: Baylor University Press, 2004), pp. 15–50.
12 This is most explicitly stated in Irvin Greenberg's essay, "The Ethics of Jewish Power," in Rosemary Radford Ruether and Marc H. Ellis (eds), *Beyond Occupation: American Jewish, Christian and Palestinian Voices for Peace* (Boston, MA: Beacon press, 1990), pp. 22–74.
13 I develop this theme—after Israel—in my *Judaism Does Not Equal Israel* (New York: New Press, 2009).
14 The transition from Zionist ideology to statehood is discussed in Meron Benvenisti, *Sacred Landscape: The Buried History of the Holy Land since 1948* (Berkeley: University of California Press, 2002), pp. 144–92.
15 For a take on the one-state/two-state debate see Anthony Lowenstein and Ahmed Moor, *After Zionism: One State for Israel and Palestine* (London: Al Saqi Books, 2012).
16 Although seemingly more a concern for Jews than for Palestinians, the possibility of such an identity collapse might precipitate an escalation in Israeli aggression. Fending off identity collapse is one of the specialties of state actors.
17 Some writers are attempting to deal with the political effects of the failure of Zionism. However, most are yet to think through to question of Jewish identity *after*. For an interesting volume on post-Zionism see Epharim Nimni, *The Challenge of Post-Zionism: Alternatives to Fundamentalist Politics in Israel* (London: Zed Books, 2003).
18 An example of this unannounced dependence runs through Judith Butler's *Parting Ways*. Although Butler's critique of Israel is extensive and brutal in its honesty, I doubt that Jews can part ways with Israel, Zionism, or the Holocaust. In any case, at least in our lifetimes, none of these will disappear. Without Butler suggesting this directly, parting ways can become an easy way out. Instead, the task seems to be

working through, contesting, and molding all three to justice. I also part company with Butler's sense that Jewish exile—as a people and as dissidents—should and can be overcome. Wrestling with Butler's analysis is yet another wrestling with the Jewish prophetic.

19 The new Israeli historians document the ethnic cleansing of Palestinians in the birth of Israel. For a summary of their findings see Ilan Pappe, *The Ethnic Cleansing of Palestine* (London: Oneworld, 2006).

7

The Spirit of Zionism

Derrida, Ruah, *and the Purloined Birthright*

Christopher Wise

Introduction

The Derridean concept of spirit/specter as an occult pharmakon is indebted not only to the Hebraic notion of *ruah* [רוח] but also to the Egyptian *heka*, Soninke *ñaxamala*, Mandé *nyama*, and many other comparable Egypto-African renditions of the word, some that are historically prior to the Hebraic *ruah*. I will argue here that Derrida elides these related African concepts in order to accord Judaism a place of special prominence within the history of European philosophy.

Because his readers in the West tend to be unaware of the ancient history and cultures of Africa and the Middle East, they seldom challenge his assumptions regarding the exceptional status of Judaism, especially as a world religion prefiguring all other related cultures and religious groups from these regions. For instance, Derrida promotes the mythical notion that Judaism is "the single source" of all the Abrahamic faiths, reinforcing orthodox Judeo-Christian doctrines about the unique role of Judaism in the history of monotheism.[1] This notion, coterminous with the *idée reçue* that the biblical patriarch Abraham inaugurated the rite of circumcision as a sign of the first covenant, is not only historically inaccurate, it also serves to bury the memory of Egypto-African contributions to what Derrida calls the "abrahamo-philosophical."[2] While Derrida rarely professed his religious beliefs in any unambiguous or dogmatic sense, he also declined to historicize privileged theological concepts like *ruah*, the Abrahamic, the messianic Jew, and messianicity, promoting instead these loaded religious signifiers as if they were appropriate for all peoples everywhere.

The exalted status accorded to the concept of the messianic in Derrida's later writings, both in its overtly theological sense as historical "messianism" and in its allegedly more "neutral" or universal sense as "messianicity," reinforces troubling mythologies of blood nobility that are influential not only among messianic Zionists in Israel and the Occupied Territories but also among militant and fundamentalist Christians in the US. Archaic myths about specially chosen peoples, elected on the basis of the exceptional blood that flows in their veins, are not merely peripheral concerns of the major Abrahamic traditions but are inextricable from their histories and most basic doctrines, including Christianity and Islam. Given the fact that all three of the Abrahamic traditions evolved within a particular geographical setting, one that was impacted by more than 4,000 years of Afro-Egyptian civilization, there is little reason to be surprised that Abrahamic traditions did not escape the influence of Ancient Egypt. If it is important to honor a cultural heritage for the vital role it has played throughout human history, it does not follow that it is advisable to advocate the use of theological concepts drawn from that heritage for international political debate.

In historicizing concepts like *ruah* and messianicity, particularly in relation to their African and Egyptian counterparts, some of which precede Judaism, Christianity, and Islam, I will limit myself here to two observations. First, Derrida's attempt to extend to Judaism a privileged status within the history of European philosophy should be recognized for what it was—a form of special pleading on behalf of a particular ethnic group at the expense of other non-European peoples, especially African and Middle Eastern ones. Second, Derrida militates in favor of a theocratic rather than secular solution to the Palestinian–Israeli conflict, one that is articulated in favor of a particular historical tradition, sometimes posited as an ethnic identity and sometimes as a religion.[3] In fact, the very concept of the "secular" is for Derrida always already a religious one.[4] Despite my reservations about Derrida's political views, my criticisms here and elsewhere are offered not to discourage a careful critical study of Derrida's writings, but in order to affirm their historical importance and even extend their reach, thereby making deconstruction more accessible, especially to scholars in African and Middle Eastern studies.[5]

The element of the *Pharmakon*

Not long after 9/11, I taught in the American Studies and Islamic Studies Graduate Programs at the University of Jordan in Amman. One weekend, I drove out to the southern end of the Dead Sea to visit Lot's Cave, the legendary grotto where Abraham's nephew holed up with his daughters following the destruction of Sodom. The students in the programs were predominately Muslim, and when I asked them if they had ever visited the site, my question was greeted with polite if not embarrassed silence. My Muslim students rejected the story of Lot's Cave and therefore had no interest in visiting the grotto, whereas my Christian students preferred that I had not mentioned it at all. In the tale as recounted in Genesis, Lot's daughters lost their husbands in the fire and, since they longed to have children, they plied their father with wine in order to fornicate with him. My Muslim students remarked that the "Prophet Lut," as he is known in Islam, was a Prophet of God. As such, it was not possible that he could be attributed with such shameful behavior. In fact, this was one of those false stories in the Bible that the "Israelis" had inserted against the will of God. I asked my students why the "Israelis" would have done this, and the answer I received fascinated me.

In the Book of Genesis, both of Lot's daughters conceive children after fornicating with their father. The sons of Lot's daughters are Ben-Ami, who becomes the father of the Ammonites, and Moab, who becomes the father of the Moabites. Both of these tribes, along with the Philistines and others, are competitors with the Israelites for the land that God promises to Abraham. The "Israelis" inserted this false and ignoble genealogy, I was told, in order to discredit the claims of their competitors to the land of Palestine.

The exchange was very awkward for my Christian students. In fact, the Old Testament is rarely discussed in most Jordanian churches or in public schools where religious education is compulsory for Muslim and Christian children alike. At the time, I was also at work on translation projects in West African literature, after having lived in Burkina Faso, where I taught at the Université de Ouagadougou. In West African literature, I had already encountered many tales of unusual and ignoble genealogies, although in this context they were usually promoted in order to suggest the pure blood lines of Arab descendants of the Prophet Muhammad, as opposed to the "merely" black and pre-Islamic inhabitants of the Sahel. This is precisely the theme of Yambo Ouologuem's classic novel, *The Duty of Violence* (1968). It is also echoed in the oral epics of Mandé and Songhay griots, as well as the medieval manuscripts of Timbuktu, such as Al Hajj Mahmud Kati's *Tarikh al fattash*. In the latter, for instance, Kati tells the story of a giant named "Waj" (or "Og") who is a friend of the Prophet Noah, and who survives the flood by standing on the highest peak of a mountain, where the water rises to the level of his chin. Waj survives by eating fish, and when the waters at last recede he falls into a deep sleep. In his sleep, Waj lets loose a tremendous nocturnal emission which forms a small pool. In the meantime, Noah's ark has landed and the servant girls on the ark are sent to gather firewood. Thinking the pool of Waj's sperm is a nice spot for an afternoon swim, the girls dive into the pool and all of them later end up pregnant. Their offspring, we are told, is a local tribe known as the Sorkho. The context of the story is that the Askiya Muhammad, who is the "King" of the Songhay, is attempting to determine which indigenous tribes may be licitly enslaved and their lands confiscated, especially on behalf of the Sharifs; that is, the noble blood heirs of the Prophet Muhammad, who hail from the cities of Mecca and Medina.[6] What is always at stake in these stories of tribal origin is the question of blood, its pure or impure transmission.

In Cheick Oumar Sissoko's cinematic tribute to the Book of Genesis, entitled *La genèse* (1999), the popular Mandé singer Salif Keita was cast in the role of Esau, the brother of Jacob who sells his birthright for a bowl of soup. Sissoko's casting of Keita was an apt choice, given the well-known biography of Mali's most popular singer, whose decision to become a musician in the 1960s led to his being disowned by his family. As a member of the Mandé nobility and descendant of Sundiata Keita, the founder of the Mandé Dynasty of the thirteenth and fourteenth centuries, Salif Keita deeply embarrassed his family and debased himself by violating the cultural taboo of turning himself into a "griot," or a Mandé praise singer, who belongs to a lower caste known as the *nyamakala*. Among the Mandé, the Keita family does not sing but is normally the venerated object of the praise songs of the griot. In Sissoko's film, as well as in the biblical narrative, Esau loses his birthright because he eats from a bowl of soup that the author of the Book of Genesis describes as "red red" in color (Gen. 25.30). This abhorrent act defiles Esau, henceforth according him a lower status than his younger brother Jacob. Although quite ancient, the biblical tale of Jacob and Esau is historically preceded by the far more ancient Egyptian tale of rivalry between the gods Seth and Horus, a conflict referred to by contemporary Egyptologists as the "Hamlet constellation" or the Egyptian "monomyth."[7] In the Egyptian variant of this tale, the younger Horus similarly overcomes his adversary Seth by feeding him a polluted meal. With the help of his mother Isis, Horus ejaculates into a piece of lettuce, which is then fed to his uncle as a salad garnish. When his uncle Seth realizes that he has unwittingly eaten the bodily fluids of Horus, he is compelled to acknowledge the superior status of his nephew Horus—the rightful, albeit younger, heir of Osiris, relinquishing his claim to be ruler of Egypt.

For more than 4,000 years, the story of Seth and Horus's battle for prestige was re-enacted along the various temples of the Nile as the single, most enduring rite of the ancient Egyptians. The public enactment of this rite has its origins in customs that long precede the composition of its biblical counterpart. Throughout West Africa, the oldest narratives of the griot's origins echo the biblical and Egyptian versions of the "Hamlet constellation" in many significant ways. The most commonly told version of the origins of the griot entails a story of two brothers who journey across the Sahel zone when the younger of the two falls ill from starvation.[8] The older brother feels compassion for his dying sibling, informing him that he will go and look for something to feed him. After several hours, the older brother at last returns with a portion of meat which he feeds to his younger brother, hence restoring him to health. As the two brothers continue their journey, the younger brother is surprised to see that his older brother now limps and that blood drips from his brother's leg. When he realizes that his older brother has fed him his own flesh and blood to save his life, he is horrified by what he himself has done (in fact, he feels that he has defiled himself by eating his brother's flesh) and yet he also feels deep gratitude to the brother who saved his life. As a result, the younger brother is now compelled to sing the praises of his older brother, who in contrast retains his noble status.

The Mandé nobleman is literally the man of pure blood, in contrast to the griot who has been contaminated with the toxic fluids of the other. So poisonous is the body of the griot that he was seldom buried in the ground, where his body could poison and ruin the crops, but inside the trunk of a hollowed-out baobab tree.[9] Concerns about the preservation of one's noble status by refraining from the consumption of the bodily fluids of the other are widely reiterated in West African oral traditions, some directly influenced by Ancient Egyptian civilization. This dynamic is also evident in the Christian sacrament of communion, wherein one ritually consumes the flesh and bodily fluids of Jesus Christ, therein demonstrating one's subservience and fidelity to Christ as Lord. It was for this reason that many figures in the ancient African world, such as the Neo-Platonist author Apuleius, who wrote *The Golden Ass*, associated Christianity with the practice of sorcery and therefore rejected it.[10]

The Songhay, who speak a "Nilo-Sahelian" language, are very much aware of their historical relation to Ancient Egypt, which is repeatedly acknowledged in their oral and written traditions. In *The Epic of Askia Mohammed*, a version of the Songhay griot epic transcribed by Thomas Hale from a performance by Nouhou Malio, the culminating moment occurs when the son of the Askiya (or "king") reveals that he is not a man of pure blood—because his mother hailed from a low or "contaminated" caste—when he drinks from a bowl of fetid water. His father, the Askiya, who had formerly overlooked his son's impure blood line, now insults him by alluding to the polluted breast milk of his mother.[11] Although the parallels of this story and the Ancient Egyptian monomyth are too extensive to explore here, it is worth noting the obvious similarities between this prominent Songhay narrative and the similar tale told in Genesis 25.30.

My point in this context is that it is not only people of Jewish origin who have expressed concerns about preserving the integrity of their maternal blood heritage, but many other African and Middle Eastern peoples through the ages. In fact, this ancient theme is one of the most enduring aspects of the historical cultures of all the regions that came into contact with the Ancient Egyptians, including the founders of the Jewish religion and the Songhay people. Not unlike the custom of ritual circumcision, which led Freud to ponder the historical indebtedness of psychoanalysis to Judaism, the anxiety over preserving one's "pure" blood nobility, linked to the sentimental notion that some historical groups are uniquely chosen peoples whereas others are not, due to their "impure" blood lines, are hardly specific to Judaism as a religion but originate from within a cultural matrix that is far older than Judaism, a relatively recent religion in comparison to that of the Ancient Egyptians. The West African griot who sings praises to the higher caste nobility is also a ritual circumciser who performs at name-giving ceremonies, not unlike the Jewish *mohel*. Excavations of Roderick and Susan MacIntosh at Jeno-Jenne, which is West Africa's oldest known city, show that the griot tradition extends thousands of years into the past, and that Jenno-Jenne was in contact with Ancient Egyptian civilization.

While Sahelian beliefs about language are comparable to Judaic ones, they are far closer to articulations of Judaism that prevailed prior to the reformation that was inaugurated by Maimonides, as well as Philo's earlier attempts to wed Judeo-Christianity to Platonism, both of which Derrida criticizes.[12] As mentioned above, *ruah* is the Hebraic word for "spirit," which is prefigured by the Egyptian *heka*, and which is coterminous with the Soninke *ñaxamala*, Mandé *nyama*, Fulfulde *nyaama*, etc. None of these ancient terms for "spirit" (from Latin *spiritus*) suggest a concept that is underwritten by any transcendental ground, imagined to be a truly existing yet intangible essence, as described, for instance, in Plato's *Phaedrus*. The African and Middle Eastern concept of "spirit"—an oral utterance or, literally, a vapor or wet-wind—in each of these cases is not external to what Plato construed as the realm of becoming, but refers to an actual fluid of the body that is believed to be a lethal and occult substance. This is why all those who consume this highly dangerous fluid imagine that they are menaced with the possible loss of their noble status. When the bodily fluids of the other intermingle with one's own bodily fluids, the actual composition of the body is imagined to undergo a transformation. The substance that enters into one's body, a leaky receptacle of material fluids, can bring about great harm, but it can also be a great boon in certain circumstances. The liquid *pharmakon* in all of these systems of thought is neither good nor evil in itself, but is potentially both at the same time, depending on what is done with it. What should be clear is that *ruah*, the Hebraic word for "spirit," is not an untranslatable shibboleth, but is comparable to, if not interchangeable with, a vast array of Egyptian and African concepts of spirit, both ancient and contemporary.

It is not coincidental that Derrida's most complex and extended discussion of the autonomy of the specter is articulated in a careful close reading of Shakespeare's *Hamlet*, essentially a retelling of the Osiris monomyth, or the "Hamlet constellation." The cosmic duel of Horus and Seth was re-enacted along the banks of the Nile for thousands of years prior to the Abrahamic dispensation, but also prior to the rise of Platonic logocentrism in Greece (as well as North Africa). In fact, this rite was staged far longer than its Christian counterpart, the sacrament of communion. Among the Ancient Egyptians, the spoken word was also an occult substance, imbued with magical properties and devoid of metaphysical reality. The Egyptian *heka*, a word that means both "word" and "magic," was a dangerous, even deadly force, composed primarily of bodily fluids, especially maternal blood. Like the "bifid" Hebraic term *ruah* (or "spirit"), which can also become the volcanic *ruah ra'a* (or "evil spirit"), the Egyptian *heka* carries within it both the potential to enact great good and great evil. Herman Te Velde points out that the Egyptian concept *heka* may similarly be employed for evil purposes: "The Egyptians were aware that unordered creative energy was also at work [in the universe]," Te Velde notes. "Sometimes we read of evil *heka* or the need of protecting oneself against the *heka* of others."[13]

Derrida likewise speaks of *ruah* and its ever-possible transformation into *ruah ra'a* or "evil spirit." There is, for Derrida, a war that always already rages within spirit or *ruah*—the war that occurs in God's very name. Spirit is a priori "divided, bifid, ambivalent, polysemic: God deconstructing."[14] In *The Egyptian Book of the Dead*, the pious scribe Ani not only swears that he has kept his vows but swears that he has never eaten human feces.[15] Among the Ancient Egyptians, those who deliberately consumed the body's fluids or waste did so in order to increase their occult power; that is, their ability to inflict harm by contaminating the body of the other, via the ears, with evil *heka*. Whereas Polonius in *Hamlet* kills his brother the King through pouring poison into his ears, the evil Egyptian sorcerer attacked his enemies through uttering lethal curses that were interlaced with the polluted fluids of his own body, words that were aimed at the ears of his victim. In the West African context, if the griot made himself taboo by eating the flesh of his brother, he also transformed himself into a man of power, especially feared by the nobility who wished to preserve their purity of blood and heart. Sahelian researchers have catalogued various meanings for the Mandé term *nyama*, including "evil or satanic; morally neutral; dangerous; polluting: energizing or animating; necessary for action; or indicative of imperfect self-control."[16] It is "a force, a power, or if one prefers, an energy, a fluid possessed by every man."[17] Quite literally, *nyama* is saliva, blood, urine, feces, and semen, terms that are in this respect interchangeable. "[T]he *pharmakon* always penetrates like a liquid," Derrida states, "it is absorbed, drunk, introduced into the inside.... Liquid is the element of the *pharmakon*."[18]

Ruah and the African trace

The examples that may also be cited in support of these comparisons, in both the extant texts of the ancient Egyptians and more recent texts of contemporary Africa (especially West Africa), are far too extensive to allow for more than a few emblematic illustrations. In addition to a concept of spirit as a kind of wet-wind and bodily fluid, Derrida also affirmed the notion of specter as the visual counterpart of spirit, stating that specter is "anything but nothing, anything but incorporeal, and anything but mere appearance."[19] "If by 'specter' I had simply meant appearance without reality and materiality," Derrida states, "I would have wasted a great deal of my own and other people's time for nothing."[20] But, "reality" here does not necessarily mean essential reality in any metaphysical sense. In contrast to Heidegger, Derrida insists that there is no "intact kernel" or concealed essence behind what appears, only the irreducible longing for the existence of "the intact kernel."[21] Derrida frequently evoked the specter of *ruah* as a repressed concept of spirit haunting Western philosophy, especially in Heidegger, but he had nothing to say about the far older Egyptian concept of *heka*, as well as African variants of spirit, such as the Soninke *ñaxamala*, the Mandé *nyama*, the Fulfulde *nyaama*, and countless related words that are well known in Northwest Africa. Derrida's sporadic references to Egypt are typically offered as glosses on dialogues by Plato, rather than as a direct engagement with any actual Egyptian text.[22] For instance, in his essay "Khora," which is a thoughtful reading of Plato's *Timaeus*, Derrida makes no reference to the Ancient Egyptian concept of nothingness, which is amply documented in Egyptian manuscripts and predates its Platonic counterpart the *khora* by thousands of years.[23] Derrida similarly declines to investigate the etymologies of concepts like *ruah*, the Abrahamic, or messianicity, in stark contrast to the inexhaustible rigor his readers have come to expect when he analyzes prominent Greek concepts like *logos*, *bios*, *zoe*, etc. Readers are simply asked to excuse his reliance upon religious signifiers like the dogmatic term *messianicity* on "pedagogical" and "rhetorical" grounds.[24]

For Derrida, the term "messianicity" refers to an irreducible and universal structure of all human communication, a provocative way of thinking about truth as the promise of what is to come. But he declines to investigate this term's controversial basis in historical doctrines of blood election, not only in Judaism but also in all of the major Abrahamic traditions. The doctrine of the Messiah or the "Anointed One" came into prominence in the aftermath of the Babylonian Captivity and is inextricable from the rise of doctrines of blood election in ancient Israel, as evident in the Prophet Ezra's insistence that Israelites with "foreign" wives and children must renounce their families of questionable blood origin (Ezra 9.1-12). Messianic doctrines are at one with the belief that a "righteous" and "pure" remnant must be preserved, if the Messiah was to come at all. In the Christian religion as well, the Messiah Jesus comes only through a Davidic blood line, or "the stem of Jesse." In the Shi'a tradition, by way of contrast, doctrines of blood election are reinscribed with reference to the figure of the Mahdi, who is believed to be a direct descendant of the Prophet Muhammad through his daughter Fatima and cousin Ali. Not coincidentally, Shi'a Muslims also embrace eschatological theologies heralding the eventual return of the now-occult Mahdi and the Messiah Jesus.

In addition to Messianic cults in the U.S. like the Branch Davidians of Waco, Texas, which has been linked to the mass murderer Timothy McVeigh, perhaps the most dangerous Messianic variants of the Abrahamic religion are the Gush Eminem, the Kookists, or the Messianic Zionists currently colonizing the Palestinian West Bank. In the case of the Messianic Zionists, the need to preserve the purity of Jewish blood is affirmed in order to facilitate the coming of the Messiah, which will occur only when all the Holy Land is reclaimed. (For many, the "promised land" includes portions of Jordan as well as the West Bank.) Even more orthodox Haredim adopt strict interpretations of blood laws, prohibiting non-Jews from donating organs or blood to Jews, the breastfeeding of Jews by non-Jews, and making other similar prohibitions. As Israeli Rabbi Yitzhak Ginsburg put it in an article that appeared in *Haaretz*, "If every single cell in a Jewish body entails divinity, and is part of God, then every strand of DNA is a part of God. Therefore, something is special about Jewish DNA."[25]

Although Derrida himself would no doubt find Ginsburg's statement problematic, my point here is that the ancient concept of the Messianic has a particularly troubled history, one that renders it unsuitable for use in international political debate. "The politically important distinction between Jewish blood and non-Jewish blood is well-known to most Israelis," Shahak and Mezvinksy state, "but is ignored by almost all those who write about Israel and its policies."[26] Shahak and Mezvinsky also observe that "only religious Jews who believe in messianic ideology have been willing to establish and live in [Palestinian] settlements."[27] The question of the interdependency of doctrines of the Messianic and blood election is complicated by the fact that the Hebraic *ruah*, like the Egyptian *heka* and the Mandé *nyama*, does not simply mean "spirit" in any transcendental sense, but the actual matter or blood of the mother. When Derrida speaks of the "maternal debt,"[28] or "the feminine figure of YHWH,"[29] which is a more obviously theological articulation of the former, he also alludes to the problematic of occulted spirit or *ruah*, which he insists is "at the heart" of all his writing.[30] The heart of the mother, which is the primordial blood source, is "wherever you save real treasure, that which is not visible on earth, that whose capital accumulates beyond the economy of the terrestrial visible."[31]

Whether one celebrates or rejects Derrida's recuperative use of Jewish theological concepts like the Messianic, *milah*, and *ruah*, these words nonetheless have particular etymologies and originate within specific historical settings that are not mysterious. They are paralleled and anticipated by countless similar terms from the ancient world, particularly from Ancient Egypt, Africa, and Mesopotamia. However, Derrida speculates that we may have no knowledge at all of the Messianic and similar theological concepts of Africa and the Middle East without the revelations of prophets like Abraham, Moses, and Ezra.[32] While Derrida states that he is not fully decided on this question, and that he "oscillates" between belief in prophetic revelation and a less dogmatic notion of belief such as the Heideggerian *Zusage*,[33] he chooses to defer the question, thereby preserving the Messianic as a *general* rather than historically particular signifier. This strategy insures that what Derrida calls the Abrahamic, or what might more accurately be called the Judaic,[34] preserves an exceptional, irreducible, and incomparable status in the history of European philosophy.

Derrida's concern is nearly always with what he calls "the abrahamo-philosophical."[35] In contrast, African philosophers, poets, and writers are often indifferent to Abrahamic themes, concepts, idioms, and obsessions, although their thought originates in the very same historical and cultural matrix that gave birth to Judaism. As the Tuareg poet Hawad puts it in his poem "Anarchy's Delirious Trek,"

> We peddle neither/the Quran of Muhammad,/nor the Gospel of Mary's son,/nor the Torah of Moses./Don't look for us in these places..../Our dreams lie further south,/where the milky wake of stars/washes into the roots of the abyss.[36]

Hawad's indifference and even *hostility* to the Abrahamic is articulated within the cultural context of a "deep Sahelian" society that bears the historical imprints of Ancient Egyptian civilization. The same may be said for the Mosiac Law, which makes its historical entry as a reaction against Egyptian religion, ironically insuring the repressed memory of the very beliefs it hoped to supersede.

One need not go so far as Freud, who argues that Moses was an Egyptian and a disgruntled disciple of the first monotheist Akhenaten. As Egyptologist Jan Assman points out, the Mosaic law preserves the memory of the religion of the Ancient Egyptians, as the repressed paganism that Moses and his followers reject. Like Christianity, Judaism came into the world as a "'counter-religion' because it rejects and repudiates everything that went before and what is outside itself as 'paganism.'"[37] In the Mosaic law, Assman points out, "Egypt represents the old, while Israel represents the new.... The same figure reproduces itself on another level with the opposition between the 'Old' and the 'New' Testaments."[38] Derrida similarly observed that Christianity always already presupposed and even required the preservation of Judaism as a condition of its very coherence. In his appreciative reading of Levinas on this question, Derrida suggested that Judaism may be construed as "the possibility of giving the Bible a context, of keeping this book readable."[39] But what is true of Judaism with respect to Christianity is also true of Egypt with respect to Judaism: "Egypt is the womb from which the chosen people emerged."[40] In fact, Jews lived for centuries in Egypt and Northwest Africa before and after the destruction of Herod's Temple, during which time they both influenced and were influenced by their cultural surroundings. When Islam arrived in West Africa over a thousand years ago, brought by Yemeni Arabs, Jews already dwelled in the land, not far from Timbuktu. As documented in the *Tarikh al fattash*, the underwater djinn Raura ibn Sāra, who was said to rule the Songhay people prior to the arrival of Islam, reputedly feared only one man, Suleyman, the son of Dawud, or Solomon, the son of David.[41] Al Hajj Mahmud Kati, the author of the medieval Songhay chronicle *Tarikh al fattash*, was a Sephardic immigrant to Timbuktu in the aftermath of the Spanish Inquisition, not unlike many other, similar, Sephardic Jews and Muslims in Northwest Africa, including Algeria.

Derrida's critique of European philosophy is articulated from within a specific literary, cultural, and historical heritage, from which figures such as the Sephardic-Songhay author Kati and various other scribes from Timbuktu, Oudane, Djenne, and Kano should not be excluded. This heritage includes but is not limited to Jewish influences and sources. Despite his North African origins, Derrida steadfastly declined to investigate the history and status of Jews in Northwest Africa, nor any Judaic theological concepts, within any context other than a European one. Derrida thus situates *ruah* in relation to dominant Western philosophical concepts, but never African or Middle Eastern concepts.

Derrida, Heidegger, and *ruah*

While the particularity of each historical articulation of the concept of "spirit" should be respected, the Hebraic articulation of this notion is not an exemplary instance in human history, as Derrida implies when he criticizes Martin Heidegger's neglect of *ruah* in *Of Spirit: Heidegger and the Question* (1989). In other words, if Heidegger is resolutely silent about the Hebraic *ruah*, which is certainly a fair criticism of Heidegger's writings, Derrida is resolutely silent in his turn about inextricably interrelated African concepts.[42] Regarding Heidegger's affiliation with the Nazi Party, Derrida comments:

> Nazism was not born in the desert. We all know this, but it has to be constantly recalled. And even if, far from any desert, it had grown like a mushroom in the silence of a European forest, it would have done so in the shadow of big trees, in the shelter of their silence or their indifference but in the same soil.[43]

Derrida locates Heidegger's comments and writing on the European concept of spirit within the historical epic that culminated in the *Shoah*, sensitively probing Heidegger's apparently calculated neglect of *ruah*. Yet, Derrida often defended Heidegger against spurious criticisms of his work on the grounds of his affiliation with the Nazi Party. In this case, however, Derrida faults Heidegger for his neglectful silence on *ruah*, linking this omission to the rise of Nazism. In *The Beast and the Sovereign, Volume I*, Derrida points out that "one is always a priori negligent."[44] He also observes that "neglect" is "an abyssal word that one should not use in a neglected or negligent way."[45] Certainly, Derrida's critique of Heidegger in *Of Spirit* is thoughtful, rigorous, and careful. But Derrida also suggests that the Messianic Jew may be construed as a universal figure for all non-European peoples, including Muslims.[46]

In *Archive Fever* (1995), Derrida similarly cites Yosif Hayim Yerushalmi's dogmatic view that "'*Only in Israel and nowhere else* is the injunction to remember felt as a religious imperative [emphasis added].'"[47] Derrida tells us that he "trembles" before this sentence and wonders if it is just. Freud, in contrast, called circumcision a "particularly clumsy invention" if it was intended to distinguish Jews from other Middle Eastern tribes, given its wide prevalence and long history in the region. "The question concerning the origin of circumcision has only one answer," Freud observes, "it comes from Egypt."[48] Sentimental notions about circumcision like Yerushalmi's may resonate with deeply felt aspects of Judaic spirituality, but they have no basis in history, and they certainly do not offer grounds to accord the State of Israel an exemplary status, especially with regard to international law.

In *Specters of Marx*, Derrida also compares the deconstructive thinker of techniques, in effect the thinker of the future who has thought beyond the limitations of the Kantian subject inscribed in UN law, to the "universal" figure of the Messianic Jew. "Jews are in all senses of this word the circumcised and the circumcisers, those who have the experience, a certain concise experience of circumcision," Derrida states. "*Anyone or no one may be a Jew* [emphasis added]."[49] John Caputo comments in his reading of Derrida on this question, "If circumcision is Jewish, it is only [Jewish] ... inasmuch as the Jew is witness to something universal, that spiritually *we are all Jews*, all called and chosen to welcome the other [emphasis added]."[50] But what is true of the "Jewish" rite of circumcision is equally true for countless tribes like the Mossi, Dogon, Woolf, Soninke, Fulani, etc. The Jewish experience of circumcision is neither more nor less "concise" than it is for those who belong to many other ethnic groups still practicing circumcision, tribal cutting, scarification, tattooing, teeth-sharpening, and other forms of totemic marking. One might very well say *"we are all Songhay, Bella, Lobi*," and so on, rather than *"we are all Jews*," substituting the name of virtually thousands of other Middle Eastern and African tribal groups in the place of the privileged signifier "Jew." But this is not what either Derrida or Caputo do. The question of Jewish identity's *unexceptional* status outside of a Euro-Christian context is never considered. While it is true that Jews have lived in Europe for centuries prior to the *Shoah*, it is also true that millions of African and Middle Eastern people now live in Europe and have also made and continue to make important contributions to European culture and civilization.

In his critique of Heidegger, Derrida not only fails to historicize and relativize the "Jewish" concept of spirit; he also states that he is "not certain that Moslems and some others wouldn't join in the concert or the hymn [emphasis added]" once the Jewish concept of *ruah* receives the recognition it deserves.[51] Judaic theology is credited for its contributions to European philosophy, wrongly elided by Heidegger, and this is indeed a cause for celebration, as Derrida suggests, since European philosophy is certainly indebted to Jewish as well as Ancient Egyptian theology. But who are these other "others," who Derrida claims will "join the hymn," beyond "the Moslem"? (Derrida does not distinguish between Sunni and Shi'a, despite the long history of warfare and antagonism between them.) It is unlikely that Derrida here means Eurocentric Judeo-Christians like Caputo, although these are the actual "others" who would most likely reach for their hymnals. On the other hand, it is difficult to imagine Arab Muslims or

Christians living in the West Bank or Gaza celebrating the promotion of the allegedly "neutral" figure of the Messianic Jew to a quasi-universal sign, or that they would not detect an evangelical impulse in this critical maneuver. It is also unlikely that these same "others" will be happy to celebrate the restoration of the Hebraic concept of *ruah* in the history of European philosophy without reference to countless African and Middle Eastern concepts of spirit that precede and parallel it.

Derrida points out that Nazism "was not born in a desert." In contrast, Abrahamic religion (in effect, a codeword for Judaism) was allegedly born in the "placeless place" of the abyssal desert, "the empty, abstract, and dry" void that is yet another word for the Platonic khora.[52] However, just as Palestine was certainly not an empty desert in 1948 ("a land without people for a people without land"), Judaism did not appear fully formed in an abyssal desert but was nurtured in the cultural matrix of Ancient Egypt, Mesopotamia, and Africa. More objective scholarship on the region, particularly in Middle Eastern and African studies as well as contemporary Egyptology, verifies the truism that Judaism like all world religions has an actual history and has been influenced by multiple cultures, religions, and political systems, including those of historical rivals that one would rather forget.

Although he lived in Algeria until he was 19, Derrida insisted that he was ill-prepared, if not incompetent, when it came to the question of African philosophy. Addressing a gathering of African philosophers at Cotonou, Benin in 1978, Derrida stated:

> I will not speak to you about the crisis in the teaching of philosophy in Africa itself, first of all because *I would have nothing to tell you about it* ... I doubt that the 'crisis' in Africa has a unity, even unity as a crisis, unless it is linked to the crisis of African unity, which is something else again. Moreover, *I have neither the means nor the pretense to teach you anything at all about the diversity of African situations.* And finally, the scene of a European or even a Euro-African coming to diagnose a crisis of African teaching before African philosophers, researchers, and teachers seems *unbearably laughable* [emphasis added].[53]

Despite his claims to the contrary, Derrida's neglect of African philosophy on the basis of its inaccessibility seems implausible, given both his personal history and his remarkable gifts as a teacher and philosopher. Derrida insists that his testimony regarding Africa is far too "limited."[54] But why such extreme modesty if not *fear* of African philosophy, particularly in a book that is ironically entitled *Who's Afraid of Philosophy?* Is it really true that Derrida lacked "the means and pretense" to critically engage African philosophy, and that the very thought that he might attempt to do so should seem to his readers "unbearably laughable"? It is possible, of course, that Derrida never discusses well-known African concepts like *heka* and *nyama*, despite their shared history with the Hebraic *ruah*, because he had never heard of them. What is certain is that he made very little effort to investigate African philosophy, which he claimed was entirely beyond his grasp. Consequently, Derrida's deconstruction of European metaphysics remains ensconced within a myopically Jewish thinking of the trace.

The Zionist Plebiscite

The task for Derrida's readers today, at least those who strive for a more just and inclusive articulation of deconstruction, is to situate the spectral idioms that haunt Derrida's discourse within the actual historical framework from which his powerful critique of Platonic logocentrism emerged. One may still love the thought of Derrida and venerate the thinker for his obviously important contributions to contemporary critical thought while recognizing that Derrida's views on Zionism did not represent what is most exemplary in his thought. A careful, close reading of Derrida's writings on the question of Zionism shows that he defended Zionism while recognizing its indefensibility in any sense other than a "realistic" or Machiavellian one. To cite Derrida himself in a lecture given in Jerusalem in 1988, "the existence [of the Israeli State], it goes without saying, must henceforth be recognized by all and definitively guaranteed."[55] In this same lecture, Derrida also states his solidarity with all those who "advocate the withdrawal of Israeli troops from the occupied territories as well as the recognition of the Palestinian's right to chose their own representatives."[56] Hence, while rejecting the military occupation of Palestine, Derrida nonetheless affirmed Israel's unquestionable right to exist as a Jewish state, though he urged critical reflection upon "its prehistory, the conditions of its recent founding, and the constitutional, legal, political foundations of its present functioning."[57]

While the move was progressive in some respects (and Derrida insisted that deconstruction was or at least should be "progressive"), it is important to note that even figures such as Ariel Sharon abandoned the ill-fated dream of colonizing Gaza and the West Bank, not out of friendship for the Palestinians but in order to save Zionism itself, or to preserve Israel's identity as a Jewish state. Sharon built the "West Bank Barrier" (in Arabic, "*jidar al-fasi al'-'unsun*" or "racial segregation wall") because he realistically calculated that demographics were not on the side of Israeli Jews. Derrida's call to withdraw Israeli troops from occupied Palestine was not necessarily a progressive gesture, but possibly linked to his desire to preserve Israel's political character as a Jewish state. Derrida's talk "Interpretations at War: Kant, the Jew, the German" is a meditation on the necessity of forgetting the violence that is always prior to the founding of any nation-state. Derrida tells his audience in Jerusalem in 1988 that those who wish to have any future at all must be somewhat indifferent to the past: "[A] nation is at the same time both memory (and forgetting pertains to the very deployment of this memory) and, in the present, promise, project, a 'desire to live together.'"[58] The nation is, for Derrida, "a *spiritual* principle [emphasis added]."[59] To belong to a nation is a matter of saying "yes" on a daily basis. It is a "daily plebiscite, just as the existence of the individual is a perpetual affirmation of life." [60] However, if the nation is "a daily plebiscite," or a matter of "yes-saying," the "yes" is also a vapor or *matter* of *ruah*—in effect, the matter *of the mother*. Derrida affirms the very *spirit* of Zionism.

In his discussion of the "constitutional, legal, [and] political foundations of [Israel's] present functioning," Derrida does not, however, deconstruct the Israeli "Law of Return," nor does he defend the Palestinian "Right of Return" encoded in UN Law.

If the Jewish nation is to survive as a nation, if it is to have any future at all, Derrida reminds his listeners, "a sort of essential indifference to the past" is unavoidable.[61] For Derrida, then, the State of Israel and the Jew residing within the State of Israel remain *shibboleths*, figures of "absolute singularity."[62] In his "Circumfession," Derrida described himself as a "little black and very Arab Jew," but he did not describe himself as a "little black and very Jewish Arab."[63] The terms "black" and "Arab" remained for Derrida adjectives that he subordinated to the sign of the "Jew." In contrast, the Palestinian Edward W. Said invoked the more neutral concept of "the secular wound," which is *not* a tribal shibboleth but a general trace that is not reducible to either Arab or Jewish identity.[64] However, in one of his last interviews conducted by the Israeli Jew Ari Shavat, Said stated, "My definition of pan-Arabism would comprise [all regional] communities within an Arab-Islamic framework. Including the Jews."[65] When Shavat responded that many Jews in Israel would find this prospect frightening because they would now become a demographic minority, Said remarked, "Yes, but you're going to be a minority anyway. In about ten years there will be demographic parity between Jews and Palestinians, and the process will go on."[66] Said went ever further than this, adding, "the Jews are a minority everywhere. They are a minority in America. They can certainly be a minority in Israel."[67]

Said's argument is Machiavellian in its own way, since though he too belonged to a religious minority in the Arab world, his status as an Arab Christian was underwritten by the existence of two billion fellow Christians living outside the region. In the case of Arab Muslims, there are twenty-one Arab Muslim nations besides Palestine and more than a billion fellow Muslims who live across the globe. There is no comparable Jewish demographic outside the region.

While instances of ethnic cleansing that are comparable to the *Shoah* have indeed occurred, as historians like Norman Finkelstein, Ward Churchill, and Noam Chomsky point out, the history of Jews in Europe provides evidence that Israeli and Diaspora Jews are rightly concerned about what might happen to them should Jews in Israel become a minority within what Said calls an "Arab-Islamic framework." Said himself shared this concern. In this same interview, he states,

> I worry about [retaliation against the Jews]. The history of minorities in the Middle East has not been as bad as Europe, but I wonder what would happen [to them]. It worries me a great deal. The question of what is going to be the fate of the Jews is very difficult for me. I really don't know. It worries me.[68]

Said was not so naive as to believe that all displaced Palestinians could return to ancestral homelands that were once confiscated by Israeli Jews. He knew very well that even many Arabs living in Israel and the Occupied Territories did not want this to occur. Yet, he emphasized the necessity of respect for international law and repeatedly stated that some sort of acknowledgment of wrongdoing on behalf of the Israelis was essential in order for the wounds of the past to heal. Following Nelson Mandela, Said's mantra was "one person, one vote." The Kantian view that every human being should be assured universal human rights because we must all put our feet *somewhere* is not reducible to the ideologies of blood election like Messianic Zionism. "Beyond even alliances with a chosen people," Derrida states, "there is no nationality or nationalism that is not religious or mythological, let us say 'mystical' in the broad sense."[69] But the birthright that is based on the fact of residency in a town or city (the liberal concept of the citizen is linked to the French word "*cité* ") is not religious in the same sense as the birthright that is predicated on the ancient Egypto-African myth of blood election. As the Israeli historian Zeev Sternhell suggests, "Those who wish Israel to be a truly liberal state or Israeli society to be open must recognize the fact that liberalism derives from the initial attempt in the seventeenth century to separate religion from politics."[70] Unlike Derrida, who never lived in Israel, Sternhell unambiguously rejects the misguided efforts of the Israeli right to merge politics and religion, insisting that "a liberal state can only be a secular state, a state in which the concept of citizenship lies at the center of collective existence [emphasis added]."[71]

Noam Chomsky has similarly remarked that "citizens of France are French, but citizens of the Jewish state may be non-Jews, either by ethnic or religious origin, or simply by choice.... *To the extent that Israel is a Jewish state, it cannot be a democratic state* [emphasis added]."[72] The Kantian "citizen" embedded in the UN charter is an emblem of the desire to escape the irrational, theocratic state. Although certainly not exempt from the ongoing need for deconstruction, this concept was forged in the Enlightenment in order to establish a political space emptied of the religious, as well as to expand the vista of individual freedom, including freedom from the *absolutely singular* requirements of religious dogma. If a liberal democratic man does not fully escape his historical basis in religion, neither does he surrender to it, nor does he tolerate the use of dogmatic religious terminology in documents of state. In the land of his birth, Derrida more progressively advocated "the effective dissociation of the political and the theological" in order to resolve Algeria's long-standing conflicts in the aftermath of French colonization.[73] What Derrida sought for Algeria is equally desirable in Israel and the Occupied Territories, and to make this case, as did Edward Said, is not tantamount to promoting the "globalatinization" or neo-hellenization of Israel-Palestine, any more than Derrida's wish to dissociate the political and the theological in the case of Algeria was globalatinizing.

Conclusion

The path to peace and security for both Palestinian Arabs and Israeli Jews will not be an easy one. The US's "realistic" and lopsided support for the Israelis has certainly done little to instill confidence in the virtues of liberal democratic idealism. Moreover, there is no sign that Israelis will soon awaken from their collective denial of the demographic realities that now confront them. But there is nothing to be gained from ignoring the fact that neither peace nor security can be achieved for either party outside the framework of current international law, which, while flawed and in need of deconstruction, is nonetheless based upon liberal democratic and republican ideals rather than regressive theologies of blood election.

Notes

1. Jacques Derrida, *Acts of Religion* (New York: Routledge, 2002), 90.
2. Jacques Derrida, *The Beast & the Sovereign, Volume I* (Chicago, IL: The University of Chicago Press, 2009), 314.
3. Derrida himself references the rhetorical tropes of the *syllepses*, which "'consist of taking one and the same word in two different senses, one of which is, or is supposed to be, the original, or at least the *literal* meaning; the other the *figurative*, or supposedly figurative, even if is not so in reality'" (*Dissemination* (Chicago, IL: The University of Chicago Press, 1981), 220). In his widely discussed criticisms of Francis Fukuyama's writings in *Specters of Marx* (1993), Derrida shows how Fukuyama sometimes evokes the concept of the democratic in terms of "actuality" (literally, liberal democratic states like France, the Netherlands, and the US) and sometimes in terms of democratic "ideality" (figuratively, the liberal democratic state as a transcendental ideal). The trope of syllepsis creates confusion in discussions of Judaism, which is often simultaneously articulated as a matter of personal identity (*literally*, Judaism as tribal affiliation) and sometimes as a matter of one's personal religion (*figuratively*, Judaism as spirituality). *Specters of Marx: The State of the Debt, the Work of Mourning, & The New International* (New York: Routledge, 1994).
4. Jacques Derrida, *Deconstruction Engaged: The Sydney Seminars*, ed. Paul Patton and Terry Smith (Sydney: Power Publications, 2001), 116.
5. It is Derrida's Zionism, rather than his Jewish identity, that makes his work less attractive for many scholars in Africa and the Middle East. In his review of my book *Derrida, Africa, and the Middle East* (2009), Shane Moran claims that I promote the "tendentiously absurd" formula that "Derrida = Jew = Zionist" ("Review, Derrida, Africa, and the Middle East," *Textual Practice*, Volume 24, Issue 2 (2010), 387). I agree with Moran that such a line of argumentation would be misguided and obviously absurd; however, this is not what I have ever suggested in any of my published writings on this question. As a white South African, Moran's concern seems to be that no individual should be trapped within a particular tribal identity or should be held to account for the past transgressions of the ethnic group into which one is born. Moran does not reflect upon Judaism's status as a prominent world religion, which is not merely a matter of tribal or ethnic identity. Comparisons of the Zionist State of Israel to Apartheid South Africa are generally not satisfying in themselves, not without reference to the interrelations of Jewish theology and Zionism. In other words, the modern State of Israel is not merely an apartheid state enforcing different laws for different ethnic or racial groups. It is also an "Abrahamic" theocracy—to momentarily adopt Derrida's terminology—that is comparable to theocratic African and Middle Eastern nations like Saudi Arabia, Iran, and Mauritania.
6. Christopher Wise, *The Timbuktu Chronicles, 1493–1599: Ta'rikh al fattish* (Trenton, NJ: Africa World Press, 2011), 52–6.
7. Jan Assman, *The Search for God in Ancient Egypt* (Ithaca, NY and London: Cornell University Press, 2001), 97.
8. Thomas Hale, *Griots and Griottes: Masters of Words and Music* (Bloomington, IN: Indiana University Press, 1998), 64.
9. Hale, *Griots and Griottes*, 92.

10 P. G. Walsh, "Introduction," in Apuleius, *The Golden Ass* (Oxford: Oxford University Press, 2008), xxxviii–xxxix.
11 Thomas Hale and Nouhou Malio, *The Epic of Askia Mohammed* (Bloomington and Indianapolis, IN: Indiana University Press, 1996), 60.
12 Derrida, *Acts of Religion*, 148–63.
13 Herman Te Velde, "The God Heka in Egyptian Theology," *Jaarbericht van het Voorasiatisch-Egyptisch Genootshap. Ex Oriente Lux*, Vol. 21 (1970), 175–86.
14 Derrida, *Acts of Religion*, 108.
15 Eva Von Dassow, *The Egyptian Book of the Dead: The Book of Going Forth By Day*, trans. Raymond Faulkner (San Francisco, CA: Chronicle Books, 2008), 134.
16 Charles Bird, Martha B. Kendall, and Kalilou Tera, "Etymologies of Nyamakala," in *Status and Identity in West Africa*, David C. Conrad and Barbara E. Frank (eds) (Bloomington and Indianapolis, IN: Indiana University Press, 1995), 28.
17 Joseph Henry, *L'ame d'un peuple africain: Les Bambara, leur vie psychique, éthique, sociale, religieuse* (Munster: Aschendorff, 1910), 27.
18 Derrida, *Dissemination*, 152.
19 Jacques Derrida, "Marx & Sons," in *Ghostly Demarcations: A Symposium on Jacques Derrida's Specters of Marx*, ed. Michael Sprinker (London and New York: Verso, 1999), 267.
20 Derrida, "Marx & Sons," 267. The Derridean concept of specter is prefigured in Ancient Egyptian literature as *"ka"* which is represented by a hieroglyphic image of two hands clapping. The *ka* refers to one's visual double such as an image in a photograph or mirror. In extant literature, the *ka* operates autonomously of one's body, especially after one's death or during sleep. For instance, the *ka* may depart from one's body in dreams in order to haunt the dreams of one's family members, friends, lovers, enemies, etc. This concept is also well known in West Africa, especially in Sufi brotherhoods like the Umarian Tidjaniyya. Equivalent West African concepts include the Fulfulde *mbeelu*, the Tidjaniyya *rahwan*, and the Mandé *ja*. See Amadou Hampaté Ba's *Kaidara: A Fulani Cosmological Epic from Mali* (Boulder, CO: Lynne Rienner, A Three Continents Book, 1988), 140–1, and John Williams Johnson's *The Epic of Son Jara: A West African Tradition* (Bloomington, IN: Indiana University Press, 1992), 132. See also my interview with the Umarian Tidjaniyya of Podor, Senegal, "The Tidjaniya of Alawar, Podor: Wise Interview 2008." This interview exists in a film version that may be viewed on the web. "The Tidjaniya of Alawar, Podor: Wise Interview 2008" by Christopher Wise and Fallou Ngom (www.youtube.com/channel/UCa5zevWfzE4Ke6epIczN4Tg). Avaliable November 1, 2013.
21 Jacques Derrida, *Ear of the Other: Otobiography, Transference, Translation* (Lincoln, NE: University of Nebraska Press, 1988), 114–15.
22 Derrida *does* briefly discuss actual Egyptian sources in the footnotes of *Dissemination*, in order to advance his provocative reading of Plato's *Phadreus*. To make his case, Derrida also cites a few French Egyptologists in his reading of Plato's tale of Thoth and Thamus. Such references stand as rare exceptions with regard to African and Middle Eastern sources that are not "Abrahamic."
23 Erik Hornung, *Conceptions of God in Ancient Egypt: The One and the Many* (Ithaca, NY: Cornell University Press, 1971), 173.
24 Derrida, "Marx & Sons," 229.
25 Israel Shahak and Norton Mezvinsky, *Jewish Fundamentalism in Israel* (London and Sterling, VA: Pluto Press, 1999), 43.

26 Shahak and Mezvinsky, *Jewish Fundamentalism in Israel*, 154.
27 Ibid., 82.
28 Jacques Derrida, *Specters of Marx: The State of the Debt, the Work of Mourning, & The New International* (New York: Routledge, 1994), 109–10.
29 Jacques Derrida, "Circumfession," in *Jacques Derrida*, Jacques Derrida and Geoffry Bennington (Chicago, IL, and London: University of Chicago Press, 1993), 155.
30 Derrida, "Marx & Sons," 231.
31 Jacques Derrida, *The Gift of Death* (Chicago, IL: The University of Chicago Press, 1995), 98.
32 John Caputo and Jacques Derrida, *Deconstruction In A Nutshell: A Conversation with Jacques Derrida* (New York: Fordham University Press, 1997), 22–3.
33 In his reading of Heidegger on the question of the *Zusage*, Derrida states that "the name of the *Zusage* ('accord, acquiescing, trust or confidence') designates that which is most irreducible, indeed most originary in thought, prior even to that questioning said by him to constitute the piety (*Frommigkeit*) of thinking" (*Acts of Religion*, 95). Derrida criticizes Heidegger for asserting that "belief *in general* has no place in the experience or the act of thinking *in general*." This is where, Derrida states, "we would have difficulty following him." Derrida's criticism of Heidegger is valid, since it is difficult to dispute that belief "in general" always already has a place in the act of thinking "in general." However, Derrida accords to the *Zusage* the particular name of the *Messianic*, a bloated religious signifier.
34 As I have argued elsewhere, Derrida's conceptions of the Abrahamic and the Messianic tend to be biased in favor of historically Judaic conceptions of these notions. For instance, the figure of Abraham in the Christian tradition occupies a lower status than the Priest Melchizedek. In the Christian tradition, this latter figure, who is believed to be uncircumcised, gives his blessing to Abraham after they partake of the rite of the Eucharist, which is far more significant in the Christian tradition than the "Abrahamic" rite of circumcision. See Genesis 14.17-20 and Hebrews 7.1-7; see also Wise *Derrida, Africa, and the Middle East* (New York: Palgrave-Macmillan, 2009), 34–5. Similarly, the Derridean notion of the "Messianic" always already refers to a structure of expectation. The Messianic is what we wait for, not what has already arrived. However, in both Christianity and Islam, the Messiah Jesus has indeed come, although Jesus is not an incarnate deity in the Islamic tradition. Derrida tends to ignore ontological distinctions which are inherent in Abrahamic traditions that are not Jewish.
35 Derrida, *The Sovereign and the Beast*, Vol. I, 314.
36 Hawad, "Anarchy's Delirious Trek," in *The Desert Shore: Literatures of the Sahel*, ed. Christopher Wise (Boulder, CO: Lynne Rienner, 2001), 117.
37 Jan Assman, *Moses, The Egyptian: The Memory of Egypt in Western Monotheism* (Cambridge, MA: Harvard University Press, 1997), 3.
38 Assman, *Moses The Egyptian*, 7.
39 Derrida, *Acts of Religion*, 91.
40 Assman, *Moses The Egyptian*, 209.
41 Wise, *The Timbuktu Chronicles*, 50.
42 Jacques Derrida, *Of Spirit: Heidegger and the Question* (Chicago, IL: The University of Chicago Press, 1989), 100–1.
43 Derrida, *Of Spirit*, 109.
44 Derrida, *The Sovereign and the Beast*, Vol. 1, 94.

45 Ibid., 95.
46 In *Sovereignties in Question*, Derrida states:
    The Jew is the *shibboleth*. Witness to the universal, but as an *absolute*, dated, marked, incised, caesuraed singularity – as the other and in the name of the other. (And I would also add that, in its fearsome political ambiguity, *shibboleth* could today name the State of Israel, the present state of the State of Israel… [The Jew is] witness to the universal as *absolute singularity* [emphasis added]" (*Sovereignties in Question: The Poetics of Paul Celan* (New York: Fordham University Press, 2005), 50–1).
47 Jacques Derrida, *Archive Fever: A Freudian Impression* (Chicago, IL: The University of Chicago Press, 1995), 76.
48 Sigmund Freud, *Moses and Monotheism* (New York: Vintage, 1939), 29.
49 Derrida, *Sovereignties in Question*, 55.
50 John Caputo, *The Prayers and Tears of Jacques Derrida* (Bloomington, IN: Indiana University Press, 1997), 262.
51 Derrida, *Of Spirit*, 111.
52 Derrida, *Specters of Marx*, 166–7.
53 Jacques Derrida, *Who's Afraid of Philosophy? Right to Philosophy, Volume I* (Stanford, CA: Stanford University Press, 2002), 108.
54 Derrida, *Who's Afraid of Philosophy?*, 108.
55 Derrida, *Acts of Religion*, 138.
56 Ibid.
57 Ibid.
58 Ibid., 185.
59 Ibid., 184.
60 Ibid., 186.
61 Ibid., 185.
62 Derrida, *Sovereignties in Question*, 50–1.
63 Derrida, "Circumfession," 58.
64 Edward W. Said, *Freud and the Non-European* (New York and London: Verso, 2003), 54.
65 Edward W. Said, "My Right of Return" (Interview with Ari Shavat), in *Power, Politics, and Culture: Interviews With Edward W. Said*, ed. Gauri Viswanathan (New York: Vintage Books, 2001), 456.
66 Said, "My Right of Return," 453.
67 Ibid.
68 Ibid.
69 Derrida, *Specters of Marx*, 91.
70 Zev Sternhel, *The Founding Myths of Israel* (Princeton, NJ: Princeton University Press, 1998), xiii.
71 Sternhel, *The Founding Myths of Israel*, xiii.
72 Noam Chomsky, "Foreword," *The Arabs and and Israel* (London: The Bodley Head, 1968), 9.
73 Derrida, *Acts of Religion*, 306.

8

Rex, or the Negation of Wandering

Ranjana Khanna

Ultimately, the paradoxical effect I wanted to describe schematically is that my suffering as a persecuted Jew ... no doubt killed in me an elementary confidence in any community, in any fusional gregariousness, whatever its nature, and beginning of course with any anti-Semitic herding that alleges ethnic, religious, or national roots.... Of course, this anxious vigilance of a stranger within, this insomniac distrust, has not failed to come up in respect to the still exemplary phenomenon that is the state of Israel.
    Jacques Derrida, "Abraham, The Other"[1] *Judeities: Questions for Jacques Derrida*, 15

Child, you must write on your typewriter a name that you choose for yourself. Like me.... You bark, yet you are not a dog. You cannot stand erect, yet you are not a dog! Write, the name will create you, the name will establish everything, a good name is better than a good body, a name is better than a posture, better than anything, every creature has a name, even a cockroach, Adolf Cockroach, creation's diadem, crown, wreath, wreath about the cockroach's head. Write a name!
                        Yoram Kaniuk, *Adam Resurrected*[2], 218–19

The Israeli state, established in 1948, does not have a written constitution, but it did establish constitutional laws. One of these sought famously to make possible an "ingathering of the exiles" that had been promised by the fifth section of Israel's *Declaration of Establishment*. In 1950, the Israeli Knesset passed The Law of Return, declaring the right of every Jew to come to Israel and to obtain Israeli citizenship, thus addressing two forms of dispersion and vulnerability. The first was the immediate context of the many refugees seeking asylum in the aftermath of the Holocaust and from European anti-Semitism more generally. This form of reversal or "negation" of diaspora was the realization of the call made by Theodor Herzl, in part in reaction to the divisive Dreyfus affair in which a French Alsatian assimilated Jew was wrongfully convicted for passing French military secrets to the Germans. Eventually, Dreyfus was called back from the penal colony in French Guiana and restored to the military.[3] Understanding the intense passions and the anti-Semitism that drove the Dreyfus affair from 1894 to 1906 as only the tip of the iceberg, Herzl called, in his *The Jewish State* in 1896, for such an ingathering, over time.[4] This was with an understanding that because of contemporary anti-Semitism, Jews would never be safe in Europe. But Herzl was not opposed to an independent Jewish state outside of the site of contemporary Israel, for example, in Argentina or Uganda, even as Palestine was certainly also desirable for him.

The second context of dispersal addressed a messianic time, as it were, and the desire to regather as a nation the scattered, wandering Jews following the destruction of the first temple by the Babylonians. Those following Ahad Ha'am's Messianic and spiritual Zionism saw Zionism as a *return from* and a *negation of* the diaspora, and thus the site of British Mandate Palestine was essential for their reasoning. The Messianic time of the spiritual Zionism of Ahad Ha'am in turn stood in contrast to the Messianism of Orthodox Jews such as Neturai Karta, who have lived in and outside Israel since 1938 and who have consistently been anti-Zionist because they believe that only the arrival of the Messiah should create a Jewish state, not the Jews themselves.[5] A double temporality of the asylum state came together, within the context of a colonial exit strategy for the British from Mandate Palestine. Thinkers as diverse as Hannah Arendt (in 1948–51) and Aimé Césaire (in 1955) called attention to the tight connection between anti-Semitism, imperialism, and totalitarianism as the context in which the Jewish state was born. This was in the same year as the establishment of the *Universal Declaration of Human Rights* in 1948.[6]

The coming together of two different temporalities of an ingathering gives some insight into why Hannah Arendt (not writing here in the context of Israel, and with great respect for the institution of asylum) refers to asylum as an anachronistic category that will continue to decline along with the nation-state. Israel was born or reborn, then, with the overt desire to bring together Jews as one people.[7]

Yoram Kaniuk's early novel *Adam Resurrected* (1971), which is both more and less than a national allegory, addresses this context of the Holocaust, the trauma of survival, and its aftermath in Israel through the staging of the border between sanity and insanity.[8] The strengths and weaknesses of the novel are that, in its efforts to contain a highly theatrical representation of insanity, it is sometimes too theatrical, stretching the novel to the limits of the form. The bulk of the novel takes place in a mental asylum in the Negev desert established by one Mrs. Seizling in 1960, an American philanthropist who encounters a woman—the elder of the Schwester twins—who, in turn, inadvertently convinces her of the need for funds for a mental asylum in Israel. She tells her that in the wasteland of the desert, "the Covenant with Abraham shall be re-enacted"[9]:

> Do you know, my dear Mrs. Seizling, why these cries, these shrieks, are heard in this land in the dead of night? ... They cry because there is no escape. The insult scorches. The knowledge, the final realization that they were simply raw material in the most advanced factory of Europe, under a sky inhabited by a God in exile, by a Stranger, this information drives us crazy. Such humiliation! So we have turned this country into the largest mental asylum on earth. I tell you that out of

these, out of the lunatics who weep in the night, will enter somebody who will enter a wadi among the rocks and be received by God in friendship and spoken to.[10]

The promise of generation is demanded through paternal sacrifice and filial piety—the promise of a future nation generated through Abraham's seed: Abraham begat Isaac; Isaac begat.... Here that promise will be enacted through the idea of reproduction in the asylum.

The most notable of the asylum's inmates is Adam Stein, who had been viciously adopted as the dog of a Nazi officer in a camp during the Holocaust. The officer had seen him as a clown some years before in his circus. Adam's mode of camp survival was, following the commands of Commandant Klein, to entertain camp prisoners (including his wife and child) with his violin on the way to their deaths in the gas chambers. He would then resume residence and life on all fours with his master Herr Commandant Klein and Klein's "real" dog, Rex, sharing food with Rex from the dog bowl. Rex is a dog who carries the name of King. He will be revisited on Adam in a different form as a dog-child, child-dog, and perhaps as the dog-child of *their* relationship, as soon to be David, the second King of Israel: Rex begat Adam; Adam begat David....

Entering into a discussion concerning Zionism, community, and its impossibility through the concept of asylum, or perhaps more accurately through the non-concept of asylum, allows for insight into this threshold term that implies an inside and an outside, a togetherness and a separation, a concealment or a fugitive element and an ever-present insistence of life in the extreme, coded between non-existence and vivid criminalization at the core of community. To bring together the notion of a political home in a state, a religiously conceived sanctuary, and a mental hospital is to collapse notions of asylum that refer to the most individuated figure, on the one hand, and, on the other, to a group that is religiously conceived and politically constituted as the instantiation of the modern nation-state.

Because of its temporal dimension, asylum foregrounds the problem of the generative within community.[11] An asylum state, imagined as growing both from within and from the outside, and the structures of the hereditary and of inheritance which dominate it, shape, on the one hand, a relation to the group through the filial relation organized through properties and property, and, on the other, the more overt transfer of property that lies within inheritance and its gift/debt problem.[12] Asylum assaults its seekers with the im/possibility of Being without such group or filial relations. But also, asylum seekers are beyond the constraints of Being anthropomorphized in the proper names of inheritance and group, or in legal (and now liberal) structures of dignity afforded through recognition, acknowledgment, and the speaking of names that comes with naturalization, documentation, incarceration, or institutionalization.[13]

Kaniuk's novel asks us to address the possibilities of being in excess of the proper name on the level of individuation and it raises the question of how the proper name betrays something about the naming of a people—something necessary, but always flawed, and, at its most extreme, potentially genocidal with the sole alternatives of death and survival upon which genocide balances. The question of the group name itself is hardly new and, in relation to "the Jew" it is there in "On the Jewish Question" where Marx teases out the difference between justice and the law, and the problem of criticizing one form of rights as dangerous ultimately to human emancipation. Acknowledging the necessity of dealing with histories of prejudice, discrimination, and genocidal violence, Marx simultaneously calls for protecting and rejecting rights premised on a liberal notion of freedom from interference. Engels addresses the same problem of inheritance with implications for the proper name and the proper noun as he unravels sexual difference in the relationship between reproduction and right, monogamy, and private property as the "world historical defeat of the female sex": Jew begat woman.

Understanding Israel and Zionism through Kaniuk's novel reveals multiple temporalities converging on the space or city of asylum and concerning who might be welcomed into it, how conditional or unconditional the hospitality granted may be, and who indeed decides given that asylum is the right of a state to grant or deny rather than a human right, which is solely to seek asylum under the conventions of the "Universal Declaration of Human Rights." If Israel's Law of Return sought to mitigate this by giving all Jews the right to refuge, Israel nonetheless retained the religious right to grant sanctuary when the state made it a requirement that proof of Jewishness would be necessary. Asylum is the negation of something that is core not only to the Jewish category of diaspora, but also to modernism, nation-state modernity, and indeed the wandering Jew as a central figure within that. If Judaism itself always imagined refuge as the end to diaspora, this was foreclosed in modernist narratives of the wandering Jew, which paradoxically made the term of racist attack into a secularized cosmopolitan virtue. Gil Anidjar in his "Mal de Sionisme (Zionist Fever)" writes:

> [Z]ionism is also the *end* of Judaism, bringing about a "new Jew," or what Benjamin Beit-Hallami has more pointedly called "the anti-Jew," who is both more and less Jewish than the Jew (the "new Jew" as opposed to the exilic "old Jew"), or simply *no longer* Jewish. Following a strict logic of the supplement, Zionism simultaneously adds to and substitutes for Judaism. To the extent that it calls for the end of exile (the Zionist concept of "negation of exile, *shilat ha-galut*"), to the extent that it embodies what Levinas has described as a way of "escaping or renouncing the fact of diaspora," Zionism also has a profoundly negative, even destructive, rapport with Judaism, a rapport that asserts itself most forcefully in the polemical rhetoric that repeatedly equates the Jews with the state of Israel (a state that continues to refer to itself as "the State of the Jewish people" in its entirety), thus claiming to represent them, but also substituting for them, putting itself instead of them—in a way that is not entirely devoid of menacing echoes—*after* them.[14]

Netta van Vliet, in her *Differend of Israel*, also writes of the contradictory nature of Israel—simultaneously a Jewish state and a modern liberal state—addressing the difficulty of bringing together two notions that stand in contradiction to each other and that confuse how the state is understood. In addition, *contra* Anidjar, she suggests that

Zionism has *not* substituted Israel for the Jews, or replaced the Old Jew with the New Jew, but rather, even if unintentionally, continually brings the two together—in many different ways. For her, Israeli Zionism insisted on being both a liberal democracy (with universal citizenry) and Jewish at the same time, marking the difference between them but also making them inseparable. If for her the Jew is supplementary to the Israeli, it highlights the problem of difference for the modern state form, which then points to the blindness to sexual difference that is revealed in the modern state form through the example, and indeed the exemplary nature, of Israel.[15]

The *differend* elaborated in van Vliet's argument could be characterized in Miriam Leonard's terms as a further elaboration of the division between Athens and Jerusalem, or the figurative relation that is set up from Roman times to the present between the Greek and the Jew from Tertullian to James Joyce: between Hellenism and Hebraism, Christianity and paganism, rationality and irrationality, secularism and religion. The geographical binary points toward a quintessential difference, one could say: the sexual difference. The oft-quoted line from James Joyce's *Ulysses* highlights the blind spot to difference as encapsulated within sexual difference—"Women's reason: Jewgreek is Greekjew. Extremes meet." While Leonard reads this quite rightly as referring to an idea of women's irrationality, one could also say that, like Molly's final soliloquy, it opens to a form of a yet to be realized feminine difference that became so important for Derrida and for Cixous's *écriture féminine*—the novel *Vivre l'Orange*, to live the orange, or to live Oran/Iran—and which plays indeed also with the sense of internal exile from a site of belonging, Oran-I, Oran-je, which is a form of acknowledging that one's nation, far from being an unqualified sanctuary, leaves one open to the whims of state sovereignty. We could understand this autobiographically as being a Jew in Oran, Algeria during the moment of the abrogation of French citizenship for Jews during the Vichy regime. Adam Stein recognizes this well when he says, speculating on the use of the term "soap" in Israel which, far from cleanliness, designates finishing someone off or the figure who deserves to be finished off through reference to rumors of Nazi soap made of Jews: "*If I am a bar of soap in the country of sanctuary, then I have come home.*"[16]

Leopold Bloom is the quintessential wandering Jew of literary modernism. It is a commonplace that modernism in general, and *Ulysses* in particular, is concerned with exile and alienation.[17] When the category of exile is debated, it is usually in the context of what type of exile, whether forced or chosen, whether it is actual or metaphorical (as discussed in Hélène Cixous's monumental *The Exile of James Joyce*) or, in the words of Robert reporting on Richard in Joyce's play Exiles, "economic" or "spiritual." Richard reads Robert's description of him:

> There are those who left her [our country] to seek the bread by which men live and there are others, nay, her most favored children, who left her to seek in other lands that food of the spirit by which a nation of human beings is sustained in life … those who left her in her hour of need.[18]

But even in *Ulysses*, the iconic text of literary modernism, the theoretical category of asylum is a useful one for addressing the text and, indeed, the relevant period of literature.

If Erich Auerbach begins and ends his *Mimesis* with odysseys—a discussion of Homer in the first chapter, and brief interludes on Joyce's *Ulysses* in his final chapter on Virginia Woolf—it is implicitly to mark the different formation of notions of exile in the history of what he understands as European literature.[19] Homer's *Odyssey* introduces the history of the world through an everyman, Odysseus, and the gods who have intervened in his history. While the epic is ostensibly about the exilic travels of Odysseus as he returns from the Trojan war, Auerbach reminds us that another temporal framework is represented, not as memory but as a temporality which is different from that of the main narrative. Odysseus becomes more typical and at the same time more specifically individuated with these tales about his and the others' pasts being narrated. While Auerbach maintains that Joyce continues to explore an everyman figure, he acknowledges the continued emphasis on particular localization. The very difficulty of Joyce's *Ulysses*, for Auerbach, is the wandering minds of many different narrative voices, which are exiled from themselves temporally by the intrusion of memories. But they are also exiled from each other by the marked separation of their worlds in spite of their specific context in Dublin. The exile then is not simply identified in the fact of Bloom the wandering Jew, necessarily an outsider, or Stephen the wandering Bard, but also as exiles unto themselves, contained within a shared space.

In the tense Circe section of *Ulysses*, Bloom, and then the others, literalize or demetaphorize situational conflict through the gendered discussion of refuges and mental asylums. They highlight the lesser mobility of women and their "confinement" of various sorts—"Rescue of fallen women Magdalen asylum"—or the outcasting of sexual normativity through Mulligan's "Dr. Bloom is bisexually abnormal. He has recently escaped from Dr Eustace's private asylum for demented gentlemen."[20]

We see another form of demetaphorization in the idea of Ireland's anti-Semitism being revealed through the lack of asylum for the Jews, and in such forms of structural conflict as that of the anonymous narrator in Cyclops, who becomes the wandering "no man" from *The Odyssey*, returning to haunt after he has been tricked and is full of the resentments of the land, of family, and of the stasis afforded by the bitter political divisions in the city. The character named The Citizen sits with his dog, called Garryowen, occasionally giving it something to eat.[21] He taunts Bloom for being a Jew while Garryowen growls at him and sniffs him, which initiates commentary about the smell of Jews:

> —And I belong to a race too, says Bloom, that is hated and persecuted. Also now. This very moment. This very instant.
> Gob, he near burnt his fingers with the butt of his old cigar.
> —Robbed, says he. Plundered. Insulted. Persecuted. Taking what belongs to us by right. At this very moment, says he, putting up his fist, sold by auction off in Morocco like slaves or cattles.
> —Are you talking about the new Jerusalem? says the citizen.
> —I'm talking about injustice, says Bloom.[22]

Ulysses becomes then a text of confinement and political tension as much as one of exile and alienated transcendence. And addressing injustice becomes a secularized labor of love precisely because a space and a name and the status of citizen are not, for Bloom, sufficient to counteract that injustice. The Jew, who in *Ulysses* carries the trace of the non-human, here exemplified through this discussion of smell, casts doubt on Irish Republican (and indeed any) nationalist discourse.

Classically, dogs recognize man when they know him to be their master. This is the lesson of Argos's recognition of Odysseus in *The Odyssey*. In the final Penelope section, Argos sees his master approaching. Weakened and soiled, he momentarily perks up when he sees Odysseus, who sheds a tear for him. And Argos, satisfied at their apparent mutual recognition, dies. Rather like the dog Levinas names Bobby, a dog who Levinas suggests may be the child of the child of the child, etc. of Argos; Argos may be the first great Kantian. Levinas suggests that Bobby, a scrawny dog who "survived in some wild patch in the region of the camp" in a forestry commando unit for Jewish prisoners in Nazi Germany in which Levinas was confined with 70 others, "was the last Kantian in Nazi Germany, without the brain needed to universalize maxims or drives."[23] In *Ulysses*, the relation between man and dog is presented otherwise; Garryowen seems to smell the trace of the animal in Bloom, the not-yet-man, or at least, the not-yet-citizen that is this modern wandering everyman.

But to return, then, from the scent to the name. Bobby, Levinas said, was "an exotic name" given "as one does with dogs." Already in *Adam Resurrected*, the reader is faced with the irony of name and the treatment of name as ironic. If Adam names himself Adam, it is in the same gesture as Commandant Klein called his dog Rex:

> Adam is a nice name. The Indians called the first man *Manu*, which means the master of intentions and great and occult ideas. The Greeks, who invented logic, who invented democracy with the help of slaves, and the modern sewage system and drama, they called man *anthropos*: in other words, the observer from above. The Romans called him *homo*, the talking animal. The Hebrew called him *Adam*, after the material—the earth or *adamah*—out of which he was fashioned, in the name of his inherited fault or infirmity, the blood coursing through him toward life and death.[24]

Adam is far from man, and Rex is far from the King, but like the King he is both before and outside the law, the beast and the sovereign.[25] Rather than establishing his being or his dignity, the name Rex rather poses the question of whether such a king can decide to make an exception to let Adam live or die (Argos begat Rex; Rex begat Adam; Adam begat David).

Years later, Adam, while in the asylum in the Negev, encounters a dog-child survivor who is brought there. The dog-child, or child-dog, who is either incarcerated in the asylum or is a symptom of Adam's trauma (or perhaps both), also plays a decisive role in Adam's life. As the dog-child seems to become more human and less dog, in part thanks to Adam's efforts to relate to him, Adam is depleted, and nears a self-induced death. He mourns the dog and seeks its trace in a typewriter he gives the dog-child to play with. The dog-child thus plays with the technology of modernity before he even speaks. He is forced by two lunatics—Adam, and Wolfowitz the Circumciser—to name himself with the typewriter. As if explaining the book's title—in Hebrew, *Adam ben Kelev* means Man, Son of Dog—he is forced to the typewriter as technology becomes, however paradoxically, less the instrument of modernity and less the means to humanity, and more the trace of the inhuman within the name it produces. Like *Ulysses*, which plays with the GOD-DOG linguistic inverse, it seems that God in the novel, and therefore the origin of all things, may have ultimately been the product of a typo rather than anything more profound. In the beginning was the word, and the word was DOG.

Writing then is always prior to speech in the way that the inhuman is always before and beyond the human. Tapping on the typewriter, the dog-child seeks to write himself into existence. Or, if he does not seek to do this, his existence may be a by-product of his play turned into labor. The name confers more and less on Garryowen, Bobby, or Argos in their masculinist parthenogenetic creation than the dog who is outside the confines of the law, who is *animot*, to use Derrida's term—a word, a non-being, that signifies without the specificity of species or sex—the trace of life, one could say.[26]

> [W]ith the first trace of the thinking of the trace in *Of Grammatology*, the whole machine that tends to replace the word "writing" in the ordinary sense by "trace" or the word "speech" by trace, had as its final purpose that writing, speech, trace are *not the proper characteristic of the human*. There is animal trace, animals write. From the beginning, the deconstruction of the *properly human*, and thus of its empire, its right, is in place. Jacques Derrida has always resisted the opposition between the human and the animal, just as he does the opposition and thus the hierarchization between man and woman; this is the absolutely permanent, archoriginary trait of his political trajectory.[27]

The inhuman trace remains even as the production of man through the technology of the typewriter is also the production of citizen. And yet, what form of injustice can be addressed by this citizen, to bring Bloom's question to the dog?

Adam has a twin brother Herbert who lives inside him, appearing on windowsills, observing him as if he were the rational super-ego that has come to taunt with his philosophical training, his mockery of Adam's clowning, his supercilious cruel professors, and his *Introduction to Ethical Theory*. All this comes with a refusal to acknowledge Adam the dog as anything other than a charlatan. The birth of the state and the birth of the asylum are conducted by foreign powers with their own idea of an ethical sense of future refuge. While on one level the gestures are philanthropic, the novel shows how they create their own forms of injustice through naming.

The mental asylum in the Negev desert is not only a tool for showing the madness that ensues after the Holocaust, and the need to restore some kind of post-traumatic order. It also exemplifies the insanity of the state and the state-form dictating that an ingathering can or should be a benign solution to the trauma and injustice of the final solution. The chief doctor, Dr. Gross, who is fascinated by Adam, admits an inability to cure him, and the apparent health of the final chapters is by no means assurance of anything. Characters can predict their own deaths to the minute, can continue to think of Adam as a sign of hope, and doctors and nurses alike can be enamored by Adam's sometimes murderous charms. Adam himself carries the trace of a dog within him, is aroused by the idea of sex in a dog's presence, or doggy sex with crowns adorning him and his sexual partner, nurse Jenny. He never addresses fully the charm and violence of his own masculinism, and neither does the novel itself address adequately the loss of the feminine that leads to the patrilineal parthenogenesis of dog-children.

The dog-child typist becomes part of the masculinist technology of the state when his random typing begins to produce words infinitely more mature and sexist than in his youth, as if he too, like Adam, accounts for his survivor's guilt by taking it out in the pleasure and pain of sexual encounter and violence. Adam also sees himself as a potential victim of sexual violence. And—together with the gang rape, real or imagined, of the Schwester twin by Bedouins, the dead Ruth and the attempted murder of another Ruth—these forms of sexual violence speak to a sense that there is little hope of reproduction outside of a masculinist parthenogenesis. About all these acts of violence against women nothing can really be said: "I didn't know what to say to the Schwester sisters when I parted from them. We gazed at one another with enormous sadness. But we did not cry. We didn't mention what had happened. We didn't mention the desert and God's revelation."[28] As if the violation of women in the novel is only a reminder that woman does not exist, we see her trace perhaps in the inhuman.

> The dog is a prisoner in the world of paradise, the machine world of Olivetti. Mr Olivetti, do you know that a certain dog in the Institute for Rehabilitation and Therapy in Arad is playing Satan's requiem on you? Mr Olivetti, I salute you from far away, from Arad, from the outdoors, from the desert. By the way, do I have a face? I'm looking at the dog now, is his face mine? Is my face the portion of suffering which explodes in his face of sunshine? What a fantastic match, like the old days: Rex and Adam, the dogs of Ilse Koch and Commandant Klein.... What passion! I once saw a woman like that, Klein's wife, in bed.... Why was she so hungry? Because of the odor of burned bones ?... And she wanted to believe that everything would change after dedicating one night to a dog.... And he? My Klein? He's alive and will yet live ... became a Jew. There is no justice in the world. Only my child is just. My dog. His fingers hover.... The sight of those fingers worshipping that cold Olivetti is somewhat endearing and human, perhaps also noble and warm. Who made this Olivetti? Other Olivettis, foreign Olivettis, made this Olivetti. Olivetti begat Olivetti who begat Olivetti who begat Olivetti.... "*I am* a dog! Adam screams. That's what you never understood. Herbert, my brother ... despite all your studies ... and Hobbes with his dog-eat-dogism, man-be-wolfism, and Rousseau and Leibniz and your Hegel and Kant ... you never understood that you were—that is, I was—a dog."[29]

Reading the novel with and against Levinas's "The Name of a Dog, or Natural Rights," about Bobby the dog, shows the banality of being a Kantian in the face of disposable life. What kind of futurity is imagined out of the form of dignity Levinas describes? What form of hospitality for a new future will leave uncompromised the trace of difference manifested in the different peoples, themselves displaced by the establishment of this asylum state?

The question is then begged: How does one say "I am Adam," "I am human," or indeed "I am animal," "I am Jew"? Derrida's work on both Judaism and the animal gives a partial answer. And why the necessity to claim the proper names and proper nouns of patrilineal descent and the properties and property which come with that? In *The Animal that therefore I am, (More to Follow)*, Derrida elaborates on the dubious status of statements of identification through an extrapolation of the "*Je suis*" or, the "more to follow." While "*Je suis*" means both "I am" and "I follow," and "more to follow" suggests a continuation of a line, they also refer to the non-presence of the I, the insistence of its past and its future (and its smell?) that haunt, such that being is opened by non-being, belonging is undone by non-belonging, and human always carries the trace of the inhuman.

In "Abraham, the Other," Derrida writes of the difficulty of claiming the name Jew for himself:

> And to speak honorably of this word jew—and by honorably I mean measuring oneself by way of what is worthy of that name or that adjective in the audible and visible forms of its syllables.... –the *j* and the *oui* (yes) of *juif* between the *suis* (am) of *je suis* (I am), *je suis juif* (I am jew), the *juste* (barely, only, just; or: righteous, just).... One would have to appeal to a force of poetic invention and memory, to a power of invention *like* the boldness of anamnesis.[30]

As Derrida himself writes, when asked to address issues related to Judaism, he almost always responds autobiographically, with all the complexities of the *je suis* enfolded into that. He reminds one of the literary repressed of Molly Bloom, whose own Sephardic Jewish background through matrilineal descent buried beneath the Roman Catholic also provides the possibility of pleasure in the "Yes," and the "I come" *Je jouis* of her final words. He writes of his childhood in Algeria and of the history of Jews in Algeria who were given citizenship in 1870 thanks to the Crémieux decrees.

Adolphe Crémieux was a French Jewish lawyer, who secured citizenship for Jews during his time in the national defense. Crémieux was also the founder of the French organization Alliance Israélite Universelle in 1860 and ran it until his death in 1880. The organization, later directed by Levinas, focused on the education and professional advancement of Jews, and set up schools, some of which still remain.[31] Derrida writes movingly of his relationship to the catholicized language of Judaism in the Algeria of his youth, circumcision which itself is bound to the cut within the autobiographical utterance, and the trauma of Jewish children like himself being expelled from schools during the Vichy regime as a consequence of a French decision rather than a German one. For him, then, the name "Jew" always carries with it the trace of modern European colonialism, as will the Holocaust and Zionism.

Herzl could imagine his Zion after the legal battle of Dreyfus with something like a belief in the possibility of representation and citizenship. Hannah Arendt could formulate her understanding of justice and evil through the Eichmann trial, noting the compromised form of victor's justice, and the problem of jurisdiction. She could not formulate a notion of a new polity, with speaking animals as Adam might say. Derrida will develop his own sense of justice partly through the Klaus Barbie trial.

These three trials of anti-Semitic violence have thus given rise to diverse notions of the just. Derrida, in "Force of Law," famously refers to Jacques Vergès, Barbie's infamous defense lawyer. The aporias of justice and the law, forms of exception and decision are theorized only with brief gestures toward Vergès. However, Derrida clearly states his admiration for the sovereign decision to put French law on trial, showing the manner in which victor's justice leads to a blindness in colonial law and in postcolonial amnesia. Vergès famously cut his teeth in Algeria where he defended Djamila Bouhired. He was critical of the amnesia that was sought following the Evian Accords whereby those involved in the struggle were not brought to trial for their acts.

Alice Kaplan's fascinating essay on Alain Finkielkraut's *Remembering in Vain*, an analysis of the Barbie Trial, forcefully shows how the notion of temporality at stake in Vergès defense was the source of such tremendous vitriol in France.[32] She explains that Barbie was tried under the law of Crimes Against Humanity, a French law that has no statute of limitations. This allowed Vergès to make a theatrical performance. Crimes brought to trial in 1987 allegedly committed during World War II were interpreted through the lens of the Algerian War (1954–62) and the Evian Accords from 1962. The contradiction in the French legal system—the fact that Barbie could be tried, but no French officer could be tried for his part in the Algerian war—showed that the whole system of law, with its claims to authority from pre-existing laws while turning a blind eye to contradiction, was flawed. His show trial, or legal rupture strategy, takes its inspiration from literary trials, and the theatrical trials of former years.[33] The colonial trace is clearly, within Vergès' logic, the inhuman trace articulated in the terms of crimes against humanity. His argument is similar to that of Aimé Césaire in *Discourse on Colonialism*:

> Yes, it would be worthwhile to study clinically, in detail, the steps taken by Hitler and Hitlerism and to reveal to the very distinguished, very humanistic, very Christian bourgeois of the twentieth century that without his being aware of it, he has a Hitler inside him, that Hitler inhabits him, that Hitler is his *demon*, that if he rails against him, he is being inconsistent and that, at bottom, what he cannot forgive Hitler for is not *crime* in itself, *the crime against man*, it is not *the humiliation of man as such*, it is the crime against the white man, the humiliation of the white man, and the fact that he applied to Europe colonialist procedures which until then had been reserved exclusively for the Arabs of Algeria, the coolies of India, and the blacks of Africa.
>
> And that is the great thing I hold against pseudo-humanism: that for too long it has diminished the rights of man, that its concept of those rights has been— and still is—narrow and fragmentary, incomplete and biased and, all things considered, sordidly racist.[34]

Vergès works then within the time frame of memory and the literary rather than in the legal time frame of most lawyers.

If Herzl sought a new state following Dreyfus, and Arendt a new Aristotelian polity that would not rest on the form of victor's justice she saw in the Eichmann trial, then Derrida would understand the political through that which haunts, the trace, the inhuman, the feminine, the Jew, the Algerian, in such a way that doubt is shed on any cohesive idea of community: Dreyfus begat Herzl; Eichmann begat Arendt begat Butler and Agamben. Barbie and Bouhired begat Vergès: Molly and Vergès begat Cixous and Derrida. Both the literary and the legal do the work of questioning the constitution of something as human and put it alongside the more prosaic and the less transcendental figurations that sometimes ensue or are presumed. There is no question of the human or of species without a question of sexual difference embedded within it, and without the repressed story of feminine labor. Futurity in the asylum marks sexual difference as the *ur*-category of difference erased through the foundational violence of patrilineal descent. There can be no adequate species-thought without acknowledging the economy of the same—the androcentric same—that persists. Thinking in asylum and planetary terms, the figure coming into the mental asylum or seeking political asylum becomes human through a process of becoming subject—forced into a recognizable form as if the inhuman state of being before those laws, and indeed after them, could be erased.[35]

Notes

1. Jacques Derrida, "Abraham, The Other" in eds. Bergo, Cohenm Zagury-Orly, *Judeities: Questions for Jacques Derrida* (New York: Fordham Unversity Press, 2007) 15.
2. Yoram Kaniuk, *Adam Resurrected* translated by Seymour Simckes (New York: Grove Press, 1971) 218-9.
3. There is some debate as to how catalytic the Dreyfus affair was in Herzl's publishing trajectory. However, given that he was a journalist for the *Neue Freie Presse* in Paris at the time, the trial certainly had some impact. For a good sense of the climate around the Dreyfus affair, see Ruth Harris, *The Man on Devil's Island: Alfred Dreyfus and the Affair That Divided France* (London: Allen Lane, 2010).
4. Theodor Herzl, *The Jewish State; An Attempt at a Modern Solution of the Jewish Question* (New York: American Zionist Emergency Council, 1946).
5. See Steven Zipperstein's *Elusive Prophet: Ahad Ha'am and the Origins of Zionism* (Berkeley: University of California Press, 1993) for more on this debate.
6. See Hannah Arendt, *The Origins of Totalitarianism* (New York: Harcourt, 1994); Aimé Césaire, *Discourse on Colonialism* (New York: Monthly Review Press, 2000).
7. See Arendt, *Origins*, 280.
8. This is somewhat different from the view held by Jean-Paul Sartre and so many thinkers of the mid- and late twentieth century who saw the figure of the Jew as a purely figurative form. Jean-Paul Sartre insisted on the Jew being a product of notions of him from the outside in *Anti-Semite and Jew* (New York: Schocken Books, 1948); and such ideas are commented upon usefully in Levinas's "Existentialisme et antisemitisme," *Les cahiers de l'Alliance israélite universelle*, 14–15 (June/July 1947): 2–3; Derrida's "Abraham, the Other" in Bettina Bergo, Joseph Cohen, and Raphael Zagury-Orly (eds), *Judeities: Questions for Jacques Derrida* (New York: Fordham University Press, 2007), 1–35 and in Emmanuel Levinas, "Être juif," *Confluences*, 15–17 (1947). On this topic, see also Sarah Hammerschlag, *The Figural Jew: Politics and Identity in Postwar French Thought* (Chicago, IL: The University of Chicago Press, 2010).
9. Kaniuk, *Adam Resurrected*, 50.

10 Kaniuk, *Adam Resurrected*, 51–2.
11 I have elaborated further on this in "Indignity," *Positions* 16:1 (2008): 39–77, and "Asylum," *Texas International Law Journal* 41:3 (2006): 471–90.
12 I am indebted to Rosalind Morris's extrapolation of the distinctions between the hereditary and inheritance in her forthcoming book.
13 I am thinking here through Paul de Man's "Anthropomorphism, and Trope in the Lyric" in *The Rhetoric of Romanticism* (New York: Columbia University Press, 1984), 239–62; and Barbara Johnson's "Anthropomorphism in Lyric and Law," *Yale Journal of Law and the Humanities* 549 (1998).
14 Gil Anidjar, "Mal de Sionisme (Zionist Fever)" in ed. Elisabeth Weber, *Living Together: Jacques Derrida's Communities of Violence and Peace* (New York: Fordham, 2012) 49–50.
15 Netta van Vliet, unpublished PhD dissertation, "The Differend of Israel," July 2012, Duke University.
16 Kaniuk, *Adam Resurrected*, 133. See also *Vivre l'Orange* (Paris: des femmes, 1979).
17 Joyce, *Ulysses* (Hollywood, FL: Simon and Brown, 2013).
18 Joyce, *Exiles. With the Author's Notes and an Introduction by Padraic Column* (London: Granada Publishing, repr. 1983), 126–7. See also Hélène Cixous, *The Exile of James Joyce* (New York: D. Lewis, 1972).
19 Erich Auerbach, *Mimesis: The Representation of Reality in Western Literature* (Princeton, NJ: Princeton University Press, 1953).
20 Joyce, *Ulysses*, 434.
21 Garryowen, literally the garden of John, refers to a place outside Limerick in Ireland which was a hospital outside the city walls.
22 Joyce, *Ulysses*, 285.
23 Emmanuel Levinas, *Difficult Freedom*, trans. Sean Hand (Baltimore, MD: Johns Hopkins University Press, 1990), 153.
24 Kaniuk, *Adam Resurrected*, 217.
25 Jacques Derrida, *The Beast and the Sovereign* Vols 1 & 2 (translated by Geoffrey Bennington) (Chicago: University of Chicago Press, 2011).
26 Jacques Derrida, *The Animal That Therefore I Am*; see also Anne Berger and Marta Segara (eds), *Demenageries: Thinking of Animals after Derrida* (Amsterdam: Rodopi, 2011).
27 Hélène Cixous, "Co-Responding Voix You," *Derrida and the Time of the Political*, 43.
28 Kaniuk, *Adam Resurrected*, 367.
29 Ibid., 201, 204.
30 Derrida, "Abraham, the Other."
31 For more on the Alliance, see Jean-Claude Kuperminc, "L'alliance israe(acute)lite universelle en Algerie," in *Juifs d'Algerie presentee au Musee d'art et d'histoire du Judaisme* (2012; Skira Flammarion, Paris), 219–21. Interestingly, Emmanuel Levinas was to become director of the Ecole Normale Orientale of the Alliance Israelite Universelle in Paris in the 1930s.
32 Alice Kaplan, "On Alain Finkielkraut's 'Remembering in Vain': The Klaus Barbie Trial and Crimes against Humanity," *Critical Inquiry* 19 (1992): 70–86.
33 See Jacques Derrida, "Force of Law"; Jacques Vergès, *Justice et Littérature* (Paris: PUF, 2011).
34 Aimé Césaire, *Discourse on Colonialism* (New York: Monthly Review Press), 36–7.
35 Thank you to Netta Van Vliet for commenting on an earlier version of this chapter.

9

The Hermeneutical Stance
Being Discharged at the Margins of Political Zionism

Santiago Zabala

The point is not simply to scatter geographically, but to derive a set of principles from scattered existence that can serve a new conception of political justice. That conception would entail a fair doctrine on the rights of refugees and a critique of nationalist modes of state violence that sustain the occupation, land confiscation, and the political imprisonment and exile of Palestinians. It would also imply a notion of cohabitation whose condition of emergence would be the end of settler colonialism. More generally formulated, it is on the basis of this conception of cohabitation that the critique of illegitimate nation-state violence can and must be waged—with no exceptions.

Judith Butler, Parting Ways, 2012

Hermeneutics, similar to deconstruction, is one of the few philosophical positions that often prompt their followers to side politically; that is, running the risk of making unforgettable civil errors. It is interesting to note how the philosopher who stressed for the first time his ontological stance is also the one who made an unforgettable political mistake: Martin Heidegger. Although the German master is not the only great philosopher in history to support a racist political ideology, he is certainly the first who comes to mind when analyzing, as we will do here, the ontological features of existence at the margins of political Zionism. Even though Heidegger had several Jewish friends and refused to ratify the dismissal of two anti-Nazi deans when he was Rector of the University of Freiburg in 1933,[1] being a member of the Nazi regime was something he remained ashamed of for the rest of his life. But to suggest, as Emmanuel Faye does, that all his writings "spread the radically racist and human life-destroying conceptions that make up the foundation of Hitlerism and Nazism"[2] is exaggerated and inaccurate. The fact that brilliant philosophers such as Hannah Arendt, Jacques Derrida, and Rainer Schürmann have developed the German master's conceptions without spreading hate is an indication that Faye was either assuming that racism is necessarily a feature of counter-Enlightenment or serving political Zionism's interest to keep anti-Semitism alive by all means.[3]

As it turns out, it is quite possible that the French intellectual was following both of the above-mentioned ideologies, bearing in mind that they belong to metaphysics; that is, the forgetfulness of Being in favor of beings. Nonetheless, Heidegger continues to be an easy political target in our intellectual world: he was Rector of the University of Freiburg in 1933 (for 11 months), criticized humanism's ontic meaning (in his exchange with Jean-Paul Sartre), and even had an affair with a Jewess (Hannah Arendt) who would later oppose the creation of the State of Israel.[4] If many contemporary Heideggerian scholars defend or are even glad he made this mistake, it is not because (as many believe) they are also racist, but rather because this discourages intellectuals from developing and furthering his philosophy.

This brief chapter is not interested in defending Heidegger or pointing out how many leftist thinkers he inspired, but rather in justifying the hermeneutical stance in favor of Palestinians and Jews in their existential conflict against political Zionism. While Palestinians are marginalized behind concrete walls, Jews (such as Noam Chomsky, Ilan Pappé, or Idith Zertal) must face an epistemological wall of dismissal, hate, and humiliation for their opposition to political Zionism. Even though the ontic consequences of the wall have finally begun to receive attention,[5] their ontological status has too often been disregarded. Being, once again, has been ignored in favor of beings. If Heidegger's ontological revolution was meant to redirect philosophy's attention toward Being, it is not for theoretical reasons as many believe, but rather for ethical ones: we are Being, not beings. The fact that today so much of Being is discharged (ignored, exploited, or left outside main conceptual frames) is a consequence of metaphysics, which can be overcome only if ontology becomes the point of departure, rather than of arrival, for philosophical investigation. Similarly to Judith Butler's scatteredness, the discharge of Being also aims toward a "political justice" of "cohabitation,"[6] but instead of belonging to a particular religious belief, it embraces numerous religions, cultures, and races. In sum, those discharged belong to the tradition of the oppressed, weak, and losers of history whose main concern has always been to strive for existence. Hermeneutic stance is not only *for* the weak, but, as we will see, *of* the weak. Before justifying this stance however, it is important to outline the ontological nature of the discharge in relation to political Zionism's metaphysical consequences.

Being discharged is not an exclusive existential condition of those who oppose political Zionism, but rather one in which the majority of the world population find themselves due to metaphysically framed (economic, religious, or civil) policies. These frames secure the correct functioning of the system for the bearers of power; that is, those interested in preserving their privileged condition. While Western democracies conserve liberal states by neutralizing political alternatives[7] and capitalism protects financial markets by creating recessions,[8] political Zionism confiscates lands in the name of true Judaism. As we know, political Zionism not only claims to represent all Jewish people, but also issues a call to return to Zion, standing for the Land of Israel in general, a return which, as Michael Marder explains in his contribution to this collection (Chapter 10), is impossible, since it "negates its very contextual embeddedness, annulling the place-ness of place as such."[9] But in order to impose these frames, Being must be interpreted as the presence of something that is present; that is, objectively. In this way, as Heidegger explained in *Being and Time*, any determination or justification of Being will depend upon its reduction and correspondence to beings; that is, in its representation. Just as democracy and capitalism claim to represent the best possible political and economic system, representing the end of history as Francis Fukuyama put it, political Zionism claims to represent the rightful owners of the Land of Israel regardless of the differences that exist on the ground. The problem with this metaphysical configuration, also named "realism" in contemporary philosophy, is not only that the ontological difference is obscured, but also that truth becomes a violent imposition that will inevitably discard, marginalize, and ignore anyone who does not belong, accept, or believe in its necessity. After decades of violent neoliberal capitalism and political Zionism, we are thus left with 80 percent of humanity living on less than $10 a day and with approximately 22 percent of former Palestine unfairly distributed between Gaza, the West Bank, and East Jerusalem. As a result, these populations are marginalized; that is, existentially discharged from the current world order.

In spite of these violent impositions, Being is not annulled but rather weakened to the point where, as Heidegger said, "within metaphysics there is nothing to Being as such";[10] that is, it becomes "the most worn-out."[11] But this does not mean that Being as a marginalized remnant ceases to exist; quite the contrary: it opens up a possibility of emancipation from metaphysics.[12] If "Being remains constantly available to us,"[13] it is not thanks to its strength but through its weakness; that is, its condition of being marginalized and discharged. A condition we must "guard" at all times, considering it is the only available alternative to the imposed political, economic, or national realism.

As Derrida pointed out,

> The remainder *is* not, it is not a Being, not a modification of that which is. Like the trace, the remaining offers itself for thought before or beyond Being. It is inaccessible to a straightforward intuitive perception (since it refers to something wholly other, it inscribes in itself something of the infinitely other), and it escapes all forms of prehension, all forms of monumentalization, and all forms of archivation. Often, like the trace, I associate it with ashes: remains without a substantial remainder, essentially, but which have to be taken account of and without which there would be neither accounting nor calculation, nor a principle of reason able to give an account or a rationale (*reddere rationem*), nor a Being as such. That is why there are *remainder effects*, in the sense of a result or a present, idealizable, ideally iterable residue.[14]

Heidegger's "worn out" Being is not very different from Derrida's remainders; both refer to the ignored existence that seems to have become "inaccessible to a straightforward intuitive perception." As it turns out, such precarious existence is not only accessible but is also a real possibility for those who do not function within framed democracies or who oppose Zionist politics. Its main feature is to strive for existence at the margins of capitalism or Israel; that is, in the slums that represent more than three-quarters of the world population and in Gaza. Although people are not forced in the same manner into the slums of Los Angeles or Gaza, they nonetheless have to face walls, which are not only meant to safeguard the functioning of the economico-political system, but most of all to keep out the discharged Being. Together with Palestinians, who have been violently marginalized and ignored, are those Jews, like the American political scientist Norman Finkelstein, who oppose political Zionism. Finkelstein, of course, has been denied tenure after teaching for six years at DePaul University and publishing acclaimed historical investigations of political Zionism's manipulation of the Holocaust.[15] Although his case cannot be compared to that of the Palestinian victims of Zionism, it is worth noting the similarity in the walls they face. As Arendt predicted, political Zionism has not only reinforced nationalism but has also created a kind of "statelessness" for an ever-increasing population, which also includes Jews.

In sum, political Zionism does not only represent "the massive dispossessions of Palestinians in 1948, the appropriation of land in 1967, and the recurrent confiscations of Palestinian lands that continues now with the building of the wall and the expansion of settlements,"[16] but also the discharge of Being. If Being must remain discharged from the standpoint of Zionist nationalists who can then proceed with their programs of occupation and segregation, then philosophy has the obligation to retrieve its remainders. But why is the hermeneutical stance suitable for advancing claims in favor of the discharge of Being?

As the philosophy of interpretation, where truth is a consequence rather than the cause of its own interpretations, hermeneutics is not concerned with facts, but rather with those beings who must submit to them. This is why throughout its history it has often provided the possibility for the oppressed beliefs and discredited positions to emancipate from the bearers of power. Contrary to descriptive philosophies driven by *theoria* in an attempt to conserve or impose a seemingly objective status quo, hermeneutics is motivated by an active *technē* in order to interpret differently. But who needs different interpretations?

Interpretation is often required by those who are at the margins of the scientific, religious, or political establishments—the "weak," the "discharged," or the "losers of history," as Walter Benjamin would say. However, history not only continues at the margins but is actually the realm where Being strives to existence. This is probably why Mike Davis emphasized in the *Planet of Slums* how slums are not simply run-down areas characterized by waste deposits, substandard housing, and spreading insecurity, but also living "populations"[17] that must be recognized precisely as living or existing. The needs of these marginal populations have been often ignored, since they fail to measure up to the frames around them, the frames of the imposed truth. As we mentioned above, these are the beings whose existence (Being) is discharged and must be recovered from forgetfulness, marginalization, and the slums. This is probably why Heidegger stressed that hermeneutics is not interested in

> taking cognizance of something and having knowledge about it, but rather an existential knowing, i.e., a being [*ein sein*]. It speaks from out of interpretation and for the sake of it ... as far as I am concerned, if this personal comment is

permitted, I think that hermeneutics is not philosophy at all, but in fact something preliminary which runs in advance of it and has its own reasons for being: what is at issue in it, what it all comes to, is not to become finished with it as quickly as possible, but rather to hold out in it as long as possible ... it wishes only to place an object which has fallen into forgetfulness before today's philosophers for their "well-disposed consideration."[18]

If hermeneutics is the philosophy *of* and *for* the discharged Being, it isn't only due to the "existential knowledge" it offers, concerning itself with ontological difference, but also because it is, itself, a "discharged discipline." Its origins are still an issue of dispute among historians: some situate the beginning in Aristotle's treatise *Peri hermeneias* (*De interpretatione*), others in Flacius, in *Clavis scripturae sacrae*, or later in the seventeenth century when Johann Dannhauer introduced for the first time the Latin word "*hermeneutica*" as a necessary requirement for those sciences that relied on the interpretation of texts. In addition, the fact that Hermes (the messenger of the gods renowned for his speed, athleticism, and swiftness, who exercised the practical activity of delivering the announcements, warnings, and prophecies of the gods of Olympus) was often accused of anarchy because the messages he transmitted were never accurate, is an indication that hermeneutics is unreliable as a discipline; after all, its inventory of topics spreads over many different cultural, historical, and intellectual contexts that render its framing in a philosophical position very difficult. This must be why Heidegger thinks that hermeneutics "runs in advance" of philosophy; that is, even before we begin to systemize our thought.

As we can see, interpretation is not philological or phenomenological as many believe, but rather ontological—concerned with the differences of existence itself. Butler recognizes this when she states that it isn't only the science of "how best to read religious texts, but how to read them in the present and how best to cross the temporal and geographical divides that characterize the conditions of their inception and their present applicability."[19] In this way hermeneutics sides with Palestinians and Jews against political Zionism in order to cross those divisions and frames that discharge, ignore, and make impossible our existence. Hermeneutics maintains interpretation possible and alive everywhere it is ignored or discharged because "Existence is never an 'object,' but rather Being—it is *there* only insofar as in each case a living 'is' it."[20] Seizing the right to interpret differently, the weak may emerge politically only if they are recognized as the discharged Being, or, in other words, the oppressed human beings. This is perhaps why Daniel Barenboim was so pleased when, after one of his concerts in Gaza City, a man told him: "We feel like the world has forgotten us. We receive aid supplies, and we're grateful for that. But the fact that you have come here with your orchestra gives us the feeling that we are human beings."[21]

Notes

1. G. Steiner, *Martin Heidegger* (Chicago, IL: The University of Chicago Press, 1991), 116–24.
2. E. Faye, *Heidegger: The Introduction of Nazism into Philosophy in Light of the Unpublished Seminars of 1933–1935*, trans. M. B. Smith (New Haven, CT: Yale University Press, 2009), 316. Faye is simply the latest study dedicated to Heidegger's Nazism, before him Victor Farias (*Heidegger And Nazism*, Philadelphia, PA: Temple University Press, 1991) and Tom Rockmore (*On Heidegger's Nazism and Philosophy*, Berkeley: University of California Press, 1991) have also tried to demonstrate the inevitable racist consequences of his philosophy.
3. Political Zionism has also used the Holocaust to justify its settlement. See N. Finkelstein, *The Holocaust Industry: Reflections on the Exploitation of Jewish Suffering* (London: Verso, 2000).
4. As Butler reminds us, although Arendt "was a Jew, she insisted that Israel ought *not* to be a Jewish state and thought its efforts to legitimate its claims to the land through state violence were racist forms of colonization that could only lead to permanent conflict." J. Butler, *Parting Ways: Jewishness and the Critique of Zionism* (New York: Columbia University Press, 2012), 35.
5. On the ontic condition of Palestinians see B. White, *Palestinians in Israel: Segregation, Discrimination and Democracy* (London: Pluto Press, 2011); I. Pappe, *The Ethnic Cleansing of Palestine* (Oxford: Oneworld, 2006); N. Chomsky and I. Pappe, *Gaza in Crisis: Reflections on Israel's War against the Palestinians*, ed. Frank Barat (Chicago, IL: Haymarket, 2011), and N. Finkelstein, *This Time We Went Too Far: Truth and Consequences of the Gaza Invasion* (New York: Or Books, 2010).
6. J. Butler, *Parting Ways: Jewishness and the Critique of Zionism* (New York: Columbia University Press, 2012), 118.
7. Political alternatives to the established neoliberal parties in the West are almost unfeasible. The Greeks were ask to vote again in 2012 since the first round did not comply with EU demands. How liberal states are imposed is exposed in G. Vattimo and S. Zabala, *Hermeneutic Communism* (New York: Columbia University Press, 2011), 51–8.
8. Financial recessions are created in order to implement unpopular reforms and render inevitable our capitalism system. See J. Stiglitz, "Global Crisis—Made in America," *Spiegel Online* (December 11, 2008).
9. See M. Marder (Chapter 10, this volume).
10. M. Heidegger, *Nietzsche*, trans. D. F. Krell (San Francisco, CA: Harper & Row, 1991), 3: 202.
11. M. Heidegger, *Basic Concepts*, trans. G. E. Aylesworth (Bloomington: Indiana University Press, 1993), 51.
12. The meaning of "remnant" and "remains" is outlined in S. Zabala, *The Remains of Being* (New York: Columbia University Press, 2009).
13. Heidegger, *Basic Concepts*, 51.
14. J. Derrida, *Paper Machine*, trans. R. Bowlby (Stanford, CA: Stanford University Press, 2005), 151–2.
15. N. Finkelstein, *The Holocaust Industry*.
16. J. Butler, *Parting Ways*, 2.
17. M. Davis, *Planet of Slums* (London: Verso: 2006), 201–2.

18 M. Heidegger, *Ontology: The Hermeneutics of Facticity*, trans. J. van Buren (Bloomington: Indiana University Press, 1999), 14–16.
19 J. Butler, *Parting Ways*, 11.
20 M. Heidegger, *Ontology: The Hermeneutics of Facticity*, 18.
21 Joachim Kronsbein and Bernhard Zand, "The Germans Are Prisoners of Their Past: Interview with Daniel Barenboim," in *Spiegel*, (also available June 6, 2012 on http://www.spiegel.de/international/world/spiegel-interview-with-daniel-barenboim-a-840129-2.html).

10

The Zionist Synecdoche

Michael Marder

> *The linguistic evil is total; it has no limit, first of all because it is entirely political. The evil stems from the fact that Zionists...do not understand the essence of language.*
>
> Jacques Derrida on Gershom Scholem, "The Eyes of Language," in *Acts of Religion*

A part for the whole: Rhetoric, representation, violence

A rhetorical figure, a strategy of political representation, an instrument of violence: here are the faces of the Zionist synecdoche. Indeed, these are the faces of Zionism as synecdoche, which means the substitution of a part for the whole (*pars pro toto*) in an unequal, if not fraudulent, exchange. Zion, a hill in the city of Jerusalem, is an over-determined, over-coded place that, instead of resting in its own semantic and physico-geographic confines, negates its very contextual embeddedness, annulling the place-ness of place as such. It is hardly possible to return to Zion, because Zion does not return, nor refer, to itself. Despite its presumed anchoring in the eternal, it is a highly mobile locale: it spreads centrifugally, displacing and imposing itself onto other places and subjects outside it, and, at the same time, draws people and events into itself, as though into a vortex. A radial point of several concentric circles, Zion stands, first, for the entire city along with its inhabitants, and, second, for the "Land of Israel." A name of excess, it is more than itself. If the areas outside Zion are—still or already—Zion, then this sacred, consecrated, separated, fetishized part, a part non-identical to itself, becomes equivalent to the whole and, in fact, convokes the idealized entity—be it the city or the country—into existence.

The semantic imperialism of the synecdoche matches its geopolitical expansionism. In the original Greek, this rhetorical device says, Συν + ἐκ + δέχομαι = I receive out of [and] *with*.... The fiction of the synecdoche is that it is simply impossible to accept the outstanding part without all the others, or without the whole which this part represents. When I receive its oversaturated meaning I get more than what I bargained for: one boasts of having bought wheels, when an entire vehicle that includes them has been purchased. Taking this expression literally would result in an absurdity, because wheels without an engine and without the rest of the car are quite useless. Yet, certain other instances of synecdoche, especially those fraudulently or ideologically constructed, merit a dissolution of the bond between my acceptance and the "bonus" I receive along with the accepted thing. In each case, the question is: Am I prepared to accept the whole Y with part X? Does the hill called Zion necessarily go along with the entire city ("eternal and indivisible," as the politico-metaphysical dogma affirms) wherein it is situated? Are the hill and the city inextricably bound to the larger territory that surrounds them, as the Zionist ideology endeavors to make us believe? And who is this "I" entitled to receive the exceptional part that is Zion? On the one hand, these are questions of Right, which is to say that they cut to the heart of the political or theological privilege the Zionist synecdoche claims for itself. On the other hand, and at the same time, they are questions of ethical commitment, intended for the subject, who assents to, but who is also free to reject, the series of synecdochic substitutions. In merely formulating these queries before anticipating a response, we have already loosened the bonds of the synecdoche that, more often than not, depends on automatic mental associations. Such loosening does not yet amount to an outright refusal; it is a still more basic negative gesture, indispensable to any critique worthy of the name, which undercuts the blind acceptance of, as much as the excess of what is accepted together with, the meaning of Zion.

The dissection of synecdoche is not its pure negation because, instead of accepting X with Y, one may opt to receive X without.... Without the "with," devoid of the problematic σuv, the hill of Zion is neither more nor less than a hill: it conforms to its geographical and historical limits (critique, we may recall in the footsteps of Kant, encloses each thing, and especially human reason, within its proper limits). Having amputated the synecdochic "with," I accept *what is* minus its idealization. To decline the semantic bonus is not so much to appeal to uninspired literalness, or to repudiate the possibility that things might be otherwise than the way they are. Rather, it is to assent to the place that would finally become what it is in all its spatio-temporal singularity and materiality, cut off from the representations of what lies beyond both the earthly horizons all around it and the transcendent horizon of the sacred. But how is it possible to receive Zion without Zionism? How, in discarding the excess of synecdochic meaning, can we ward off not only religious Zionism, of the kind Yitzchak Yaacov Reines and Abraham Kook among others propagated, but also the so-called secular, cultural or political, Zionisms that imbued Zion with the connotations of the ground for the gathering of the Jewish People?

Whether purely theological or metaphysical, it is the ideality of Zion that succumbs to the critique of the ideological apparatus Zionism has perfected. If, as early as in the Hebrew Bible, Zion refers to the city of Jerusalem *and* her inhabitants,[1] then it combines the rhetorical device of metonymy with the initial synecdoche. A place—hence, something—stands in for someone, namely for a collectivity of human beings. The strategy should not sound surprising. For instance, when the citizens of France vote in presidential elections, one expects to encounter newspaper headlines such as

"France Decides." Metonymic expressions are, to be sure, often blatantly wrong. Only voters who care to show up at the voting booths make their decisions known and, of these, the majority, as legally defined, decides who will serve as the country's next president. A cunning homogenization of all voting and non-voting citizens under the banner of an ideal object called "France" passes the choice of a group that, in absolute terms, probably comprises less than half of the population for the verdict of the entire body politic.[2]

Analogous, albeit even more daring, are the strategies of political representation in Zionism that shore up their ideological construction with the rhetorical power of synecdoche. The unwholesome substitution is, once again, double: Zionists for all Israelies, and Israel for the entire world Jewry, or the diaspora. Although a great (and steadily growing) number of Israeli citizens do not identify with the Zionist goals and aspirations, the legal, institutional, religious, and cultural shape of the polity is determined by that part which hypostatizes itself in the vacant place of the whole. The official reasons for this identification vary from the need for national unity in the face of external existential peril to the "internal" demographic threat that the non-Jewish portion of the country's population would soon outnumber ethnic Jews. Whatever the reason, the ideological construction of the entire country is fashioned in the image of the most zealous part of the contemporary Zionist movement. And so is the Israeli *idea* of the Jewish diaspora.

When it comes to the second, global synecdoche—the way Israel claims to be the steward of world Jewry—the foundations for the cunning substitution run deeper and are more closely related to the essentially metaphysical logic than in the case of intra-state political representation. Diaspora literally spells out the scattering of the seed, δια-σπορά, a condition that contravenes the metaphysical myth of a simple and originary unity, transcendentally vouchsafed by Ideas, Substance, God, Spirit, and so forth. An avowal of diaspora has been the implicit *sine qua non* of Derrida's deconstruction of Western metaphysics. The argument that the origin is not one, that it is scattered still before a coherent beginning into a multiplicity of origins, has been the hallmark of deconstruction not only in its thinking of *différance* but also, and more pertinently, in the thought of *dissémination*, which is a precise translation of "diaspora" from the Greek.[3] Conversely, Zionism, of all stripes and varieties, envisions the gathering of the diaspora in the imperial place of Zion, whether or not it receives the status of a political state. The legally enshrined "right of return," which the State of Israel a priori extends to every Jew in the world, grants virtual citizenship to those living in the diaspora. This policy considers the scatter to be inessential—a mere epiphenomenal and temporary diversion from the metaphysical unity of the people. From its perspective, the physical arrival of new Jewish immigrants in Israel is certainly desirable but it is secondary to what I have just called *virtual citizenship*, or potential belonging of world Jews to the State of Israel. The gathering of Jews from the diaspora is, first and foremost, a metaphysical endeavor of recovering a lost higher unity of the People, whose actual "return" would be nothing but the means or the sign for the accomplishment of this Messianic mission. This is why the ideology of Zionism deems world Jews as always already belonging to Israel "body and soul," whether they want it or not, as the recent controversy over the Kafka papers amply demonstrates.[4]

In brief, the global synecdoche of Israeli Jews for the whole of the Jewish people hinges upon the metaphysical unity that, for the Zionists, finds its embodiment in the place of Zion and its political expression, the Israeli State. This inclusionary and expansionist model is in sharp contrast to yet another synecdoche that actually denies certain people the right to political representation and so functions as an instrument of violence. I am referring to the idea that only one portion of all the residents in the territory stretching between the Eastern Mediterranean and the River Jordan constitutes the rightful inhabitants of the place. The expulsions of Palestinian people from their homes upon declaration of Israeli independence; the international limbo the population of the Occupied Territories has endured for decades; the uprooting of Palestinian orchards and olive trees, themselves metonymies of the people enrooted in a particular locale—these and related acts of violence are consequences of the exclusionary synecdoche that effaces and destroys much more than it reveals and constructs. This is not to say that Zionism was "blind to the presence of Arabs in Palestine"[5]; rather, it was (transcendentally) blind to the *justifications of* and the *right to* their presence. Especially after the UN Partitioning of Palestine in 1947 to 1948, the whole of Palestine's population no longer existed on the legal or political plane, even though, of course, physical existence stubbornly endured. It is in the gap between these two existences that violence struck, when that part which received the benefit of political statehood stood in for the whole by virtue of the circumstances and by dint of its own ideology.

Those in favor of a one-state solution to the Israeli–Palestinian conflict tend to encourage a different sense of the whole, far removed from synecdochic violence. When Edward Said wrote in 1999, "I see no other way than to begin now to speak about sharing the land that has thrust us together, sharing it in a truly democratic way, with equal rights for each citizen,"[6] he rhetorically re-created a shared whole, "the land," which no party would be able to represent or stand in for better than any other such party. Crucially, prior to Said's intervention, this vision had been advanced by certain members of the Zionist movement (e.g. Martin Buber and Hannah Arendt, to mention only the most readily recognizable names) whose viewpoints have, in the meanwhile, been silenced in the movement's official narrative.[7] Given the diversity of intellectual traditions upon which Zionism has drawn, it is to be expected that such radical alternatives would emerge in its midst. What matters, however, is that dissenting voices, and prominent ones at that, are marginalized within and subsequently excluded from the discourse of Zionism, thanks to the interposition of the movement's hegemonic part for the whole.[8] We would do well not to forget, then, that the Zionist synecdoche also means a synecdoche *within* Zionism and that, therefore, we are dealing with a complex of mutually reinforcing, internal and external, exclusions made possible by synecdochic substitutions. The violence of silencing a stream of thought is certainly incomparable to the violence that created a population of refugees but it could well be that the two grow out of the same root.

The blindness of language

The vertiginous superimposition of synecdoche upon synecdoche we have just witnessed creates a flurry of identifications of a part with the whole that, in naming and feigning to disclose a thing, effectively obfuscate that which is named. To a certain extent, language always induces this curious effect of blinding us to what it makes us see. When I say "tree," I make the sense of what I intend accessible to my interlocutors, while concealing a mind-boggling variety of actual trees. Words are idealities, allergic to sheer singularity. Linguistic abstraction encompasses the particulars that persist within it on the plane of mere potentiality. Quite the opposite is the case with synecdoche, where the particular interjects itself, without mediations, in the place of something larger, though not necessarily a universal. A particular hill, Zion, stands for a particular city, Jerusalem, which, in turn stands for a particular stretch of land as well as for the exceptional place where the earthly and the heavenly cities meet. The stretching of sense beyond itself, to a larger spatial circle or sphere of sacredness, blinds its addressees to *what* is contained within the material confines of the hill, the city, or the land, and, more gravely still, to *who* lives within their boundaries. The Zionist insistence on the "eternal and indivisible city" ignores explosive race-, class-, and religion-based divisions that make it appear as though several dissimilar cities are gathered under the name of Jerusalem; the term "the Land of Israel" erases the real existence of non-Jews within this idealized and spiritualized realm, and so forth. The modus operandi of the Zionist synecdoche is *concealing through naming*; it is an exaggeration of the tendency inherent in language as such and a hyperbolic idealization of particulars.

The title "The Blindness of Language" itself hides an allusion to Jacques Derrida's essay on Zionism, "The Eyes of Language: The Volcano and the Abyss."[9] In that text, Derrida offers a close reading of the 1926 letter Gershom Scholem addressed to Franz Rosenzweig on the subject of Hebrew language "revival" for the purposes of the Zionist project in Palestine under the British Mandate. The object of worry is the instrumentalization of the holy language and its harnessing for secularized "technolinguistic or technopolitical" purposes.[10] This is ultimately why Scholem believes that Zionist revivalists do not understand the essence of language and, indeed, of the sacred, which, similar to any repressed material, may return unexpectedly and with rather disastrous consequences.[11] Hence, the metaphor of the volcano, into which the hill of Zion is transfigured. Beneath the Zionist constructions the volcano is ready to erupt at any time and wipe away everything predicated upon it.

It may be true that, in keeping with Derrida's reading of Scholem, Zionists did not understand the essence of language. But they surely mastered its rhetorical strategies. Our deconstruction of the Zionist synecdoche is preoccupied with language's superficiality rather than its inner core, with what the word itself says—each time differently, depending on the part and the whole it conjoins—and with what it does. What interests us is the plurality of overlapping semantic surfaces productive of real effects "on the ground," directly feeding into modes of political representation, or violence, or both. How would Derrida's text have mutated, had it emerged from the heights of the volcano and from the depths of the abyss—the reincarnations of the pyramid and the pit in his earlier writings[12]—to the plains of rhetoric?

Let us begin at the end, with the vague announcement of the disaster, the punishment meted out by the return of the repressed sacredness of language. Following the Messianic vein of the missive he analyzes, Derrida asks, "ruin [*la perte*]—is this the punishment deserved for having secularized, profaned, ruined, for having done, in sum, the impossible itself? Or indeed the contrary, the terrifying return of the sacred? And of what, finally, would the punishment consist?"[13] The temporality of the unpredictable event of ruin, when the volcano underneath the Zionist project finally erupts, is one of the future without a horizon of projection or anticipation, as Derrida would say. The deep past of holy language, exempt from everyday use, rushes toward us from the future to-come: between the two modalities of time, bypassing the present as well as conscious representation, the event comes to pass. Yet, for us, who pursue an essentially superficial approach to the Zionist synecdoche, the event has already happened, because ruin, violence, and destruction have never ceased erupting from the multiple substitutions of a part for the whole, excluding, expelling, and silencing other, undesirable parts. There is nothing vague about this announcement of the disaster that has affected the historical present since the middle of the twentieth century.

In his epistolary confession, what Scholem finds unnerving is the disaster of secular Zionism that flirts with the "sacrifice of sacrifice," aiming to abolish sacred language qua sacred.[14] At issue is the synecdoche of secular enthusiasts, their self-hypostatization in the place of all—secular and religious—Zionists. Scholem's main concern is with the specific Zionist strategy and with the tactical advantage the secular Zionist faction has scored over their religious opponents in determining the future course of the movement. His care for the deep ontology of language is perhaps the most superficial veil concealing ideological disagreements; it is, in clinical terms, a symptom of his frustration with the usurpation of the movement by a faction that universalized its partial position and determined the very means through which, and the playing field on which, any position could be expressed. The prediction of the impending disaster is, then, a kind of revenge, though not of the repressed sacred but of the defeated Scholem himself.

It follows that the carefully staged opposition between the inner essence of language and its instrumentalization for ephemeral political purposes is itself political through and through. Scholem's polemics against politicization, relying on what presumably stays immune to the ever-changing demands of actuality, resorts to the tactics of neutralization, perfected, for instance, by all those who contrive a discourse in the name of a- or trans-historical human rights. The point of the polemics is to occupy a higher moral or religious ground so as to gain advantage in the struggle between two visions of Zionism by styling one's own vision as apolitical, or "essential": "He [Scholem] only opposes an essential Zionism or a Zionism to come to actual Zionism [*un sionisme de fait*], to the Zionism that blindly practices an 'actualization' of the sacred language without seeing the abyss."[15] In this opposition, the synecdoche revolves around the problem of temporality and, especially, around the status of the present: while actual Zionism, bent on the modernization of the Hebrew language, makes something of the past live again in the present, which it believes to represent a pinnacle of Jewish history, essential Zionism finds refuge in sacred immutability, in the deep past of pure essence and the "to-come" of its return. Whereas, for Scholem, the present has no right to stand for the entire tradition, let alone for the sacred history without history kept safe in the depths of what is essential, for Zionists, who endeavor to "actualize" the past (above all, language), the thing thus actualized must serve the demands of the present. It is not, as Derrida thinks, "difficult to know whether evil, the fall itself, consists in falling or in staying on the surface,"[16] precisely because staying on the surface is nothing but an upward Fall[17] from the deep core of essence.

This, then, is what Scholem conceals when he names the essence of language, itself made of names; that is, essentially superficial elements. He conceals, namely, a battle for legitimacy that would see only one of the Zionisms become a synecdoche for the entire movement, and he does so by masquerading political strategies and goals behind the façade of onto-theological lamentations and prophecies. An essential Zionist, he fights against the instrumental rationality of the secular and secularizing *sionisme de fait* that keeps its eye on what it wants to accomplish with language, on what it wishes to do *with* language and *through* language. But this other Zionism's untiring, ever-vigilant, all-seeing eye, symbolizing the eye of reason itself, is a figure of lucidity blind to the withdrawn essence of sacredness, to sacred language and sacred identity: "It is thus lucidity that threatens to engulf us, not blindness. The blind men that we are, *almost all of us*, live in this language, above the abyss."[18] The lucidity that blinds parallels the structure of the synecdoche, which conceals through naming, except that what we are blinded to is the metaphysical ideality of the sacred, while what is concealed from us is the raw materiality of existence. The despair oozing from Scholem's letter and from its close reading by Derrida has to do with the realization that the secularizing blindness to questions of essence does not automatically turn its subjects around to face the materiality of existence. Instead, it re-creates the idealities of language, identity, nation, and so forth, more destructive than ever before, unleashed on everything that does not exactly fit the molds invigilated by the all-seeing eye of ideology, blind only to itself.

The Phoenix-like rebirth of the Hebrew language signals the death of a certain idea of Zionism and the temporary (according to Scholem) forgetting of the sacred. But what Scholem considers to be "our language," *unsere Sprache*, is not a purely internal Jewish affair. In this instance, "our" operates an ambiguous synecdoche. Does it refer to the author of the letter and his addressee, Scholem and Rosenzweig? Does it stand for essential Zionists? For all Zionists? For the Jewish people as a whole? Or, does each of these smaller "parts" strive to equate what is properly its own with a larger political arena *in toto*? And who can describe as "ours" that language which, un-appropriable, boils at a bottom of a volcano?

The Zionist synecdoche constitutes itself thanks to a primordial exclusion of everyone who does not speak "our language." But, strangely enough, Derrida avoids discussing the marginalized others, who, excluded from the designation "our," make the rest of the letter possible.[19] He does not accentuate the only mention of the Arab people, *das arabische Volk*, in Scholem's text. The letter's author writes on the subject:

> One speaks here of many things that could make us fail. One speaks more than ever today about the Arabs. But more uncanny than the Arab people [*unheimlicher als das arabische Volk*] another threat confronts us that is a necessary consequence of the Zionist undertaking: What about the 'actualization' [*Aktualisierung*] of Hebrew?[20]

Immediately after likening the country to a volcano that "houses language," Scholem registers another much talked-about threat, "the Arabs." He will not revisit this subject because "the Arabs" are what one speaks *of*, not those one speaks *to*. Theirs is a mute threat, which does not appear to be "a *necessary* consequence of the Zionist undertaking," but which is nonetheless unavoidable insofar as they do not share "our language" and are existentially excluded from the ambiguous synecdoche of the possessive form. It is, however, an uncanny threat because the ones who experience it have reified the source of the perceived danger: "the Arabs" are—Scholem reports in his letter—objects of conversations, not subjects deemed capable of responding. What would be the sense of talking to, let alone negotiating with, someone who does not speak "our language" (obviously, besides Hebrew, at stake in this expression is the language of "our" customs, mores, religious injunctions, moral precepts) and who poses the much-discussed threat to "us"?

To be fair, Arab people are not as uncanny, in Scholem's view, as the real cause of his worries. An implicit hierarchy of dangerousness emerges from the letter's outset. The least uncanny is the common object of conversations, the Arab threat; second come the enemies one can still talk to, the Zionist revivalists who intend to "actualize" Hebrew and secularize the Zionist project; third, and most uncanny, is the mute menace inherent in language itself, reduced to a means of communication, to the detriment of the highly unstable and explosive trace of its sacredness. Arab people are the least uncanny in this scheme of things because they do not have to be excluded from the linguistic community, as Scholem envisions it. An alternative would have been to introduce a language that belongs to no one, neither "ours" nor "theirs"; that is to say, Esperanto, instead of Hebrew, which remains "pregnant with catastrophes."[21] Scholem proves to be more secular than the secularizing revivalists of Hebrew, since he is willing to adopt an altogether different political or public language in the region, on condition that the sacredness of "our language" would not be contaminated with the pragmatic considerations of the everyday. Although it is metaphysically and onto-theologically inspired, the proposal for such differentiation of functions expresses Enlightenment precepts on the separation of Church and State that would allow for the co-existence, in the public sphere, of groups adhering to distinct religions. Whether he wants it or not, at the hands of Scholem, secularization ceases to be an "empty expression."[22] Its sense made more ample, it internally transfigures the blindness of language, not quite championing a new lucidity but making possible a sober paradigm of true sharing. The Zionist synecdoche loses steam: its power of concealment, which is also concealment as power, wanes. Zionism deconstructs itself, thrusting itself open to the other.

The language of blindness

A self-deconstructive vein has always run through the Zionist movement, which included proponents of the Jewish–Arab union in Palestine, or what has come to be known as the "bi-national state solution." Silenced by means of the hegemonic Zionist synecdoche, they, like Scholem, were analogous to biblical prophets, the harsh social critics who warned the powers that be of the impending doom. It is our ethical duty to heed their voices drowned in the mad rush of violence they vehemently denounced.

One such voice belongs to Nathan Chofshi, the anarchist and pacifist President of the Palestine branch of the War Resisters' International. Writing in 1946, exactly 20 years after Scholem's letter to Rosenzweig, for the monthly publication *Be'ayot* (*Problems*) of the movement *Ichud* (*Union*), Chofshi seems to echo the sentiment of this earlier missive. His article, entitled "Into the Abyss," outlines the dangerous path predicted in 1926. The abyss into which Jews in Palestine are now plunging has nothing to do with the secularization of Hebrew but, rather, with the ideology of violence prevalent in the Zionist movement. Especially telling and evocative of Scholem is the pairing of the abyss and the volcano, boiling over with contempt for the Arab other: "Without an understanding with our Arab neighbors, we are building on a volcano and our whole work is in jeopardy."[23] As though he were a seismologist, Chofshi probes the grounds of Zion and finds them volcanic, ready to give way under "our" feet and to spew out fountains of deadly hatred. But the eruption is not only anticipated; it has already come to pass and its ongoing happening overshadows everything noted in "Into the Abyss."

"The disaster has happened" is the opening sentence of Chofshi's text,[24] in stark contrast to Scholem's deferral of the traumatic event to an indefinite future. Later on, the disaster will be assigned an exact date "November 1, 1945," the day or the night when the Jewish Resistance Movement in Palestine carried out a series of sabotage operations, involving "[e]xplosions and destruction, blood and fire, dead, wounded, and 'prisoners.'"[25] Writing to express his dismay with the events of that fateful Night of the Trains, Chofshi denounces, in the first instance, the decision of the Zionist zealots to resort to "redemptive" violence for the achievement of their goals. The star of redemption has gone awry, in the literal sense of disaster, of which Chofshi, who describes November 1 as an "ill-starred day"[26]—we might say, a day indistinguishable from a starless night—is all too aware. The singular catastrophe is a metonymy of violence, with the attendant glorification of heroic sacrifice and demonstration of brute force. A bizarre demonstration, it dismantles, above all, the phenomenal grounds of the world: there is nothing to be seen in the scarce light of the disastrous day. It neither discloses anything nor, even, conceals through the act of naming but withdraws the conditions of possibility for seeing and for living in a place whose non-Jewish inhabitants are not as much as acknowledged.[27] Violence is the language of blindness.

Let us pause over this paradox for a moment: a demonstration of sorts—that of violent force, or of "Jewish power"[28]—erases its own phenomenality, de-monstrates itself and, by the same token, blinds those who exhibit this non-phenomenon as well as those against whom force is applied. As Chofshi implies, these dangerous, blindness-inducing manifestations are not, by any means, limited to the "terrorist gangs" that finally attained success in the 1940s. Rather, they are crucial to the aspirations of Zionist zealots who, "with Jabotinsky at their head," clamor for a Jewish state, a Jewish army, and "all ... other manifestations of physical power."[29] Among other things, the Jewish state will have been, for Chofshi, the apogee of the language of blindness, a Moloch demanding constant sacrifice, "endless suffering and bloodshed."[30] Institutionalized violence, indispensable to any political state, would not, in this instance, have the luxury of drawing the curtain of normalcy all around itself, because of the volcanic ground, on which the state will have established itself, the ground of the non-recognition and brutal suppression of the people with whom the land was to be shared. Hence, the axiom of the political abyss: the more manifest physical power and its avatars (the army, the state, etc.), the less visible the world wherein they unfold.

"Blind" is a word that recurs with remarkable consistency in Chofshi's concise text. It is "blind believers in violence" who are "leading us into the terrible abyss with the song of redemption and salvation on their lips." Theirs is a "blind faith" in "our 'strong hand'."[31] Aside from its obvious rhetorical weight, what, in the text's economy, justifies this recurrence? The effects of violence are, strictly speaking, blinding to the extent that they preclude discussion, dialogue, and *logos*; they do not permit us to "see" the phenomena of power and undercut the possibility of a political phenomenology. The Zionist synecdoche relies on the prosthesis of an unshakable faith in the righteousness of the Zionist cause, which is not up for discussion with the dissenting Jewish voices. "But if some level-headed man," Chofshi writes, "takes the risk of raising his voice and uttering a warning against this disastrous path ..., he is told to keep quiet and is accused of indifference to the sufferings of his persecuted and stricken people—and there the 'discussion' ends."[32] Coupled with the unwillingness to acknowledge the existence of—let alone to speak to—the Arab neighbors, the absence of dialogue among different factions of the Jewish population in the 1940s Palestine amounted to the absolute obscurity, the disastrous (starless or ill-starred) blindness, whence the State of Israel was born. How to shed light onto this disaster without falling into its abysses, that is, without succumbing to the vicious cycle of violence?

It would be futile to oppose lucidity to the abysses of blindness, as Chofshi's recounting of a typical conversation with a young Zionist enthusiast shows.[33] Instead, we are treated to an astute comparison of the metonymy of Zion as it is with what it should have been, had the place of Zion, along with everything it stands for, as a powerful synecdoche, represented a pillar of justice: "'Zion shall be redeemed with judgment, and her converts with righteousness,'—that is not an abstract vision, but a practical possibility."[34] What would it mean for a particular place to become an abode of justice, "redeemed with judgment" and righteousness, as Isaiah—whom Chofshi echoes—prophesies? Far from a utopian vision piercing the veil of blindness at the end of history, this other metonymy was "a practical possibility," a scenario that could still be enacted at the time when "Into the Abyss" was composed, in January 1946. Were this possibility seized upon and converted into historical reality, Zion would have turned into a genuinely unique place no longer obeying the logic of territorial appropriation. A place of co-existence outside the exclusive purview of a single identity, or, indeed, of any identity; a place of ultimate hospitality beyond the rigidity of the nation-state; a place of ethico-political resolve free of the trappings of heroism and the manipulative discourse of sacrifices.

In Chofshi's crisp formulation, the alternatives are clear enough: illusory redemption through violence and expropriation of the other versus lasting redemption through judgment that gives to the other her due and pursues "far-reaching opportunities of action in peace."[35] Although the disaster had already struck, it was still not too late to opt for the other metonymy of Zion as the place of justice within the concentric circles of its synecdoche. Over thirteen years later Chofshi will nonetheless suspect that violence irreparably mars this metonymic relation, in keeping with a paradox he discovers in the Book of Isaiah. And he will confide his suspicions in Martin Buber, to whom he writes in the autumn of 1959:

> With all my heart I live in accordance with the teachings of our later prophets; sometimes, however, I face a mystery that confuses me. In Isaiah 11 we find the wonderful picture of the fulfillment of the vision of true peace.... And how horrified I am when I come to this horrible verse at the end of the same chapter: "They shall pounce on the back of Philistia to the west and together plunder the people of the east; Edom and Moab shall be subject to them, and the children of Ammon shall obey." (11:14) ... How much encouragement it contains for Ben Gurion and his ilk, who have the cause of peace on their lips but a sharp sword in their hands.[36]

The language of blindness persists in the midst of the most luminous vision of justice. Why?

In his response, Buber resorts to a classical technique of biblical criticism, explaining that the "plunder section" of the narrative was a much later insertion, datable to the time of Babylonian exile.[37] This analysis notwithstanding, tradition passes the text on as a unified whole, which is also how it is read and received. Assuming that the two parts of Isaiah 11 are coherent, what if their puzzling co-belonging is a necessary effect of synecdoche? What if, in its exemplarity, the *pars pro toto* of the synecdoche remains violent and imperialistic, even when the part that stands in for the whole metonymizes justice and peace? With the "vision of true peace" achieved in the gathering place of Zion, to which Isaiah 11:12 points, the exemplary embodiment of justice and, especially, of truth gains the indisputable right to fight, plunder, and vanquish those who fall short of this vision. "Ben Gurion and his ilk," including the current political and ideological authorities of Israel, have learned the lesson of the Zionist synecdoche to the letter: they have realized that *pars pro toto* means *pars contra omnes*: the "part for the whole" is the "part against all." (The current Israeli siege mentality is a direct consequence of this speculative inversion, anticipated in synecdochic instability.) It is, finally, this semantic simultaneity that permits them to tout peace with "a sharp sword in their hands."

The part in a synecdochic relation to the whole boasts a quasi-miraculous capacity to absorb, vicariously, the power of what it stands for. Such symbolic investiture, then, permits it to assert its superiority vis-à-vis all the other parts comprising the whole, from which it alone stands out. The saving grace of synecdoche lies in the reinterpretation of this relation with the view to the inferiority of the exceptional part, the assumed impossibility of living up to the high demands its position imposes upon it. *Pars pro toto* would not be reversible into *pars contra omnes* if the preposition "*pro*" conveyed not a fraudulent exchange of the lesser for the greater, but a part that is "for"—at the service of, entirely dedicated to—all the others. Only then would the hyperbolic non-identity, or the symbolic excessiveness, of the synecdoche pave the way to the fullness of sense, as much as to the metonymic plentitude of being and justice. And only then, in Zion's self-divestment for the sake of the other, in its being *for* the singular Palestinian other, would the biblical prophecy, too, be fulfilled, so that Zion would be filled with justice and righteousness, מלא ציון, משפט וצדקה (Isaiah 33:5).

Notes

1 "Zion," in *Dictionary of the Old Testament: Wisdom, Poetry & Writings*, Temper Longman III and Peter Enns (eds) (Nottingham and Madison, NY: IPV Academic, 2008), 936.
2 Carl Schmitt outlined these and other machinations of democratic representation in *Legality and Legitimacy*, trans. J. Seitzer (Durham, NC and London: Duke University Press, 2004).
3 John Caputo, *The Prayers and Tears of Jacques Derrida: Religion without Religion* (Bloomington and Indianapolis: Indiana University Press, 1997), 230. See also Jarod Hayes, "Queering Roots, Queering Diaspora," in *Rites of Return: Diaspora Poetics and the Politics of Memory*, Marianne Hirsch and Nancy Miller (eds) (New York: Columbia University Press, 2011), pp. 72–87.
4 Judith Butler, "Who Owns Kafka?" *London Review of Books*, Vol. 33, No. 5, March 2011, 3–8. http://www.lrb.co.uk/v33/n05/judith-butler/who-owns-kafka (retrieved on April 17, 2012).
5 Zeev Sternhell, *The Founding Myths of Israel*, trans. David Maisel (Princeton, NJ: Princeton University Press, 1999), 43.
6 Edward Said, "The One-State Solution," *The New York Times*, January 10, 1999. http://www.nytimes.com/1999/01/10/magazine/the-one-state-solution.html?pagewanted=all&src=pm (retrieved on April 17, 2012).
7 Refer, for example, to Martin Buber, *A Land of Two Peoples: Martin Buber on Jews and Arabs*, ed. Paul Mendes-Flohr (Chicago, IL: The University of Chicago Press, 2005).
8 "The territorial decision in the Zionist movement has a general significance, because the dispersed Jewish people is often presented as a case of 'nonterritorial nationalism.' We noted the positions of Magnes and Buber who opposed a territorial solution to the partition debate of 1937. Hannah Arendt maintained, after the State of Israel was established, that the Jews are a nation even in the absence of territory. On the other hand, the Zionist ethos was *entirely* one of territory." Itzhak Galnoor, *The Partition of Palestine: Decision Crossroads in the Zionist Movement* (Albany, NY: SUNY Press, 1995), 256, emphasis added.
9 For a close reading of Derrida's text, refer to Dana Hollander, *Exemplarity and Chosenness: Rosenzweig and Derrida on the Nation of Philosophy* (Stanford, CA:

Stanford University Press, 2008). See especially the section entitled "Derrida and the Scholem-Rosenzweig Debate on Sacred Language and Translation," 147–55.
10   Jacques Derrida, "The Eyes of Language: The Abyss and the Vulcano," in *Acts of Religion*, ed. Gil Anidjar (New York and London: Routledge, 2002), 195.
11   Derrida, "The Eyes of Language," 195; cf. the epigraph.
12   Cf. Jacques Derrida, "The Pit and the Pyramid: Introduction to Hegel's Semiology," in *Margins of Philosophy*, trans. Alan Bass (Chicago, IL and London: The University of Chicago Press, 1982), 69–108.
13   Derrida, "The Eyes of Language," 224.
14   Ibid., 217.
15   Ibid., 197.
16   Ibid., 202–3.
17   I owe this term to Terry Eagleton, who mentioned it at a recent lecture on "Jesus and Tragedy" at the Washington National Cathedral on March 25, 2012.
18   Derrida, "The Eyes of Language," 197.
19   After all, this might not be surprising in light of Christopher Wise's analysis of Derrida's at times ambivalent relation to Zionism and the failure to criticize it, for instance, in *Specters of Marx*. Cf. Christopher Wise, *Derrida, Africa, and the Middle East* (London and New York: Palgrave Macmillan, 2009), 54ff.
20   Gershom Scholem, "Confession on the Subject of Our Language, A Letter to Franz Rosenzweig, December 26, 1926," in *Acts of Religion*, ed. Gil Anidjar (New York and London: Routledge, 2002), 226.
21   Scholem, "Confession on the Subject of Our Language," 227.
22   Derrida, "The Eyes of Language," 217.
23   Natan Chofshi, "Into the Abyss," in *Towards Union in Palestine: Essays on Zionism and Jewish-Arab Cooperation*, M. Buber, J. L. Magnes, and E. Simon (eds) (Westport, CT: Greenwood Press, 1972), 38.
24   Chofshi, "Into the Abyss," 37.
25   Ibid.
26   Ibid.
27   "There is an Arab people in this country and there are Arab people in the Middle East all round us. The British and Americans are taking account of these peoples in making their plans here, and we Jews have to take account of them, too" (Chofshi, "Into the Abyss," 40).
28   Chofshi, "Into the Abyss," 37.
29   Ibid., 38.
30   Ibid., 40.
31   Ibid., 38.
32   Ibid., 37.
33   Ibid., 38.
34   Ibid., 38.
35   Ibid., 38.
36   Natan Chofshi, "Letter 697. Nathan Chofshi to Martin Buber, Herzlia, October 11, 1959," in *The Letters of Martin Buber: A Life of Dialogue*, Nahum Glatzer and Paul Mendes-Flohr (eds) (New York: Schocken Books, 1991), 632.
37   Martin Buber, "Letter 698. Martin Buber to Nathan Chofshi, Jerusalem, November 8, 1959," in *The Letters of Martin Buber: A Life of Dialogue*, Nahum Glatzer and Paul Mendes-Flohr (eds) (New York: Schocken Books, 1991), 632.

11

Sharing Humanity

Towards Peaceful Coexistence in Difference

Luce Irigaray

I do not think that conflicts by which humanity is torn today can be resolved only in the present and in an almost immediate way, as some politicians seem to believe and try to convince us. Hence, the proliferation of meetings and treaties that end in nothing, and the theatrical handshakes of political representatives that are accompanied by various sorts of bombing, killing innocent citizens. All these things contribute to worsening the situation and increasing violence, instead of paving the way for the resolution of the crisis. More often than not this is the symptom of an age-old cultural construction that makes two peoples incompatible with one another and unable to contract whatever kind of bilateral agreement. And all the attempts to bring them together and create current relations often complicate matters and render them insoluble. To reach something worthwhile it would be necessary that each people puts in question its own history, convictions, manners of being, and acting. But who is capable of such a behavior, what is more as a people, that is, at a collective level?

The lasting Arab–Israeli conflict is one of the most glaring examples of a conflict that cannot find a solution in terms of a bilateral agreement. Even the manner of designating it renders this impossible, because the eventual partners are not situated at the same level. The Palestinian people is designated as "Arab"—that is, by referring only to a territorial, cultural, and linguistic origin—whereas the word "Israeli" refers to a people with these sorts of characteristics, but also to a State. How could entities that are so different contract with one another? They do not have the same juridical status. And how could it be possible to ask Palestinian people to act in a civil manner without the recognition of their civil identity as citizens of a State and, moreover, depriving them of what defines them as belonging to a territory and a tradition? How could they react differently from angry children who have no means to make themselves heard? Is anything left to them other than suicidal violence?

In reality, the Arab–Israeli problem is a sort of dramatic caricature of what can happen between different peoples and cultures in a global context, with the additional complexity of the expropriation from a territory, that is, from a part of the Earth which would have been allocated by God himself to a people with the consequential right to expel from it another people, which also believes in God. How could a people lacking both the earth and the heavens, the place of a natural life but also that of a spiritual life, enjoy a peaceful existence without revolting against the people which deprives it of all? On the other hand, how could a people which suffered the Holocaust renounce finding refuge in a land that they believe to be assigned to them by God? The problem seems really insuperable as it is in the present. And it is still made worse by the fact that the Americans give economic, military, political, and even religious support to the Israelis, so that one of the world's leading economic and nuclear powers supports Israel, whereas Palestinians lack the land, money, arms, and rights, including those of human recognition and dignity. The only possibility with regard to such an incredible confrontation is to try to analyze and deconstruct the situation as it happened, and to wonder about humanity itself in order to find the way to approach the problem. A problem that is particularly obvious and to which media coverage is given in the Arab–Israeli case, but that exists and will increase in a context of world coexistence. This must compel us to return to the question: What does it mean to be a human? In terms of the monotheistic traditions, we ought to go back to the myth of the lost Eden as the result of a will of humanity to appropriate the divine knowledge before cultivating humanity as such. We ought to recover our nudity in the garden and wonder whether and how we can start to construct our human development again, each one and together.

Passing from natural belonging to civil coexistence

No doubt, we cannot act in public places only according to our nature, which needs to be cultivated to make us capable of living in society. The first means to pass from a natural state to a social state are civil rights. They define the manner in which we can and must behave to share with others at a public level. This function of civil rights is still largely ignored and, furthermore, civil rights are not established in the same way in all countries and cultures, something that does not favor a world coexistence between individuals. In fact, civil rights should guarantee the status of all citizens and regulate the relations between them and their State, but also among them as humans, even across every boundary.

The crucial function of civil rights is thwarted at least by two things linked together: (1) the family is assumed to be a place where natural belonging must remain independent of the civil law; and (2) the universality of the law is supposed to be neutral. Now, such a neutrality does not take into consideration the sexuate nature of the citizens and thus cannot be of use in ensuring either the passage from natural to civil identity or the coexistence among citizens belonging to different identities. To build a human community, we must rethink and redefine civil rights that take into account the real and concrete identity of persons, especially with regard to their sexuate belonging. In other words, we must rethink the civil code as a tool towards the elaboration of a not neuter but embodied universal, essential for making possible a world coexistence. We have not yet reached such a stage. And the extension of family strictly speaking to all sorts of families—political, religious, cultural, etc.—prevents us from worrying about that. We are thus lacking a culture of our instincts and drives, which we transfer onto public behaviors such as domination and dependence that are all the more strong since they are cut off from their natural regulations and do not appear as mere instincts or drives. Political, cultural, religious choices may, then, be thought of as idealistic, moral, disinterested, etc., even though they are dictated by our uneducated instincts or drives. This situation does not allow either for a sound and just governance or for a private and public adequate coexistence between citizens. The frontiers between natural and civil belonging are blurred and a correct education lacks for both. It is all the more so because persons are compared to undifferentiated unities of various family entities, or peoples, without considering their most living relational aspect: their sexuate identity. The citizens are supposed to remain sexless children who need authoritarian heads of family and values capable of governing them.

Obviously, this cannot contribute towards a world community of human beings. Nevertheless, more often than not our political, religious, and cultural organizations stop at this stage and they will not evolve until our sexuate identity is taken into consideration, especially with regard to the civil code. This means that citizens must be recognized as sexuate persons and not as neutral individuals, that life itself and its determinations must be taken into account and regulated by civil rights. Citizens must compose a society or a nation as living beings who are responsible for themselves and for their relations with the others. A thing that requires an appropriate civil code that represents the rights and duties of citizens before any representative power. Between the rulers and the citizens a civil code must intervene which protects the citizens from abuses of power by the State, but also expresses their duties towards the state and other citizens, including the citizens of other countries.

In order to act in this way, the civil code must reflect citizens both in their majority and in their reality. I think that sexuate identity is the main aspect starting from which the civil code has to be modified towards a possible universal governance. Whatever its apparent neutrality, the law is still currently drawn up in terms that correspond to the necessities and the perspectives of masculine subjectivity alone. Beyond the fact that it privileges the right to possess material or spiritual goods over the respect for persons—that is, the relation to objects over the relation between subjects—it does not suit the natural qualities of every identity or a human coexistence. This is especially obvious concerning the legal status and framework required by the female body and subjectivity, the main guardians of human life. Women often still lack a civil responsibility with respect to their pregnancy, more generally to their love life, and such a lack goes against a governance that cares about life. A woman cannot remain under the guardianship of the State, especially a warlike State, without the possibility to oppose her own rights, but also duties, to the power of this State.

Now, the legal problem of pregnancy and sexual relations remains unsolved in most countries and this leads to the civil irresponsibility of women considered to be minors under the guardianship of the fathers of various sorts of families. Such a thing is in contradiction with the rules of a democratic system at the service of living beings, and it bears witness to the interference of other kinds of values: natural, cultural, or religious. A real democratic governing, moreover at a world level, cannot exist in this case. Only a platform of civil rights appropriate to the different types of persons can ensure its operation. Of course, the number of types must remain limited and based on some general criteria. Sexuate belonging appears to be the most universal of them. It is surprising that past democracies have not yet dealt with this question enough. They have deemed it sufficient to grant to women economic or social equality without caring about their own identity, notably their bodily identity. This may be explained by the fact that democracy was first established by men and was, above all, concerned with their relations, especially their respective relations, to things which served as measures to assess their secular or spiritual public roles and functions. When the relation to money more and more substituted the relation to things, its apparent neutral nature contributed to the neutralization of persons themselves who became sorts of equivalent pieces on the political scene. What then matter are only some characteristics of humanity that may or may not make possible coexisting, but not humans as such, whose first quality is to be sexuate living beings.

Reminding politicians of our sexuate belonging seems derisory in an epoch or in a situation in which money matters above all. However, a democratic and peaceful behavior and governance cannot be based only on money or goods, and such a simplistic conception of democracy does not help women to become full citizens, nor does it contribute towards the regulation of the relationships among citizens, especially citizens who are different—at the level of sex, of generation, but also of culture, of country, etc. It also maintains a confusion in the roles of politics and religion in the administration of the city, one caring more about the goods and the other more about the persons. What, according to Hegel, was the role of women inside the family home has become a sort of interference of the churches or of religious leaders or beliefs into political governance. Given the patriarchal character of the religious authorities, this intrusion does not contribute to granting women full citizenship. Furthermore, it prevents us from reaching the world democracy that we need today because the various religions have not elaborated their relation to the Absolute in the same way, and this represents an important cause of conflicts and wars between citizens and between peoples—notably in the case of the Arab–Israeli problem. It is thus urgent for us to define a platform of civil rights that allows for a democratic existence and coexistence among all citizens at a national, but also at a world level.

Democracy cannot correspond to the plan of one leader, one people, one culture, but must be concerned with the real existence of living beings who are neither sexless nor all similar and who have to deal with difference at the level of humanity itself. If the civil code must act as a mediator and a guarantee of neutrality in the exchanges between the political representatives and the citizens, and also among the citizens themselves, this does not mean that it must reduce persons to asexual individuals. Civil rights must provide all living citizens with an appropriate guarantee and corresponding duties that are defined in a general way that is understandable by every citizen.

What could religious membership in intercultural context be?

Although an appropriate civil code is essential to a peaceful coexistence, it does not meet all the needs of human accomplishment. It is a framework or a structure that permits the individuals to pass from natural life to civil life and to coexist with mutual respect. It is a sort of second skin that we must don to protect ourselves, but also to protect others, from immediate natural impulses or impetuses that do not fit civil behaviors and exchanges. Personally, I think that a civil identity ought to intervene also in the family home and that the family ought to be composed of civil, and not only natural, members who respect one another as such, even if their relations are more comprehensive than they can be in the public sphere. To be more comprehensive does not amount to being less respectful or less differentiated. Civil rights have to protect all members of the family from giving up their own individuality and growth for the sake of the family unit. This necessity has not yet been taken into consideration enough, and they are above all the women who lack both this protection and the responsibility connected with a civil identity. Furthermore, this lack of civil regulation within the family strictly speaking spreads into all sorts of family—political, religious, cultural, etc.—and does not allow for coexistence among them, especially at a world level.

In past times, especially in matriarchal times, family law ruled over the city, and a governance separated from natural ties and belonging did not exist. The Sophocles's tragedy *Antigone*, the significance of which cannot be limited to an evolution of Greek culture, tells us about the passage from this sort of governance to an organization of the city regulated by laws more or less arbitrary with respect to life. The concern for life was then confined to the family home and confided to women, whereas men were entrusted with governing the city through rules presumed to be extraneous to natural life. The family order was ensured by the care of life, its natural environment, and the respect for the gods who preserve living beings, as well as the context these need for their survival and natural growth. Family itself was the place where nature as such and the divine were maintained and cultivated. The worship of the dead and ancestry had an important place in the family religion of which women had charge.

This worship enlarged the family strictly speaking and ensured the family tradition. Thus a family could represent not only a people but also its culture. Such a culture remained linked to life notably through the worship of the dead which has to be carried out to preserve the cosmic harmony and the natural environment of living beings, as it is explained in the tragedy *Antigone*—a concern that seems to be ignored by those who regularly pollute the Earth with corpses by means of more and more sophisticated and high-performance arms. Antigone must provide her brother Polynice with a burial to preserve balance between the cosmic elements, of which different gods are the guardians, a balance that is harmed by a corpse which remains without burial. Antigone must also accomplish the rite of passage from an earthly sojourn to the sojourn of the dead for her brother because this ritual is a part of the matriarchal tradition that recommends protecting the members of the family, especially the youngest son—and, for me, Palestinians represent younger members of the human family in relation to Israeli—from becoming whatever anonymous corpse after death. The rite of passage must be accomplished towards a sexuate body in order to preserve the dead from disintegrating into mere inanimate matter. The sex is thus recognized as a decisive part of the person, which has to be taken into consideration to protect individuation even after death.

Before intervening in desire, love, or procreation, that is, in sexual behaviors strictly speaking, the sex contributes to the individuation of individuals, determining their identity. This explains why Antigone cannot marry her fiancé Hemon before recognizing the sexuate identity of her brother, especially as different from hers. Her individuation as a woman requires her to distinguish herself from belonging to both the same blood and the same sex as her brother already within the family. In the absence of such differentiation, the body and the sex somehow or other will remain split, which has something to do with the separation between the body and the soul that harms the fulfillment of our humanity and of our exchanges as humans. Indeed, beyond the fact that it corresponds to the relational aspect of our natural belonging, sexuate identity is a universal one and contributes towards coexistence among all humans—whatever their culture, tradition, religion, color, etc.—on the condition that the difference between masculine and feminine sexuate identities be recognized and cultivated as such, first in the family home.

Unfortunately, patriarchal families—be they natural, political, cultural, or religious—have not taken into account the sexuate belonging of individuals enough, and have contributed in this way towards the production of sociocultural substitutes that are totally incompatible, and a loss of individuation for the individuals, as well as the loss of the constant regulation of relations among them, that can be ensured by a respectful civil coexistence of men with women. Besides, patriarchal traditions have caused damage to women by preventing them from having a share in the elaboration of culture because they were enclosed in the family home and assigned to the natural part of the human accomplishment. Even the religious role that they had within the family became, little by little, assumed by public institutions which put the stress on masculine authorities and values here and now and on another life in the beyond instead of on the cultivation of our terrestrial existence, an existence more and more threatened by money, technology, and culture(s) that barely care about life itself and its development.

If the cultivation of life was not completely achieved in matriarchal times, these at least safeguarded an organization and a culture, including at the religious level, that were in continuity with life and the becoming of living beings. Patriarchy, instead, cut them off from their living roots and, as the chorus in the *Antigone* tragedy proclaims, the works of men, then, can lead to the best but also to the worst because they are largely arbitrary and partial with respect to life. To impose them from on high—in the form of laws, ideal or religious commandments—runs the risk of harming the growth of the living. One could even say: this has damaged life itself, its environment, and its sharing.

Thus, in particular at a world level, the various rulers must be cautious in their use of patriarchal cultures so as to preserve a possibility for citizens to recover their living roots and to undertake their cultivation and sharing again. This requires the elaboration of another culture about which political and religious leaders do not care enough. Then, there is a stopping at criticizing and even at waging war against other peoples and regimes or at resorting to ideology, a sort of enslavement of life that can sometimes be still more paralyzing than religion. A moralistic repression of consciousness is also frequent in our societies today. All that shows an absence of appropriate culture in my opinion, as is the case when democracy is reduced to equality at an economic level, with the prevalence of claims against people who have a higher salary or more goods without consideration for the human value or merit of each one, as was the case at the establishment of Greek democracy. The relations among persons are then assessed only in quantitative terms and not in terms of qualities and respective domains of competence that are necessary for running a society. Furthermore, as they are valued in a quantitative way, the relations also become competitive and conflicting.

How could a peaceful coexistence take place without implementing the aptitudes of all citizens for running the community? For ages, the masculine requirements and aptitudes, what is more drawn only from certain traditions, have been privileged under the guise of universal individuals and means of governing and exchanging. This could explain why a democratic culture is still lacking and world conflicts remain insurmountable. All the citizens of the world have not yet been invited to express their opinion and contribute towards cultural elaboration. Now, more and more, the skills of all, and especially of women, to organize the relations between people, as well as to care about life and the environment, prove to be crucial for the natural and spiritual survival and growth of humanity. Women have been locked up within the family home and their existence has been divided up into natural tasks and religious duties. It becomes ever more obvious that public life needs feminine aptitudes to develop towards a democratic world culture. The question is not one of showing that women are capable of behaving as men, even in waging war, but of providing society and governance with their own qualities and values, including a specific understanding of religious values more compatible with a civil and democratic sharing of the world. The persistent interest in Antigone's character shows that she upheld values that are essential to govern a country.

In search of an international democratic style

A certain way of dealing with everything that exists, particularly with human beings, prevented human coexistence from being realized. In order to emerge from a maternal and natural origin, man—in particular, but not only, Western man—did not recognize the difference of the other part of humanity and did not attempt to enter into relations with it by accepting the partial nature of his masculine condition. Instead he endeavored to dominate the world by gathering everything together according to his own perspective and by guaranteeing such a totality with supreme values, authorities, or divinity. All that was accomplished according to his own necessities and abilities, but was presumed to correspond to the reality and the truth of all and for all. Every person who did not share the same point of view was expelled from the community and either deported from the city or enclosed within private places. Governing was based on sameness and only a scale of values with respect to the same—or the Same— was accepted. Difference(s), thus, amounted to quantitative evaluation of the aptitude to approach the perfect model which ruled over all the imperfect copies of it. The perfection to be respected and attained would then be an Idea or its embodiment: for example, Truth, Goodness, or God. Such an organization of the world and such a model of becoming seem to be incompatible with a universal coexistence. Now it still lays down the law in most of the so-called democratic systems. And it is not only because it is possible for people to elect their president or other political representatives that democracy is really at work. Beyond the fact that popular opinion can be manipulated, in particular by the media, but also by the political parties or candidates, electing one person instead of a program amounts to entrusting the government of the country to a head who represents the One presumed to secure the unity of the community. In fact, citizens can only trust and obey the decisions of the representatives who have been elected. Could this correspond to a democratic governing?

Yet, electing various points of a program would fit a model of democratic governance better. In that case, the political running would embody more faithfully what citizens want, and less the personal positions, even the ambitions, of a sort of householder. This requires a political education on the part of citizens, and the ability to listen to them and serve the needs and demands of all citizens on the part of those who take charge of the realization of the program. Such a way of governing could begin to resemble a democracy. We are still far from this, and our so-called democratic programs more often than not amount to the result of a game of more or less obvious strategies bringing into conflict persons, various cultural groups or countries that aspire to exercise power and promise everything and nothing during election campaigns, even caricaturing dramatically the situation, just to come to power. Citizens are somehow or other held hostage of such ambitions and competitions, and the hopes that they had invested in their candidates are often dashed. Hence, changes of rulers that correspond to rejection more than to true objectives and the fact that everyone loses from sight the correct means to form a human community and the adequate cultivation of energy that this requires. Hence, also, the fact that religious Absolutes, elaborated in various incompatible ways, may substitute for a democratic governance.

The impasses of past democracies become henceforth apparent and presidential, and even legislative, elections become more and more dependent on seduction and media tactics which are used to emphasize conflicts instead of working towards their pacification, so much so that democracy is discredited. Finally, citizens even renounce their right to vote because they no longer have confidence in the candidates and their discourses. It is urgent to take this situation into account in order to prevent it from getting worse and so-called democratic governances from giving rise to totalitarian tendencies or risks of intractable conflicts that may spread into regions, continents, and the whole world, as is the case with the Arab–Israeli conflict.

The bases of culture itself are to be questioned, especially the way of forming a whole and managing it. This always amounted to gathering together all the things from the outside, and even from on high. How can citizens constitute a human community if the relations among them are not considered, whereas this could be a really democratic means to elaborate policy? Perhaps this results from the manner in which patriarchy has appropriated power. It substituted more or less arbitrary laws based on property for the ties that organized matriarchal communities. Patriarchal governance did not really care about the living links between the persons. Instead, it broke them off in order to impose an artificially built authority that ended in a society made up of only a part of humanity transformed in more or less neuter or neutralized members. In reality a sort of phallic order took the place of natural ties related to family or genealogy. Artificial links founded on codes and possession of goods—among other things of power—substituted for natural links assimilated to mere links of blood without acknowledging that sexuate belonging takes part in them. Instead of establishing his authority in partnership with the other part of humanity, with woman, by sharing respective belongings and aptitudes, man has separated natural power and constructed power, decreeing that this latter concerned cultural and public domains, whereas the former was confined to the sphere of private and family life, of which patriarchy has neglected the civic and religious specific potentials.

Humanity became split into two parts defined according to their duties in the service of patriarchal governance without thinking about their relations to natural belonging: on the one hand, a material presumed sexless bodily part, and, on the other hand, a sexuate part, blindly assimilated to the spiritual aspect of humanity. This prevented both men and women from developing their sexuate identity and the relationships between them as the basis of a human coexistence in difference, at the private level and the public level, and, consequently, a universal human sharing from taking place. In fact, our past and current regimes misjudge the citizenship and partnership of women as women and therefore have to manage without the feminine qualities required to preserve life itself and its essential environment, but also to establish civil relations among all citizens and to ensure the social weaving of a democratic community. More and more, the lack of a feminine participation in governing comes to light, while some values prove to be crucial for a democratic exercise, and first for a possible future for humanity and its earthly dwelling. Their absence is too little interpreted as the outcome of the assignation of women to the care of natural life within the family home. I will present some of these values that seem to be necessary today to govern not only a country but the whole world, values which could, among other things, be of use in preventing or in calming down the politically insoluble conflicts.

Feminine aptitudes suitable for building a world culture

It is urgent in our times to be concerned about the preservation and the care of life itself. All regimes, and especially democracies, must worry about this first. Certainly, women have protected life inside the family home, but their task was undervalued at the public and the cultural levels. And if political authorities begin to get worried about the future of our planet and its ecosystems, they still neglect the fact that humans themselves are in danger. No doubt, the State often encourages women to give birth, but it does not care enough about the life of the children when they enter public life, notably in the case of conflicts. Moreover, bringing a child into the world is still considered to be a natural process, which does not call for a highly developed subjectivity. What culture has really understood what sharing her blood and her breath with the fetus means for a woman? Do not some religious commandments or rituals borrow from what happens between a woman and the child with whom she is pregnant? Must a culture of nature be considered inferior to a culture of spirit, which aims at separating off from nature and dominating it? Must we value more a symbolic construction, which might divide us, than life itself? And could not a cultivation of life represent the seed of a new culture that humanity needs today, a culture of which women could be the prophets and in which they would have a leading part, including at the spiritual and religious levels?

Women can also have a role of privileged protagonists in a culture of hospitality that is crucial in our age. The most ancient traditions of hospitality are feminine and presuppose a mutual right to get housing and protection from one another: the term *hôte* (guest) designates both the one who gives and the one who receives hospitality in several languages, such as French. The meaning that we attribute today to the term hospitality is rather recent: "a charity which consists in free welcoming, housing and feeding the indigent and the traveller" (cf. dictionary *Le Robert*). This more hierarchic and paternalistic understanding, implicitly related to money, corresponds to the hospitality we should practice in our times. We are no longer living in times when all the children of our mother nature had a duty to give one another hospitality. Perhaps we came to that because the hospitality a woman offers inside the family home remained ignored at a public level. Is she not asked to freely be in the house and feed all the members of the family, and even the potential guests? Are not her gestures the unrecognized basis of hospitality? No doubt, feminine hospitality is still more secret and intimate: a woman gives hospitality within her own body to her lover and the future child. What could be the sense of a culture of hospitality if it ignores the original hospitality that allows humanity to love, to be born, that is, to exist? Does not this hospitality involve an ethics which goes beyond that which is advocated in public life? Does not the feminine practice of hospitality represent a value to be considered and extended outside the family strictly speaking? Would current conflicts, in particular the Arab–Israeli conflict, be possible if feminine hospitality would spread into and shape civil life? And does not a world culture require such an evolution?

Another value for which we want today is proximity between people. Even shopkeepers exploit this lack, appealing in their advertising campaign to "*your* local store," a formulation that is successful, given that people feel a little lost in a world that becomes too big, too complicated, and too cold. Meetings between neighbors or associations of citizens are also increasing because they allow people to gather together. Perhaps this results from the fact that the family—even all sorts of families—is losing its vocation for being the first place of intimacy and is becoming a mere space of familiarity. Such a familiarity, often reduced to a sharing of habits and customs, proves to be disappointing and, moreover, no longer meets the requirements of our age. Henceforth, we have to coexist with other cultures and ways of behaving, and what seemed to be obvious in a single culture or tradition is now called into question at any moment. Thus, it is urgent to discover and cultivate another sort of proximity between us, a human intimacy. What do wars look like for those who found this universal human intimacy? Once more, women can act as guides on that occasion if they become conscious of their potential and if their role is more valued by society. A woman, who shares with the other within herself in love and in motherhood, has an experience of intimacy that exceeds a spatial or cultural proximity. Her aptitude for sharing can lead us to discover a way of relating to each human other on this side and beyond any political, cultural, or religious connivance as is required in our age of blending of peoples and traditions.

This is all the more so because the sharing that a woman offers within herself does not exclude difference, beginning with that of the lover or of the son. Difference takes place in nature itself which deals with it, including at a bodily level, whereas constructed cultures more often than not do not tolerate difference(s). We all share humanity, whatever our differences may be. However, this human sharing cannot take place because secondary differences divide us: cultural or religious differences, combined with differences of sex, of age, of color, etc., as well as almost all the quantitative differences that are often substitutes for natural difference, especially sexuate difference. A woman, who remains closer to nature, is more capable of a sharing in natural differences which compose humankind, in particular the vertical difference of genealogy and the horizontal difference between man and woman. Such an aptitude is especially crucial in our times, and the ability of women to share in difference can open up a path towards a peaceful coexistence on a world scale, including between the Palaestinian people and the Israeli people.

To conclude

We have a long way to go to attain and embody a world sharing that would avoid murderous conflicts. Instead of stopping at criticizing the current ways of governing and behaving of other peoples and traditions, we ought first to wonder about what we called democracy up until now. We must recognize that a democratic governance can be neither imagined nor exercised by only a part of humanity in the name of the whole world. Democratic leaders often invite us to remember the material aspect of our lives. However, they generally reduce it to an economic element without considering our natural belonging and our sexuate embodiment. They do not realize that asexual individuals cannot achieve a democratic coexistence: in reality, they correspond to a sort of idealistic and capitalistic construction which cannot act towards a world coexistence.

If democracies are in crisis in our epoch, if they are unable to solve their own problems or those arising from the relations with other countries and traditions, it is because their foundations have nothing to do with living peoples. The political representatives govern abstract beings animated by more or less abstract games of for or against which are disconnected from their real needs or desires and are lacking any regulation, in particular at the level of energy; hence, the proliferation of conflicts resulting in chaos. Instead of basing their authority on the condemnation of others, notably of other regimes, and resorting to media tactics and demagogic rhetoric to appeal to citizens, democratic rulers ought to contribute towards the individuation of individuals so that they become capable of governing, beginning with governing themselves. Before sentencing others for terrorism, it would be advisable to analyze what remains somehow or other terrorist in our own democracies, in ourselves, in our way of thinking, speaking, and acting.

Perhaps something of a democratic process occurred in Greek times on the part of men, because this process was required to win a masculine subjectivity with respect to the maternal origin. But, having failed to pave the way to a civil coexistence with the other part of humanity, beginning with the mother herself, the true aim of democracy has been forgotten. It has thus evolved towards a loss of individuation instead of its acquisition, and has prevented a democratic governance from taking place. We must return to our initial belonging, our natural belonging, and learn how to cultivate it in a human way. We must give up all the constructed identities and values that have divided us from ourselves and among us, and make way for a becoming of humanity which is shareable by all with respect for our mutual differences. In the entire world, they are only men and women, from various ages, colors, countries, cultures, traditions, socio-economic backgrounds, etc. Starting from this difference, which is both universal and proper to each one, we can begin to build a world culture with rights and human growth suitable for all.

Index

"Abraham, the Other" (Derrida, Jacques) 142
Abrahamic faiths 113–14, 119, 120, 121, 124, 128n. 5, 129n. 22, 130n. 34
Adam Resurrected (Kaniuk, Yoram) 134–6, 139–41
African philosophy 124
Ahmadinejad, Mahmoud 18, 19
alienation 76, 77, 80, 81, 84, 85–6, 92, 137
Alliance Israélite Universelle 142, 144n. 8, 145n. 31
Anidjar, Gil
  "Mal de Sionisme (Zionist Fever)" 136
Animal that therefore I am, (More to Follow) The (Derrida, Jacques) 142
anti-Semitism xv, xvi, 1–6, 11, 25, 26–7, 36, 37, 38, 39, 40, 41, 43, 44, 45, 52n. 6, 53n. 12, 72n. 1, 84, 86, 99, 133–4, 138, 147
anti-Zionism 15–21, 58–60, 68, 100
Antigone (Sophocles) 173–5
Arabs xii, xv, 6, 12n. 4, 17, 18, 28, 43, 45, 46, 47, 48, 62, 63, 78, 115, 121, 123, 126, 127, 143, 158, 162, 163, 164, 167n. 27, 169
Archive Fever (Derrida, Jacques) 122–3
Arendt, Hannah 25, 27, 28, 29, 30, 31, 32, 33, 34, 37, 38, 39, 40, 41, 42, 43, 44, 45, 46, 47, 48, 49, 50, 51, 52, 52n. 6, 53n. 12, 54n. 28, 55n. 29, 55n. 30, 75, 78, 80, 83, 85, 86, 87, 88, 89, 90, 91, 92, 93, 96n. 52, 134, 142, 143, 144, 147, 148, 150, 152, 158, 166n. 8
  alienation and 85–6
  asylum and 134
  Benjamin, Walter and 30–1, 32, 86, 93
  Christianity and 85, 91–3
  cohabitation and 31–3

"Decline of the Rights of Man and the End of the Nation-State, The" 46, 49, 54n. 28, 55n. 29
denationalization and 46–7
Eichmann in Jerusalem 32, 37–8, 43, 45, 75, 87–91
Europe and 28, 29, 39, 40, 42, 43–5, 46, 49, 51, 55n. 28, 86
federation and 28, 42, 47–51
Human Condiiton, The 42, 55n. 29, 85, 92
human rights and 45, 46, 49–51, 54n. 28, 86, 87, 89–90
Jewish army and 44, 45, 51
"Jewish History Revised" 29
Jewish thought and 29–30, 51, 52n. 6
Jewish Writings 39
Jewishness and 25, 28, 38–43, 44–5, 51, 86
justice and 28, 31, 38, 41, 51, 54n. 28, 90–1, 142, 143
messianism and 29–30
nation-state, the and 28, 29, 37, 39, 40, 41, 42, 45–9, 50, 51, 52, 54n. 28, 55n. 29, 86, 88, 90, 134
nationalism and 28, 37, 40–52, 52n. 6, 150, 166n. 8
On Revolution 50, 85
Origins of Totalitarianism, The 28, 39, 45, 49, 52, 86–7, 89
paradox and 33, 34, 42, 45–6, 51, 88, 90
pluralization and 32–4
political theology and 85–93
political thinking of 37, 45
racism and 43
Scholem, Gershom and 28–30, 31, 37–42, 45, 51, 52n. 6, 86, 91
sovereignty and 28, 42, 45, 46, 48, 49, 51, 52

statelessness and 28–9, 35, 40, 41, 45–7, 49, 51–2, 86, 89–90, 150
"Zionism Reconsidered" 46, 48
Argentina 61, 69, 70, 71, 89, 134
assimilationism 37, 39, 40, 43
asylum 133–6, 137, 138, 139, 140, 141, 144
Auerbach, Erich 138
  Mimesis 138

Barbie, Klaus 142–3, 144
Bauer, Bruno 76, 78–9, 80, 81, 86, 88, 89, 90, 95n. 42, 96n. 52
  "Capacity of the Contemporary Jews and Christians to Become Free, The" 78, 79
  "Jewish Question, The" 78–9, 83–4
  "Trumpet of the Last Judgment over Hegel, an Atheist and Antichrist" 83
Being xii–xiv, 135, 148–51
Being and Time (Heidegger, Martin) 149
Benjamin, Walter 20, 30–1, 32, 35, 36, 86, 93, 150
  Illuminations 31
  "Theses on the Philosophy of History" 30–1
bi-national state 9, 27–8, 45, 48, 163
blood election 119–20, 126–7
Blumenberg, Hans 77
Book of Isaiah 165
Brasillach, Robert 11
Breivik, Anders Behring 1–3
British Empire, the 64–5
Buber, Martin 28, 39, 45, 48, 92, 97n. 75, 158, 165, 166n. 8
Butler, Judith 110n. 18, 144, 148, 151, 152n. 4
  Frames of War: When Is Life Grievable? 35

"Capacity of the Contemporary Jews and Christians to Become Free, The" (Bauer, Bruno) 78, 79
China 57, 65, 71, 72
Chofshi, Nathan 163–5
  "Into the Abyss" 163–5
Christianity 1, 5, 23, 63, 74n. 24, 75–8, 79, 91–3, 94n. 9, 96n. 52, 108, 114, 116, 117, 121, 130n. 34, 137 *see also* Christians
  communion and 116
  Feuerbach, Ludwig and 84
  Hegel, Georg and 81–3
  Marx, Karl and 84–5, 95n. 42
Christians 3, 4, 5, 7, 10, 12, 12n. 2, 20, 61, 63, 64, 65, 66, 67, 75, 76, 77, 78, 79, 80, 84–5, 91–2, 93, 96n. 42, 96n. 52, 113, 114–15, 118, 120, 123, 124, 126, 130n. 34, 143 *see also* Christianity
Christians United for Israel 12n. 2
circumcision 113, 117, 123, 130n. 34, 142
civil code 170–1, 172, 173
civil rights 5, 80, 170–3
Civilizational state 72
Cixous, Hélène 144
  Exile of James Joyce, The 137
  Vivre l'Orange 137
cohabitation 26, 27–8, 29, 30, 31–3, 34, 36, 148
Cohen, Hermann 53n. 6, 92
  "Deutschtum and Judentum" 44
Cohen brothers
  Serious Man, A 21
colonialism 18, 26, 29, 36, 57–8, 66–7, 78, 142, 143
conflict resolution 71, 169–70
counter-religion 121
Crémieux, Adolphe 142
criticisms xiv–xv, 24–5, 26–7, 28, 37, 38, 43, 45, 48, 75, 78, 83, 89, 92, 96n. 52, 104, 114, 122, 128n. 3, 130n. 33, 165
Croatia 3
cultural gentrification 7
Czechoslovakia 12n. 10

Davis, Mike
  Planet of Slums 150
"Debate over Judaism from Kant to Young Hegelians, The" (Tomasoni, Francesco) 81, 95n. 42
"Decline of the Rights of Man and the End of the Nation-State, The" (Arendt, Hannah) 46, 49, 54n. 28, 55n. 29

decolonization 57, 59–62
deconstruction xii–xiv, xv, xvi, 20, 99,
    100, 101, 102, 103, 105, 107, 108,
    109, 114, 124, 125, 127, 140, 147,
    157, 159
demetaphorization 138
democracy xv, 16, 24, 28, 36, 60, 80, 137,
    139, 149, 172, 175–7, 179–80
denationalization 46–7
Derrida, Jacques xi, xii, xiii, 20, 92,
    113–14, 117, 118–27, 128n. 3, 128n.
    5, 129n. 20, 129n. 22, 130n. 33,
    130n. 34, 131n. 46, 137, 140, 142–4,
    147, 149, 157, 167n. 19
  "Abraham, the Other" 142
  Animal that therefore I am, (More to Follow) The 142
  Archive Fever 122–3
  "Eyes of Language: The Volcano and the Abyss, The" 159–62
  "Force of Law" 143
  "Khora" 119
  Of Spirit: Heidegger and the Question 122–3
  Specters of Marx 123, 128n. 3, 167n. 19
"Deutschtum and Judentum" (Cohen, Hermann) 44
diaspora xiii, 28–30, 59, 62, 67, 68, 101,
    102, 133, 134, 136, 157
  negation of 133–6
Differend of Israel (van Vliet, Netta) 136–7
dispossession 30, 33, 34, 35, 36, 51, 58,
    62, 67–8, 69, 70, 73n. 3, 74n. 24,
    106, 150 *see also* refugees *and* statelessness
dissemination xiii
Dreyfus affair, the 133–4, 142–3, 144,
    144n. 3

East Jerusalem 6, 7, 9, 18, 106, 149
economic crisis 10
egoism 80, 83–4, 88, 89–90, 91, 93, 96n. 52
Egypt 17, 58, 62, 63, 87, 104, 113, 114,
    116–19, 120, 121, 123, 124, 127,
    129n. 20, 129n. 22
Eichmann in Jerusalem (Arendt, Hannah)
    32, 37–8, 43, 45, 75, 87–91
Ellis, Marc 57, 58–9, 67, 70

Epic of Askia Mohammed, The (Hale, Thomas and Malio, Nouhou) 117
"Essence of Christianity" (Feuerbach, Ludwig) 83–4, 95n. 37
ethnic cleansing 7, 16, 106, 108, 126
EU (European Union) 3, 12n. 2, 72, 152
European politics 10–11, 70
European Union (EU) 3, 12n. 2, 72, 152
exile xiii, xiv, 26, 28, 29, 30, 33, 40, 46, 51,
    108, 111n. 18, 133, 134, 136, 137–8,
    165
Exile of James Joyce, The (Cixous, Hélène)
    137
"Eyes of Language: The Volcano and the Abyss, The" (Derrida, Jacques)
    159–62

Farias, Victor 20
fascism xv, 1, 10, 11, 15–16, 17, 29, 38, 40,
    41, 42, 44, 46, 51, 53n. 6
Faye, Emmanuel 20, 147
federation 28, 42, 47–51
Feuerbach, Ludwig 83–4, 92, 95n. 37, 96n.
    52, 97n. 75
  "Essence of Christianity" 83–4
Fini, Gianfranco 15–16
Finkelstein, Norman 19, 126, 150
"Force of Law" (Derrida, Jacques) 143
Frames of War: When Is Life Grievable?
    (Butler, Judith) 35
French Revolution 4, 5, 50, 57, 58, 66,
    76, 88
fundamentalism 1, 2, 3, 4, 11, 113

Gaza Strip, the 8, 17
genealogy 24, 115–17, 119–20, 177,
    179 *see also* blood election *and* inheritance
genese, La (1999) 115–16
global linear thinking 67
governance 61, 62, 66, 71–2, 93, 171, 172,
    173, 175, 176, 177, 179, 180 *see also* nation-state
griots 115–17, 118

Ha'am, Ahad 134
Hagee, John 12n. 2
  Jerusalem Countdown 12n. 2

Hale, Thomas and Malio Nouhou
  Epic of Askia Mohammed, The 117
Hamlet (Shakespeare, William) 118
"Hamlet constellation" 116, 118
Hebrew 21, 43, 59, 103, 104, 139, 159, 161–2, 163 *see also* language
Hegel, Georg xiii, 76, 78, 80, 81–3, 89, 90, 91–2, 94n. 25, 95n. 42, 96n. 52, 97n. 66, 172
  Lectures on the Philosophy of Religion 81, 82–3
  Phenomenology of Spirit 53n. 18
  "Spirit of Christianity and its Fate, The" 81–2, 91
Heidegger, Martin xiii, 19–20, 50, 85, 119, 122–3, 130n. 33, 147–51
  Being and Time 149
heka 113, 117, 118, 119, 120, 124
Henri-Levy, Bernard 3
  Left in Dark Times, The 3
hermeneutics 20, 147–51
Herzl, Theodor 25, 65–6, 67, 69, 73n. 4, 133, 142–3, 144, 144n. 3
  Jewish State, The 73n. 4, 134
historical amnesia 35
historical materialism 31
Hitler, Adolf 1, 2, 4, 11, 12n. 2, 15, 19, 21, 44, 61, 70, 143 *see also* Nazism
Holocaust, the 5, 12n. 2, 15, 19, 68, 88, 91–2, 100, 102, 103, 108, 109, 110n. 4, 110n. 11, 110n. 18, 133, 134, 135, 140, 142, 150, 152n. 3, 170 see also *Eichmann in Jerusalem*
  theology 104–7
"holy basin" 7–8
Homer 5
  Odyssey 138, 139
homophobia 3, 8
Horus, story of 116, 118
hospitality 136, 141, 165, 178
Human Condition, The (Arendt, Hannah) 42, 55n. 29, 85, 92
human rights xv, 40, 45, 46, 61, 79, 80, 93, 126, 134, 136, 160 *see also* rights of man
  Arendt, Hannah and 49–51, 54n. 28, 86, 87, 89–90

identity 1, 2, 3, 10, 26, 4–5, 41, 42, 59, 85, 86, 99–104, 106–7, 109, 109n. 1, 110n. 16, 110n. 17, 114, 123, 125, 126, 128n. 3, 128n. 5, 161, 164–5, 166, 169, 171–3 *see also* naming *and* synecdoche
  sexuate 170–4, 177
ideology xii, xiii, xiv, xvi, 1, 3, 57, 61, 70, 76, 79, 80, 88, 106, 108, 110n. 14, 120, 147, 156, 157, 158, 161, 163, 175
Illuminations (Benjamin, Walter) 31
immigration 1–3, 10–11, 44, 54n. 27, 61
inheritance 15, 38, 135–6 *see also* blood election *and* genealogy
"Into the Abyss" (Chofshi, Nathan) 163–5
Iran xv, 12n. 1, 17, 18, 19, 20, 57, 64, 65, 71, 128n. 5, 137
Iraq 64, 65, 70, 71
Isaiah, Book of 165
Israel, State of xi, xii, xiii, xiv, xv, xvi, 2, 6, 7, 8, 9, 10, 11, 12, 12n. 2, 12n. 4, 15, 16, 17, 18, 19, 20, 21, 23, 24, 25, 26, 27, 28, 29, 30, 35, 36, 37, 39, 41, 42, 43, 45, 46, 48, 51, 55n. 29, 57, 58, 59, 60, 61, 62, 66, 67, 68, 69, 70, 71, 72, 86, 88, 89, 100, 101–2, 105–6, 107, 108, 109, 110n. 18, 113, 114, 119, 120, 121, 122, 123, 126, 127, 128n. 5, 131n. 46, 134, 135, 136–7, 148, 149, 152n. 4, 155, 157, 158, 159, 164, 165, 166n. 8, 169, 170, 172, 174, 176, 178, 179 *see also* nation-state, the
  anti-Semitism and 3–5
  asylum and 133–6
  bureaucracy and 8
  creation of xv, 15, 58–62, 64–5, 70–1
  criticisms of 24–7
  decolonization and 59–60
  Derrida, Jacques and 125–6
  dissolution of 108 *see also* destruction of *under* Jews
  exceptionalism and xv, 27
  God and 103–4
  Holocaust, the and 19
  Iran and 19
  Judaism and 59–60, 157–8

Law of Return and 133, 136
legitimacy of 18–19
modernism and 137
multiculturalism and 2
occupation and xii, 6–9, 17–18
Palestine and 27, 36, 101, 106, 108
politics of 17–18, 21
settlements and 6–9, 17–18
state violence and 25–6, 163–5
Tutu, Desmond (bishop) and 59–60
"West Bank Barrier" and 125
Italy xv, 15–16

Jerusalem xiii, 2, 6, 7–8, 32, 43, 64, 69, 71, 88, 90, 91, 101, 106, 108, 125, 137, 138, 155, 156, 159 *see also* East Jerusalem
Jerusalem Countdown (Hagee, John) 12n. 2
"Jewish History Revised" (Arendt, Hannah) 29
"Jewish Question, The" (Bauer, Bruno) 78–9, 83–4, 89
Jewish Resistance Movement 163
Jewish State, The (Herzl, Theodor) 73n. 4, 134
Jewish Writings (Arendt, Hannah) 39
Jewishness 5, 17, 18, 23, 25–6, 27, 33, 36, 38, 102, 103, 136 *see also* Jews *and* Judaism
  Arendt, Hannah and 25, 28, 38–43, 44–5, 51, 86
Jews xii, xiv, xv, xvi, 2, 3, 4, 5, 6, 7, 12n. 2, 16, 17, 20–1, 25, 26, 27, 28, 30, 32, 36, 37, 38, 39, 40, 41, 42, 43, 44, 45, 46, 47, 48, 49, 50, 51, 53n. 6, 53n. 12, 59, 60, 61, 63, 64, 65, 66, 67, 68, 69, 70, 73n. 13, 75, 77, 78, 79, 81, 83, 84, 86, 87, 88, 89, 90, 91, 92, 99–109, 109n. 3, 110n. 7, 110n. 16, 110n. 18, 120, 121, 122, 123, 125, 126, 127, 134, 136, 137, 138, 142, 148, 150, 151, 157, 158, 163, 166n. 8, 167n. 27 *see also* Jewishness *and* Judaism
  abstract 40–1
  anti-Zionism and xv–xvi, 15
  circumcision and 123
  destruction of 103, 105
  emancipation and 5, 40
  empowerment and 105–6
  Europe and 43–4
  Exodus and 63
  geography and 102–3
  Iberian peninsular expulsion of 63
  identity and 4–5, 99–104, 106–7
  as minority 126
  prophetic impulse and 104–8
  Tutu, Desmond (bishop) and 59
  violence and 25
Jews of Conscience 108–9
Joyce, James 137
  Ulysses 137–40
Judaism xv–xvi, 25, 26, 28, 31, 39, 41, 42, 43, 57, 67, 68–70, 75–85, 91, 92, 93, 94n. 9, 94n. 25, 95n. 37, 95n. 42, 96n. 52, 97n. 75, 102, 117, 119, 121, 124, 128n. 3, 128n. 5, 136, 148 *see also* Jewishness *and* Jews
  Abrahamic faiths and 113
  Bauer, Bruno and 78–80, 83–4
  as counter-religion 121
  Derrida, Jacques and 113–14, 121–4, 142
  Feuerbach, Ludwig and 84
  genealogy and 117
  Hegel, Georg and 81–3
  influence on 124
  Israel and 59–60
  Kant, Immanuel and 81
  Marx, Karl and 78–85
  Mendelsohn, Moses and 81
  Rosenzweig, Franz and 28
justice xii–xiv, xvi, 20, 25, 26, 27, 29, 31, 36, 38, 41, 44, 51, 54n. 28, 90, 91, 101, 107, 109, 111n. 18, 136, 142–3, 148, 164, 165, 166

Kaniuk, Yoram
  Adam Resurrected 134–6, 139–41
Kant, Immanuel 33, 44, 45, 79, 81, 83, 89, 125, 141, 156
  Religion in the Boundaries of Mere Reason 81
Kaplan, Alice 143
Karta, Neturai 134

Kati, Al Hajj Mahmud 122
Tarikh al fattash 115, 121–2
Keita, Salif 115
"Khora" (Derrida, Jacques) 119
kibbutzim 17, 45

lamella 4
"Latin" America 18, 61–2 *see also* South America
Law of Return 125, 133, 136
Lectures on the Philosophy of Religion (Hegel, Georg) 81, 82–3
Left in Dark Times, The (Henri-Levy, Bernard) 3
Lemon Tree (Riklis, Eran) xi–xii
Leonard, Miriam 137
Levinas, Emmanuel 92, 121, 136, 139, 142, 145n. 31
  "Name of a Dog, or Natural Rights, The" 141
liberalism 1, 27, 127
Lot's cave, story of 114–15
Lyotard, Jean-François 92, 99–100, 109n. 3

Major Trends in Jewish Mysticism (Scholem, Gershom) 29
Makdisi, Saree
  Palestine Inside Out: An Everyday Occupation 8
"Mal de Sionisme (Zionist Fever)" (Anidjar, Gil) 136
Malio, Nouhou and Hale, Thomas
  Epic of Askia Mohammed, The 117
"Manifest Destiny" 66
Marx, Karl 75, 78–87, 89, 90, 92, 93, 95n. 42, 96n. 46
  "On the Jewish Question" 75, 78–87, 91, 136
matriarchies 173–4, 177
Mendelsohn, Moses 40, 81
Messianic Zionism 120, 126, 134
messianicity *see* messianism
messianism 29–30, 35, 44, 54n. 21, 85, 92, 93, 96n. 42, 113–14, 119–21, 126, 130n. 33, 130n. 34, 134, 157
metaphysics of presence, the xiii
Mimesis (Auerbach, Erich) 138

monotheism 6, 7, 77, 84, 101, 113, 121, 170
multiculturalism 1–2, 10–11, 34, 71
Museum of Tolerance 7
Muslims 2, 7, 12n. 4, 63–4, 114, 115, 120, 122, 123, 126
mythology xi, xiv, 15–18, 20, 99, 100–1, 113, 116, 117, 118, 127, 157, 170

Nakba 16, 18, 47
"Name of a Dog, or Natural Rights, The" (Levinas, Emmanuel) 141
naming 135–42, 159, 161, 163 *see also* identity
nation-state, the 6, 26, 28–9, 46–8, 58, 60, 61–2, 63–72, 73n. 2, 77, 78, 86, 88, 90, 125, 134, 135, 136, 165 *see also* decolonization
  alternatives to 71–2
  Arendt, Hannah and 28, 29, 37, 39, 40, 41, 42, 45–9, 50, 51, 52, 54n. 28, 55n. 29, 86, 88, 90, 134
  coloniality and 57
  creation of 57–8
  Derrida, Jacques and 125
  dispossession and 68
  Europe and 57–8, 61, 70
  history of 64–71
  national subjects 66
  nationalism and 69–70
  US and 57–8, 66
nationalism xv, 8, 25, 28, 37, 40–52, 53n. 6, 60, 67, 69–70, 74n. 22, 127, 150, 166n. 8
Nazism xv, 2, 4, 5, 17, 29, 32, 37, 43, 52, 61, 86, 87–9, 104, 124, 135, 137, 139
  Heidegger, Martin and 19–20, 122, 147, 152n. 2
neutrality xiv–xv, 8, 69, 124, 170, 171, 172
neutralization xiv, 11, 148, 160, 172, 177
Night of the Trains 163
Normalization (Simecka, Milan) 12n. 10
Northwest Africa 119, 121, 122 *see also* West Africa
nyama 113, 117, 118–19, 120, 124

Odyssey (Homer) 138, 139
Of Spirit: Heidegger and the Question (Derrida, Jacques) 122–3

On Revolution (Arendt, Hannah) 50, 85
"On the Jewish Question" (Marx, Karl) 75, 78–87, 91, 136
one-state solution 101, 106–7, 158
ontology 20, 26, 33, 34, 35, 49, 50, 51, 93, 148–51, 160 *see also* Being
"Operation Cast Lead" 17, 19
Origins of Totalitarianism, The (Arendt, Hannah) 28, 39, 45, 49, 52, 86–7, 89
other, the xii, 11, 33, 35, 89, 92, 116–18, 123, 131n. 46, 165–6, 162, 165, 166, 179

Palestine xi, xii, xiii, xiv, xv, 2, 6, 7, 8–9, 15, 16, 19, 26, 27, 28, 29, 35, 36, 39, 42, 45, 46, 52, 54n. 27, 57, 60, 62, 64, 67, 68, 69, 71, 72, 100, 101, 102, 105–6, 108, 109, 115, 120, 124, 125, 126, 127, 134, 149, 159, 163, 164, 169–70, see also *Nakba*
  evictions and 8–9, 47, 150, 158
  Israel and 27, 36, 59, 101, 106
  Israeli occupations and 8–9, 17–18, 27, 108
  knowledge of 17
Palestine Inside Out: An Everyday Occupation (Makdisi, Saree) 8
pan-Arabism 126
Pappe, Ilan 15, 16–17, 148
paradoxes 2, 3, 4, 26, 33, 37, 42, 45, 51, 62, 67, 69, 74n. 22, 75, 76, 88, 90, 104, 105, 136, 140, 163, 165
patriarchies 113, 172, 174–7
peace 3, 7, 8, 9, 11, 57, 68, 71, 99, 107, 109, 127, 165, 170, 172, 173, 175, 179
pensiero debole xii
Peterson, Erik 77
Phenomenology of Spirit (Hegel, Georg) 53n. 18
philosophy xiii, 19, 20, 33, 44, 45, 77, 85, 97n. 75, 113, 114, 119, 121, 122, 123, 124, 148, 149, 150, 151, 152n. 2
Planet of Slums (Davis, Mike) 150
pluralization 31–4
pluri-national state 61, 71

political theology 75–8
  Arendt, Hannah and 85–93
  Marx, Karl and 78–85, 93
politics 2, 3, 4, 7, 9, 10, 11, 15–16, 17, 18, 19, 21, 25, 75–6, 27, 29, 30, 31, 33, 36, 37, 41, 42, 47, 50, 51, 52, 70, 76, 77, 82, 85, 93, 94n. 9, 105, 108, 127, 148–50, 172
Presse, Die 4
Prior, Michael 58, 67–8
private sphere, the 23, 79–81
Progressive Jews 25, 108–9
public sphere, the 23–4, 27, 36, 79–81, 162, 173
punishment 29, 81–2, 87, 107, 160
Purgatorium, the 6

race 5, 17, 20, 58, 60, 63–4, 66, 138, 159
racism xv, 2, 3, 10–12, 16, 17, 18, 21, 25, 41, 43, 45, 53n. 6, 58, 63, 66, 68, 108, 125, 128n. 5, 136, 143, 147, 148, 152n. 2, 152n. 4
Raz-Krakotzkin, Amnon 30
"realism" 149
Reformation, the 76
refugees 17, 18, 26, 28–9, 35, 40, 45, 47, 51, 52, 133, 158 *see also* dispossession *and* statelessness
religion xvi, 7, 23–4, 26, 36, 44, 60, 75, 76, 77, 78, 79–84, 85, 88, 89, 91, 92, 93, 94n. 25, 96n. 52, 101, 108, 113, 114, 117, 120, 121, 124, 127, 128n. 3, 128n. 5, 137, 148, 159, 162, 172, 173, 174, 175 *see also* Christianity *and* Judaism
Religion in the Boundaries of Mere Reason (Kant, Immanuel) 81
rights of man 37, 49, 55n. 29, 78, 80, 90, 143 *see also* human rights
Riklis, Eran
  Lemon Tree xi–xii
Rosenzweig, Franz 20, 92, 97n. 75, 159, 161, 163
  Star of Redemption, The 28
ruah 113, 114, 117–20, 122–5

Said, Edward 28, 29, 32, 126, 127, 158
Samuel xiv, xvin. 6

Schmitt, Carl xiv, 67, 75, 76–7, 90, 93
Scholem, Gershom 28–30, 31, 37–42,
    45, 50, 51, 53n. 6, 86, 91, 159–62,
    163
  Major Trends in Jewish Mysticism 29
secularization 24, 66–9, 75–7, 85, 162,
    163
Serbia 3
Serious Man, A (Cohen brothers) 21
Seth, story of 116, 118
sexual difference 10, 136, 137, 144
sexuate identity 170–4, 177, 179
Shakespeare, William
  Hamlet 118
Sharon, Ariel 125
shibboleths 118, 126, 131n. 46
Shoah, the xv, 16, 17, 20, 78, 122, 123, 126
  see also Holocaust, the
Simecka, Milan
  Normalization 12n. 10
Simon Wiesenthal Center 7
Sissoko, Cheick Oumar 115–16
Songhay, the 115, 117, 121–2, 123
Sophocles
  Antigone 173–5
sous rature xii
South America 61, 65, 71 *see also* "Latin"
    America
sovereignty 26, 28, 42, 45, 46, 48, 49, 51,
    52, 68, 76–7, 83, 137
Specters of Marx (Derrida, Jacques) 123,
    128n. 3, 167n. 19
spirit *see ruah*
"Spirit of Christianity and its Fate, The"
    (Hegel, Georg) 81–2, 91
Star of Redemption, The (Rosenzweig,
    Franz) 28
statelessness xi, xiv, 28, 29, 35, 37, 39,
    40, 41, 45–7, 49, 51–2, 54n. 28,
    55n. 29, 86, 89–90, 93, 150 *see also*
    dispossession *and* refugees
  Jewish 51, 86, 107
Sternhell, Zeev 127
synecdoche 155–62, 164–6

Tarikh al fattash (Kati, Al Hajj Mahmud)
    115, 121–2
terrorism 11, 17, 18, 19, 164, 180

theology 5, 75–8, 81, 85, 86, 91, 95n. 42,
    104, 105, 106, 107, 123, 128n. 5 *see
    also* political theology
"Theses on the Philosophy of History"
    (Benjamin, Walter) 30–1
Tomasoni, Francesco 81
  "Debate over Judaism from Kant to
    Young Hegelians, The" 81, 95n. 42
trauma xii, 1, 35, 134, 139, 140, 142, 163
"Trumpet of the Last Judgment over
    Hegel, an Atheist and Antichrist"
    (Bauer, Bruno) 83
Turkey 3, 57, 65, 69, 70, 72
Tutu, Desmond (bishop) 59–60
two-state solution 7, 71, 101, 106–7

Ulysses (Joyce, James) 137–40
"under erasure" xii
United States of America 2, 3, 12n. 2,
    16–18, 40, 45, 57, 58, 59, 60, 61, 62,
    64, 65, 66, 70, 71, 73n. 13, 80, 108,
    109, 113, 127, 128n. 3
universalization 32, 33, 36

van Vliet, Netta
  Differend of Israel 136–7
Vatican, the 8
Vergès, Jacques 143, 144
violence xi–xii, 3, 9, 24, 25, 26, 27, 36, 46,
    51, 61, 70, 93, 101, 125, 136, 141,
    143, 144, 147, 152n. 4, 155, 158,
    159, 160, 163–5, 169
virtual citizenship 157
Vivre l'Orange (Cixous, Hélène) 137

wandering Jew 134, 136, 137, 138
weak thought xii
West, the xiii, 1, 2, 5, 10, 15, 16–17, 18,
    19, 60, 61, 62, 63, 64, 66, 67, 68,
    69, 70, 71, 72, 73n. 3, 73n. 13, 74n.
    22, 75, 113, 119, 122, 148, 152n. 7,
    157, 175
West Africa 115–16, 117, 118, 121,
    122, 129n. 20 *see also* African
    philosophy *and* Northwest Africa
West Bank xi, 6–7, 8, 9, 101, 106, 108,
    120, 124, 125, 149
"West Bank Barrier" 125

women xiv, 1, 5, 10, 137, 138, 141, 180
    aptitudes of 177–9
    role of 171–5, 177
World War II 15, 28, 61, 64, 143

Zion 64, 69, 71, 99, 142, 148, 155–8, 159, 163, 164–5, 166
Zionism xi, xii, xiii, xiv, xv, xvi, 3, 15, 16, 20, 21, 23, 25, 26, 28, 29, 30, 31, 36, 37, 39, 40, 41, 44, 45, 46, 48, 53n. 6, 57, 59, 60, 61, 62, 63, 65, 66, 67, 68, 69, 70, 72, 73n. 13, 74n. 22, 86, 88, 99–102, 104, 105, 106, 107, 108, 109, 110n. 7, 110n. 18, 125, 126, 128n. 5, 134, 135, 137, 137, 142, 147, 148, 149, 150, 151, 152n. 3, 155, 156, 157, 158, 159, 160, 161, 162, 167n. 19
"Zionism Reconsidered" (Arendt, Hannah) 46, 48

www.ingramcontent.com/pod-product-compliance
Lightning Source LLC
Chambersburg PA
CBHW061830300426
44115CB00013B/2318